Traditional Music in Modern Java

Traditional Music in Modern Java

GAMELAN IN A CHANGING SOCIETY

Judith Becker

PUBLISHED WITH THE SUPPORT OF
THE MAURICE J. SULLIVAN & FAMILY FUND
IN THE UNIVERSITY OF HAWAII FOUNDATION

The University Press of Hawaii
Honolulu

A cassette tape recording of examples of Javanese music,
prepared by the author, may be obtained from The
University Press of Hawaii. For information, please
write to: Marketing Department, The University
Press of Hawaii, 2840 Kolowalu Street, Honolulu,
Hawaii 96822.

Library of Congress Cataloging in Publication Data

Becker, Judith O
　　Traditional music in modern Java.

　　Bibliography: p.
　　Includes index.
　　1. Gamelan.　2. Music, Javanese—History and
criticism.　I. Title.
ML1251.J4B4　　　　789′.01′095982　　　　80-19180
ISBN 0-8248-0563-1

To Pete

Contents

Figures

Preface

The traditional arts in Java appear to be thriving. A *wayang kulit* performance can be heard nearly every night in the larger towns. *Wayang orang* companies in Surakarta and Semarang perform every evening of the week. Gamelan clubs seem to spring up, like mushrooms, overnight. Inexpensive comic books of the favorite wayang stories are sold by hawkers who set up makeshift stalls by the roadside. Large outdoor theaters have been built to hold the thousands who come to see modernized versions of the old wayang stories. Government culture bureaus report that there are more *dhalangs* per population today than ever before. The overall effect is one of a great deal, an almost overwhelming amount of artistic activity.

However, if one spends time with persons involved in these activities, they communicate an unmistakable depression or malaise. The source of the depression is often difficult to specify. A direct question elicits only a vague reply: "It's not like it used to be"; "Nowadays, nobody works hard at [playing the gamelan], [dancing]"; "young people are not interested in gamelan any more"; "The old masters were more profound than those today"; "The new gamelan pieces are all only children's songs." Many of the statements reflect a certain Javanese style of discourse and might be dismissed as merely conventional. Yet, underlying the linguistic convention is the fact that Java's musicians are troubled by *something*.

A certain amount of the unhappiness can be attributed to simple economic need. Like many other segments of the population, the musician in Java does not earn enough to support himself. Beyond this, however, the arts in Java are in a troubled state. The ill-defined complaints of the village musician parallel the articulate and self-searching appraisals of the intellectuals who often appear on lecture platforms or write articles for popular newspapers.

The problem is that a gulf has developed between the aspirations of the modern Indonesian nation and the ethos and rationale embodied in the music of the gamelan. The government and many of the people are eager to become a twentieth-century nation, to obliterate the last traces of a king-subject mentality, and to overcome the deep-seated animism/ancestor worship/Hindu-Buddhism that is still the religious cast of many nominal Moslems in Java. Many government leaders and most intellectuals would change the world view of the people from a basically mystical, nonrational, awesome one in which outward appearances can never be trusted, inner reality is hidden, and unseen forces operate on all aspects of one's life to a rational approach to the universe in which things are what they seem to be, unseen forces are either ignored or disbelieved, and the destiny of the individual and the nation can be controlled. The world of the gamelan, surrounded by mysticism, otherworldliness, and inwardness, has no logical place or meaningful function within the context of the modern Indonesian nation.

The situation is one of "cultural dissonance," a term used by Leonard Meyer in *Music, The Arts, and Ideas* to describe a situation in which "an organism, a scientific theory, or [in this case] a set of stylistic norms ceases to be consonant with its environment." If the dissonant element is to survive, it must undergo changes of a rather radical nature.

Such changes are occurring, and can be demonstrated in some of the modern gamelan compositions. While innovation is necessary and inevitable, it is not surprising that modern gamelan compositions stimulate an ongoing controversy and debate.

Acknowledgments

I shall begin where most acknowledgments end, with my husband. It was as his wife that I was able to spend more than two years in Java. His tireless collecting of research materials on Javanese arts reduced my library trips to a bare minimum. His ability to elucidate instantly and at great length on such fine points as the definition of *candrasangkala* made him an invaluable, ever-available, and free research assistant. His painstaking reading of the various drafts of this study prevented many pitfalls of style and meaning.

To the subjects of this study, Ki Wasitodipuro of Yogyakarta and Ki Nartosabdho of Semarang, I am grateful for their helpfulness and generosity. While not fully understanding my purposes or my motives, they offered me all the material at their disposal and, what is more important, their time and goodwill as well.

To my gamelan teachers, Hardjo Susilo of the University of Hawaii, Pak Sumardjo, formerly of Yogyakarta now residing in Malang, and Sulaiman Gitosaprodjo, formerly of Surakarta now residing in Malang, I owe all the understanding I have of the practice of gamelan music.

To my teachers of Indonesian and Javanese, Amran Halim of Palembang and Soeséno Kartomihardjo and Imam Hanafi of IKIP (Institute Keguruan dan Ilmu Pendidikan) Malang, I am greatly indebted. Without their help all the Indonesian and Javanese language materials used in this study would have remained inaccessible.

To William P. Malm, who has been my mentor, my guide, and my friend for many years, I owe deep gratitude.

For a critical reading of the entire manuscript I wish to thank my friends and colleagues Robbins Burling, Allan Keiler, and Hardjo Susilo.

I am grateful to Martha Krieg for her talent and for her care in drawing the figures in the text.

Special thanks are due the successive directors of the Center for South and Southeast Asian Studies at the University of Michigan for their continuing support, moral and financial, without which this study would not have been written.

Finally, I wish to give thanks to the Ford Foundation Jakarta, who unintentionally supported the research for this study. By hiring my husband as a linguistic consultant at IKIP Malang, they provided me with travel expenses, a house, a car, servants, language teachers, baggage allowance, schooling for my children, music lessons, research assistants, funds for books and manuscripts, as well as a prestigious connection that opened doors that might otherwise have been closed to me.

Note on Orthography

In contemporary Java there are at least four spelling systems in everyday use: the Dutch romanization of Javanese words, the old Indonesian romanization, the new Indonesian romanization, and the Javanese romanization. Multiformity of spellings is commonplace. Variant orthographies have sometimes resulted in a great diversity of acceptable spellings for one word. In the course of doing research for this study, the following spellings were encountered for the Central Javanese city: Yogyakarta, Jogjakarta, Djodjakarta, Djojakarta, Jogdjakarta, and with the prefix *nga*, Ngajogjakarta. It seemed appropriate for the purposes of this study to attempt to be consistent in the matter of spellings even though no such consistency exists in Java.

In 1972 the Indonesian government instituted a spelling reform that has been adopted by all schools in Indonesia and by the press. I will follow this new Indonesian orthography, except when quoting texts using older spellings.

A special problem arises with the Javanese vowel [ɒ] (the sound of *aw* in *law*), which in Javanese romanization is spelled variously *a* and *o*. As the vowel is rounded, I have chosen to use the *o* alternant in the names Ki Wasitodipuro and Ki Nartosabdho where the medial and final *o* are the sound [ɒ].

A different problem occurs in the name of the city Surabaya, pronounced by the Javanese Surɒbɒjɒ. While consistency demands that I write it Suroboyo, the reader's convenience demands that I retain the conventional spelling.

Indonesian words do not, as a rule, carry any diacritical markings. On Javanese words, however, diacritical markings present yet another difficulty. There is no generally accepted method for assigning diacritical markings, and different editors and writers use different systems. Some writers have chosen to solve the problem by eliminating all diacritical markings on Javanese words. In this study, I have arbitrarily chosen as the model for diacritical markings the Javanese dictionary *Baoesastra Djawa* by W. J. S. Poerwadarminta.

In romanized Javanese the letter *e* represents two phonemes. Unmarked *e* is pronounced [ə]. (Marked *e* represents two allophones: *é* is [e], and *è* is [ɛ].) The letter *t* is pronounced [ṭ], while *th* (the same as ṭ in some representations) is pronounced [t]. The letter *d* parallels the letter *t*. *D* is pronounced [ḍ], and *dh* (same as ḍ) is pronounced [d].

Note on Transcription

All the musical examples in the text have been represented in Javanese cipher notation and Western staff notation. Every notational system developed has inherent limitations, because of the fact that there is no adequate way to translate musical sound into written symbols. Notational systems presuppose experience with the actual sound of the music. The use of the two systems of notation in this study is an attempt to convey to as wide an audience as possible as much musical information as possible. However, without actually hearing the sounds, the notations alone are inadequate.

In Javanese gamelan music two different, unrelated tuning systems are used, the *sléndro* system, which has a total of five tones per octave, and the *pélog* system, which has a total of seven tones per octave. Many sets of gamelan instruments in Java are only *sléndro* sets or only *pélog* sets. Much of the repertoire of gamelan music can be played with only one or the other of the two tuning systems. A complete set of gamelan instruments, including both tuning systems, has a pair of instruments for each instrumental type, one of the pair manifesting the *sléndro* tuning system, the other manifesting the *pélog* tuning system. As the tunings are unrelated, *sléndro* instruments and *pélog* instruments are never played simultaneously. In Java there is no concept of a standard tuning or of a particular pitch level corresponding to a fixed number of vibrations per second. Also, there is no concept of a fixed intervallic distance between any sequence of pitches. Thus while each individual set of instruments, *pélog* or *sléndro*, is carefully tuned within the set, no two sets of instruments manifest exactly the same tuning. This means that the intervallic structure of each gamelan differs in some respect from the intervallic structure of every other gamelan. The concept of a fixed intervallic distance between the notes of a scale is such a fundamental aspect of Western music that it is often difficult for Westerners to conceive of a music system in which intervallic structure does not have the same meaning or importance. The various tunings of different gamelan are, in Java, a source of pleasure and interest to the listener, and the ethos, or *rasa*, of the tuning of a particular gamelan is often a subject of pleasurable discussion and contemplation.

Typical tunings of a *sléndro* scale and a *pélog* scale expressed in the cents system are given below:

Sléndro

Pitch level	1		2		3		5		6		i̇ (upper octave)
Interval between pitch levels		220		280		236		242		248	

Pélog

Pitch level	1		2		3		4		5		6		7		i̇ *
Interval		120		144		297		117		126		155		246		

As neither the *sléndro* system nor the *pélog* system can be accurately transcribed on a Western five-lined staff, I have chosen to follow the compromise used by other Western musicologists. The *sléndro* scale is transcribed as follows:

pitch level   1 2 3 5 6

The *pélog* scale is transcribed as follows:

pitch level   1 2 3 4 5 6 7

---

*The tunings given here are taken from an article by Mantle Hood on Javanese music in the *Harvard Dictionary of Music*, 2nd rev. ed. (Cambridge, Mass.: Harvard University Press, 1969), p. 436. The cents system was devised by A. J. Ellis (1814–1890) as a method of measuring intervals. The cent is equal to 1/100 of the semitone of the well-tempered scale. A semitone equals 100 cents, a whole tone equals 200 cents.

1

An Introduction to Gamelan Music

Gamelan is a generic term for a Javanese musical ensemble of gongs and metal xylophones. A gamelan may consist of only a few gongs kept in a special room, rarely taken out, struck only a few times and returned. A gamelan may consist of twenty-five instruments, including fiddles, flutes, and zithers, and may be played almost daily.

Gamelan music can be defined by the internal features of instrumentation, musical structure, and form. In addition, specifically musical aspects of gamelan are related to and interact with the cultural environment of the gamelan including the history of gongmaking, the political and intellectual history of Java, and the uses of gamelan music in Java.

Knobbed gongs, the core instruments of the gamelan, are found in northeastern Burma, in Thailand, Laos, Cambodia, and Malaysia, in the islands of Indonesia (Sumatra, Java, Bali, Lombok, Kalimantan, Sulawesi), and in the southern Philippine island of Mindanao. Gongs and their makers, the gongsmiths, have supernatural significance in Southeast Asia. The sound of the gong is not an acoustic phenomenon of vibrating air, but a voice. All the forces operating beyond and behind the visible world find ways to speak to man. In Java, gongs are the favored way. Because of this special function, gongs are highly respected and feared. An insult to a gong is fraught with danger. "Once, the Susuhunan of Solo took the gong with him to his place of residence—or, as some will have it, it was stolen by a Solonese. All the tigers from South-Kadiri then flocked after the gong, and the district of Surakarta suffered from a veritable plague of tigers. The gong was therefore brought back to Lodaya in great haste, and the plague of tigers immediately ceased. No European is allowed to touch this gong. One civil servant, who ventured nevertheless to touch it, died soon afterwards."[1]

The blacksmith, the gongmaker, a humble figure in Western mythology, assumes the highest place among mortal men in Southeast Asian myths. From northern Burma a myth portrays him as a priest and leader of men. "... in modern Kachin [Burma] origin stories N'gawn Wa [who is at once the first parent of men and the creator of the earth] is unquestionably a blacksmith. He forges the earth and the terms used to describe the process are those of a Kachin smithy. ... Myth as we have seen makes the archtype *gumlao* leader a priest, a blacksmith, and the child of a levirate wife of an elder brother in a chiefly lineage."[2]

In Java, ancient literature relates him to the gods. "The word for 'smith' is pandé [expert], he is addressed as empu or kyai [lord, master] and these old terms are in accordance with still existing notions and associations. His craft is not looked upon as an ordinary profane trade, but it is veiled in mystery. ... The passages in the old Javanese chronicles where the smith is mentioned repeatedly give the impression that in ancient Java the roles of prince and of smith more or less overlap; ... The genealogies of the smiths, as of the princes, go back to the gods."[3]

Today, Javanese gongsmiths still prepare ritual offerings to the gods before undertaking the spiritually charged activity of gongmaking.

As mentioned earlier, a gamelan may include only a few basic instruments or a large number of instruments. Most of the instruments of the gamelan are made of bronze, an alloy of tin and copper, and are set on or hung from wooden frames.[4] Figure 1 illustrates the basic instrumental types, and the listing that follows describes the complement of instruments found in a large, Central Javanese gamelan. The order of the listing is as follows: first the instruments that play least frequently and are the most important structurally (through the *kethuk*), then the families of bronze instruments (*saron, bonang, gendèr*), stringed instruments and flutes, and finally the drums.

gong ageng/gedhé: The largest hanging gong. One or two in each gamelan. Approximately one yard in diameter.

gong siyem/suwuk: A hanging gong smaller than the *gong ageng*. Approximately two feet in diameter.

kenong: A set of large pot gongs on a wooden frame. There is a wide variety in the number of individual *kenong* found within one gamelan, from as few as two or three up to twelve. The greater number is not always considered desirable.[5] Each *kenong* is approximately fifteen inches across and ten inches high.

kempul: A set of hanging gongs smaller than the *siyem*. Again a wide latitude can be found in the total number of gongs within one gamelan, from as few as two to as many as eleven. Each *kempul* is approximately seventeen inches in diameter.

kethuk: A small pot gong on a wooden frame. A *kethuk* is approximately nine inches in diameter. One or two are usually found in a gamelan.

kempyang: A pair of small pot gongs set on a wooden frame. These gongs are smaller than the *kethuk*.

saron demung: A xylophone-type instrument with thick, heavy keys mounted on a low, wooden frame. The largest of the *saron* family, the instrument is approximately one yard long.

saron barung: The middle-sized instrument of the *saron* family. The instrument is approximately two and a half feet long.

saron peking/panerus: The smallest of the *saron* family, approximately two feet long.

bonang barung: A set of pot gongs mounted on a wooden frame in two parallel rows. The middle-sized instrument of the *bonang* family. The largest *bonang* (*panembung*) is not usually represented. The instrument is approximately five feet long.

bonang panerus: The smallest member of the *bonang* family. Approximately four and a half feet long.

slènthem: The member of the *gendèr* family with the largest keys. The thin, bronze keys are suspended over tube resonators. The instrument is approximately two and a half feet long.

gendèr barung: The middle-sized member of the *gendèr* family. Approximately forty-two inches long.

gendèr panerus: The member of the *gendèr* family with the smallest keys. The instrument is approximately one yard long.

gambang: A wooden xylophone. Approximately four feet long.

celempung: A zither. Approximately one yard long.

rebab: Two-stringed, bowed fiddle. Approximately forty-two inches long.

suling: Bamboo flute. Approximately twenty-one inches long.

kendhang gendhing/gedhé: The largest of the drums, used either alone or in conjunction with the *ketipung*. Approximately twenty-eight inches long and fifteen inches across.

ketipung: Smallest of the drums. Approximately eighteen inches long and nine inches across.

batangan/ciblon: A drum used for playing rhythmic patterns to accompany dance. Also substituted for the other drums in certain sections of long compositions. Approximately twenty-seven inches long and one foot across.

bedhug: A large, hanging drum. Approximately twenty-nine inches long and sixteen inches across.

The gamelan participates in a wide variety of activities in Java, some of which could be classified as artistic, while others more properly belong to ritual. Rarely is gamelan music heard in a concert situation with no other activity occurring simultaneously. More commonly, gamelan music

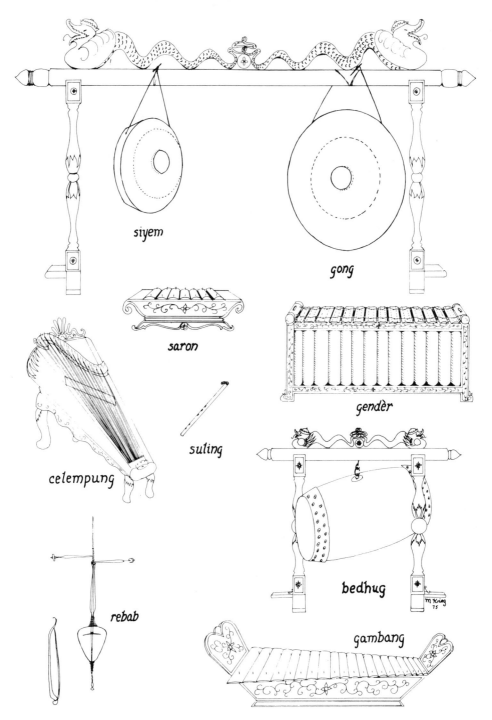

Fig. 1. Guide to the Gamelan.

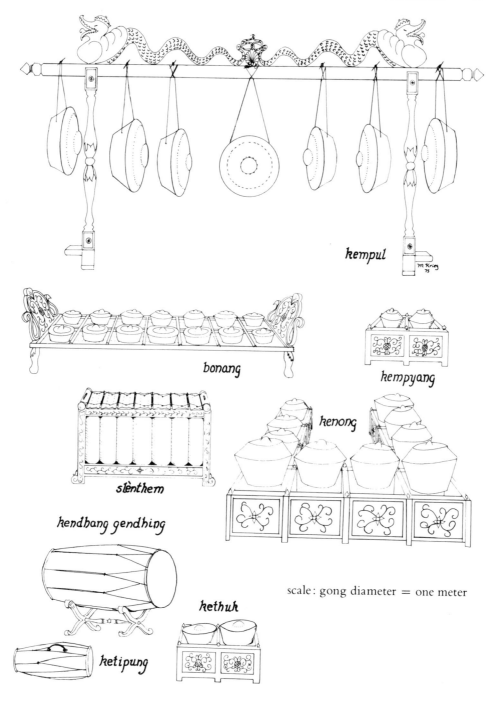

kempul

bonang

kempyang

kenong

slènthem

kendhang gendhing

hethuk

ketipung

scale: gong diameter = one meter

enhances a ritual or accompanies a drama. Music, dance, poetry, and drama are often not separable except on an analytic level. A specific piece brings to mind a particular dance form, or the appearance of a certain character on stage implies a certain composition. Poems are associated with traditional melodies, and particular dance movements imply particular drum patterns. In a similar manner, the various roles within the arts are ill-defined, with participants crossing from one role to another with ease. An actor-dancer in a professional theater company is as much at home playing in the gamelan as acting on stage.

Neither songs, dances, dramas, nor music are "arts" in the Western sense of the word. The person who sings, or plays, or dances is not an "artist," not someone in a special category apart from other people. In theory, anyone can dance, or sing, or play an instrument. Some are simply better at it or have had better training than others. The arts are not considered vehicles for personal expression, media through which the individual presents his personal world view. On the contrary, it is the performer/creator who is the vehicle through which the traditions are continually renewed and vitalized. A wall mural in a village will be communally and sequentially painted, one person in his spare moments taking up the portrait of a mythic figure where someone else left off. During a musical performance, one musician slips easily into the spot left vacant by another who has left momentarily for a bite to eat. There is practically no opportunity within the traditional arts for one individual to become a "star." The arts are deeply communal and nonindividualistic. This is in part due to the fact that traditional arts are still to some extent rituals, semirituals, or at least bear the hallmarks of a ritual origin. In essence, the traditional arts in Java are communal expressions of cultural ideals, aspirations, and world views.

Within a single artistic form it is possible to see a range of uses and functions. For example, the most famous Javanese dramatic form, the *wayang kulit*, or shadow-puppet-play, is sometimes pure ritual, usually semiritualistic, and sometimes largely entertainment. All the characters are portrayed by delicately carved and painted flat leather puppets whose arms are articulated by sticks and whose shadows are projected on a screen. The puppeteer, *dhalang*, manipulates all the puppets, speaks for each character, controls the accompanying gamelan, and intermittently sings passages from Old Javanese poetry.[6]

Wayang kulit in a purely ritual form occurs every day of the year in East Java at Mount Kawi. On the side of Mount Kawi is the tomb of a holy man. The tomb and the adjoining mountainside are felt to be spiritually charged and magically powerful. On either side of the stone steps leading to the tomb are resting houses for pilgrims, restaurants, food vendors' stalls, beggars, and sheds for *wayang kulit* performances. Day in day out, year after year, the shadow-play performances go on. The *dhalang* sits before the lighted screen, puppets arranged on either side of him, a gamelan playing behind him, and acts out the epic stories. Only one factor distinguishes these performances from any other *wayang kulit* performance. There is no audience. The performances are commissioned either to give thanks for a boon or to induce the gods to grant one. They are for an unseen audience, and no one in the bustling crowd on Mount Kawi pays the slightest attention.

At the other extreme of the ritual-entertainment spectrum are the highly publicized *sendratari* performances of stories from the *Ramayana*[7] given during the summer months on a huge stage erected before the tenth-century temple complex, Prambanan. *Sendratari* is a recently developed form derived from *wayang orang*. *Wayang orang* portrays the same epic stories as does *wayang kulit*, but live actors substitute for leather puppets. The role of the *dhalang* is reduced to singing only the fixed passages of Old Javanese poetry and narrative transitions. The gamelan accompaniment is essentially the same as in *wayang kulit*. In *sendratari*, the *wayang orang* format is shortened to only two hours, all the dialog is omitted, and the story is told entirely through dance gestures. Since the vocabulary of dance comes nowhere near the complexity and subtlety of the vocabulary of speech, the philosophic overtones of *wayang orang* are absent. Also lost is the element of speech-play, beautifully composed phrases or clever puns and innuendoes. What is gained is a visually arresting, fast-moving, and easily comprehensible theatrical form which contains many elements from earlier forms such as dance gesture, costumes, story format, and gamelan. This new form is popular with foreign tourists in Java as well as with many urban Javanese who feel the old forms are boring, interminably drawn-out, and expressive of an outmoded, out-of-date philosophy.

Wayang kulit, wayang orang, and *sendratari* are all related by story, plot format, and their basis in Hindu-Javanese religious philosophy. Secular theatrical forms with quite different origins and development also are accompanied by gamelan, sometimes playing the same repertoire as is found in the more prestigious wayang forms. Lower class theatrical forms such as East Javanese *ludruk* and Jakarta *lenong*, considered by upper-class Javanese to be vulgar and tasteless, are performed in modern dress without the stylized movements of wayang theatrical forms. Still, one finds within *ludruk* and *lenong* the same integration of music, poetry, and dance characteristic of all Javanese theater.

Every ludruk performance is a collection of examples of the following genre: ngrémo [dance], dagelan [jokes], selingan [interludes], tjerita [story].

> Every ludruk performance opens with a dance called the "ngrémo" that is performed by a man dressed in bizarre black men's or women's clothes. . . . After the ngrémo, the dagelan begins; a single clown sings, soliloquizes, then engages in a dialogue with a second clown, all of which leads into a comic skit. After the dagelan a female impersonator sings and dances. This is the selingan. After the selingan the tjerita begins. That is usually a melodramatic story with many comic episodes. Selingan by female impersonators are presented between scenes of the melodrama. In commercial performances the ngrémo lasts about half-an-hour, dagelan about an hour, melodrama about two hours, and all the selingan together consume another hour; so the total performance lasts about four and a half hours.[8]

Though no longer rural, Jakarta audiences still support the rural theater form *lenong*.

> In the villages, lenong performances usually open with a song, a dance or a dance-fight [*pentjak*]. . . . A song or dance is dedicated to the person in the audience who perhaps has flung a piece of paper, a handkerchief or something else up on stage with a request for a specific song along with the name of the person requesting. . . . Song requests like this are done in exactly the same way by the clown figures Pétruk or Garèng in wajang kulit. . . . As each character appears for the first time, he recites a poem [*pantun*] as a kind of introduction, while half-walking, half-dancing. . . . Also grief or lamentation is expressed in song. . . . In those villages which still play old-style lenong, the audience can also join in the dancing on the stage.[9]

Wayang kulit, *wayang orang*, *sendratari*, *ludruk*, and *lenong* are all events which include drama, dance, song, and gamelan. Music unites with other art forms in one integrated event.

Today, there are signs of a trend away from the total integration of former times. No longer is all gamelan playing within the context of a larger event.

Radio broadcasts of gamelan music are becoming more and more popular. The range of functions from ritual to secular entertainment also applies to radio broadcasts. Once every thirty-five days, at the coincidence of the five-day-week Javanese calendar with the Arabic seven-day-week calendar, Jum'at-Legi, the palace gamelan in Yogyakarta, broadcasts a performance of traditional gamelan pieces. These broadcasts are widely listened to not only for the beauty of the music, but also for the nourishment of the spirit. The coincidence of the two calendars and the playing of traditional pieces on an honored, sacred gamelan creates a hallowed moment in time. At the other end of the spectrum are the regular *mono suko*, or "listener's choice" broadcasts, by the government Radio Republic Indonesia stations. Traditional restrictions against the playing of pieces in certain modes at certain times of the day or night are disregarded. *Mono suko* rehearsals and broadcasts often have an air of frivolity unthinkable at a ritualized, palace gamelan performance.

The gamelan ensembles connected with these different kinds of events vary immensely. The accompaniment for East Javanese *réog*, an exorcistic trance ritual with a minimal plot, may be accompanied by a few iron gongs, a *serunai* (double-reed oboe), two rusty bonang kettles and a rough-hewn drum. A Central Javanese court gamelan may have ten times as many instruments, made of the highest quality bronze, with elaborately carved and gilded frames. The smaller, more primitive ensembles are becoming the victims of progress. When buying a gamelan, the individual or the *kampung* (neighborhood unit) will try to acquire a large, Central Javanese style gamelan if at all possible. The larger number of instruments are more expensive. Rather than have a smaller ensemble, the purchaser will sacrifice having bronze instruments and substitute iron instruments disguised with gold paint, so strong is the social pressure to have a "standard" Central Javanese gamelan.

Most of the music played by the various gamelan ensembles is traditional and anonymous. The age of any composition is impossible to determine. The question of age reflects a view of history characteristic of Western musicology and its associated written tradition that is irrelevant here. Within an oral tradition, no two performances are ever alike. Each gamelan, or each director of a gamelan, adds to or subtracts from the version he learned. Certain stylistic practices become fashionable at certain times and in certain localities. Thus a composition may develop distinct differences from one area to another over a period of time. A piece is never fixed, but involved in a continual process of re-creation with every performance, even with every repetition. It is this process of continual renewal that is summed up by the adage that within an oral tradition all music is contemporary. Change is not new to the music of the gamelan, but is an integral part of the whole music system. Oral traditions are based upon change. Only when music becomes notated is the process of continual creation arrested.

Gamelan music is changing today. The aim of this study is to examine closely some of the changes that are taking place, relating those changes to the larger societal framework, in order to gain some understanding of those changes. The works of two Javanese composers, Ki Wasitodipuro and Ki Nartosabdho, have been chosen for study in the belief that their compositions embody the general direction of gamelan change occurring today. At least 95 percent of the gamelan music one hears all over Java is traditional, whether Central Javanese style, Surabaya style, Banyumas style, and so forth. It might be possible to discount the remaining 5 percent were it not for one very important factor. The Javanese themselves are very much interested in new gamelan music. A concert of new pieces by a popular composer will be well attended, covered by the major newspapers, the subject of descriptive or philosophical reviews (seldom critical reviews) in news magazines, and the topic of countless discussions by those in attendance as well as those who were not present. A concert of new pieces given in Jakarta is read about and discussed the next day in East Java, four hundred miles away. Traditional performances do not, as a rule, receive comparable attention from the press.

The new gamelan music is not only interesting in itself, but it serves as an indicator of social change, as a societal barometer. In Java, new gamelan pieces are called *kreasi baru* or "new creations." The mirrored image of the changing environment found in *kreasi baru* is sometimes hazy, sometimes clear. The following chapters will delineate the close yet subtle interrelationships between the Javanese gamelan music system and its social matrix.

2

From Oral to Written Tradition in Javanese Music

The introduction of notation to enable the teaching of gamelan pieces seems to be a catalyst around which many changes are developing. Formerly found exclusively at the courts of Yogyakarta and Surakarta, notation is now widespread throughout central and eastern Java. Unlike other types of borrowings such as musical instruments, which are relatively easy to incorporate and absorb, notation is not an object but a technology that implies its own theory. Notation presupposes a linear concept of time, necessitates decisions as to what should be notated, and forces a perceptual bias on the user. The implicit bias of any given notational system is all the more powerful because the user is unaware of the implications of the new technology and therefore offers no conscious resistance.

Gamelan music appears to be relatively untouched by Western influence. Except for a few experiments, there is no evidence of gamelan tunings inclining away from the traditional *pélog* and *sléndro* systems toward diatonic scales. Foreign instruments only rarely find their way into the gamelan.[1] The traditional modal structures, *pathet*, within whose framework new pieces are created, show no signs of disintegration. The most popular and most frequently played pieces are still traditional pieces such as *Pangkur* or *Gambir Sawit*, pieces known by generations of Javanese. Yet the most pervasive, penetrating, and ultimately the most insidious type of Western influence goes largely unnoticed, namely, notation.

Musical notation systems first appeared in Java at the courts of Yogyakarta and Surakarta in the second half of the nineteenth century. The time of their appearance deserves careful attention. Why were notation systems introduced at that late date? Writing has been known in Java since at least the fifth century A.D. (a Sanskrit inscription from Taruna,

West Java), and the earliest known literary work in Javanese (from about A.D. 700) is the manuscript "Candakarana,"[2] based upon the Indian manuscript "Dasanama." This was the era of Indian influence in Java that extended to literature, the adoption of Indian writing systems and epics, aspects of politics and government, and to music theory. One occasionally finds in Javanese theoretical writings direct paraphrasing of Indian music theory such as the following: "According to former technical terms, there is that which is called *nada*, that which is heard by the ears of mankind. There are nada which are manifested and those which are unmanifested. Manifested nada are of two kinds, one is called *swara*, the other *swabawa*. Swara is clear, smooth and beautiful. Swabawa is not clear, not smooth and beautiful. Nada which is unmanifested is called *nada anahata*, that is tone within the heart, or sound within quietude . . . "[3]

Until about A.D. 1000 India was a center of influence and prestige for all Southeast Asia. Javanese musicians borrowed from Indian music what was felt to be useful to them: instruments, which have mostly disappeared, and technical terms and theory, which still remain. There is no evidence of any early system of musical notation borrowed from India. Had one been in use in India, it would probably have been borrowed too. The ready acceptance, wide use, and long life of an Indian-based script in Java indicates the receptivity of the Javanese to writing systems from outside. But Javanese music used no notation system and continued to flourish and develop without benefit of any written record.

A thousand years later, in Central Java, there was suddenly a great deal of experimental use of musical notation systems. Why at that time and in that particular area? A visit to the palaces of Surakarta and Yogyakarta suggests the answer. Nineteenth-century European furniture, ornate statues, china and crystal, European chandeliers, Italian floor tiles, large portraits of ancestors, grandfather clocks, and gilded mirrors are found in abundance in all the noble residences. It was a period when things European, especially Dutch, were the fashion and were acquired by all who had the means to do so. Among the nobility, the Dutch had replaced the Indians of an earlier era as prestigious models. Dutch people—not only government officials but visiting artists, scholars, and businessmen—were frequent visitors at the palaces. There was ample opportunity for the members of the court, including the musicians, to become familiar with European modes of thought, European biases about music, and European musical notation systems.[4] Professor Ir. Purbodiningrat writes:

> European pieces already have been notated, that is the reason why old pieces at this time are still available and can be studied by whoever can read the notation. It is otherwise with Javanese pieces. How can one know

the intentions and feelings of the composer when he wrote the piece?...
There arose in Jogjakarta the idea of having a notation system for gamelan
pieces motivated by the feeling that it would be a shame if the old pieces
are no longer known by our people, and the connection the pieces have
with the development of our people. Therefore, beginning in the nineteenth
century a notation system for Javanese gamelan pieces was being searched
for.[5]

The same concern is expressed on the title page of a book of notated
gamelan pieces presented by the Sultan of Yogyakarta to the Royal Batavia
Society in 1932: "By command of his Highness...for the purpose of
saving the original and ancient musical melodies from being lost...."[6]

Why, after many hundreds of years of gamelan playing, did certain
people at the court of Yogyakarta suddenly become concerned about
old pieces being forgotten? The reason is that neither the Dutch nor the
Javanese themselves understood oral traditions in which through a process
of continual re-creation every piece is at once contemporary and the
cumulative result of ageless tradition. Each performance is both unique and
a summation of all previous performances of that piece as known to those
particular players. Past and present coexist in the moment of performance.
The concern for preserving old compositions is a European concern reflecting European reliance upon notation. Since the use of notation became
widespread in the art music tradition in Europe, a piece unwritten is indeed
soon lost and forgotten. Oral traditions have greater continuity; an unwritten composition may persist in similar form for generations, or it may
slowly and subtly evolve into some other piece or form. The idea of preserving a gamelan piece as it manifests itself at one particular point in history
and in one particular locale is not an indigenous concept. It was introduced
by foreigners who mistakenly believed that a gamelan piece is a fixed
entity which, if captured in notation, would be preserved from extinction.
The irony is that by accepting this Western view of their own music,
Javanese musicians are contributing to making it, in fact, the case.

As many as seven or more different experiments with notation were
attempted between the years 1886 and 1942. One, the *Kepatihan* system,
came to dominate all others and, with slight variations, is the basis of all
contemporary notation.[7]

The initial question faced by those developing notation systems
must have been, Of all the different polyphonic lines of the gamelan, which
shall be chosen for notation? Gamelan music is composed of a series of
layers of melody, increasing in density in proportion to the higher registers
of the instruments. Most traditional Western music is not constructed in
this way, but rather has a main melody with supporting, but subordinate
harmonic structure. Western notation was developed to accommodate

European musical structure. Where is the main "melody" in a Javanese gamelan piece? In a series of polyphonic layers this is not at all clear. The part or parts emphasized in any given performance depends upon many different factors, such as (1) geographical area (Yogyakarta musicians often emphasize saron melodies, Surakarta musicians often emphasize the melodies of the gendèr barung, rebab, and gambang); (2) the relative strength of the members of the gamelan (a gamelan with a weak bonang player will not play *gendhing bonangan*, which lay stress on the bonang parts); (3) the style of music being played (dance pieces tend to have strong saron parts; concert and radio pieces usually feature the softer instruments); (4) the placement of microphones (e.g., the modern practice of putting a microphone in front of the *pesindhèn* [singer] sometimes reduces the gamelan to an accompaniment for a female soloist). There is nothing in the traditional practice of gamelan to indicate emphasis of one part over another. On the contrary, musicians will often say that ideally all parts should be equal. Given an impossible choice, a compromise solution was accepted. A middle register part of medium density was designated as the "melody," the part to be notated. Since this part was singled out by notation and placed in a special focus, a new word had to be found to designate that part. The word now in use is *balungan*, or framework, a word still not in general use and familiar in this meaning only to those who have had contact directly or indirectly with the music conservatory in Surakarta, the Akademi Seni Karawitan Indonesia.

One of the early attempts of notating gamelan music was the system known as *titilaras rantè*, or "chain" notation, developed in Surakarta in 1888 by Kyai Demang Gunasantika, the head musician at the home of a nobleman of Surakarta. (See figures 2 and 3.) Of all the notation experiments, *titilaras rantè* most closely resembles Western notation. As in all other Javanese notations, more than just the "melody" has been notated. The inadequacy of notating only one out of many polyphonic lines is obvious. In *titilaras rantè*, the kenong and gong parts were added. The gong is of central importance in marking the melodic period and the kenong is important in marking a primary subdivision of the gong unit.

Soon after the appearance of *titilaras rantè* in Surakarta, another system, known as *titilaras andha*, or "ladder" notation,[8] was developed about 1890 at the palace of the Sultan in Yogyakarta. The original model for this type of notation is not known but the resemblance to lute and guitar tablature is striking. (See figure 4.) This system gives more information than *titilaras rantè*. In addition to the saron and kenong parts it includes the kethuk, kempul, and kendhang parts.

At about the same time, 1890, the first step toward the development of *Kepatihan* notation was taken. A nobleman, Radèn Mas Tumenggung

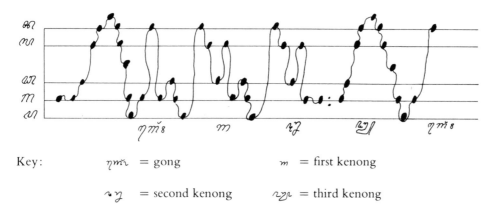

Key: ŋm̃ĩ = gong   m = first kenong

        ∿ŋ = second kenong   ᷅ᵹ᷄ = third kenong

FIG. 2. *Titilaras rantè.* "Chain" notation, for saron, kenong, and gong, first used about 1888. The composition is *Ladrang Gléyong,* Pélog Pathet Nem. Horizontal lines represent the keys of the sléndro saron. Reading from the bottom to the top as left to right on the instrument, in *Kepatihan* notation read the lines as pitch levels 1 2 3 5 6. The note between lines three and four is pitch level 4. The note above the staff is pitch level 7. The notation begins with the *buka,* introduction.

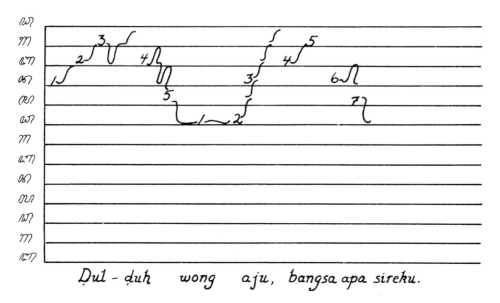

Ḍul - ḍuh   wong   aju,   bangsa apa sireku.

FIG. 3. *Titilaras rantè pesindhèn.* "Chain" notation for female vocalist, *pesindhèn,* first used about 1888. The composition is *Sekar-ageng Sastrasurendra.* The horizontal lines represent the pitch levels of the keys of the gendèr. The wavy lines between notes indicate melodic ornamentation. The text is written below the staff. (Fig. 2 and 3 are from Soetandija, *Gending Emeng minggah Ladrang Nalongsa dan Ladrang Wreda-Muspra.* Master's thesis, Akademi Seni Karawitan Indonesia, Surakarta, p. 26.)

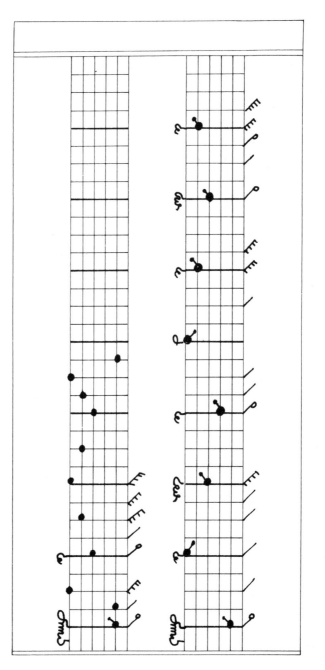

FIG. 4. *Titilaras andha.* "Ladder" notation, called by Kunst the "Jogja kraton checkered script notation," first used about 1890. The composition is *Gendhing Gunung Sari*, Sléndro Pathet Manyura. *Titilaras andha* is read from top to bottom, left to right. The vertical lines represent the keys of the saron, the horizontal lines represent rhythmic pulses. Symbols to the left of the staff are:

$\frac{9}{3}$ = gong $\frac{9}{3}$ = kempul   ℰ = kethuk   ϙ = kenong

Figures to the right of the staff are drum notation:

ℱ = tak   / = dung   ℙ = dang

(From Kunst, *Music in Java*, p. 493.)

Wreksadiningrat, living in the royal residence known as the Kepatihan in Surakarta (thus the name for the notation) worked out a system of numbering the keys of the gamelan instruments. A number refers to a pitch level of one of the Javanese scales. (See figure 5.) The pitch levels of the scale are represented by the keys of the gamelan instruments: five pitch levels per octave for the *sléndro* scale, numbered 1, 2, 3, 5, and 6, and seven pitch levels per octave for the *pélog* scale, numbered 1, 2, 3, 4, 5, 6, and 7. The keys of the *pélog* saron demung manifest the following pitch levels of the *pélog* scale:

1	2	3	4	5	6	7

Thus the first four-note phrase after the *buka* (introduction played in this case by another instrument) would be played by the musician at the saron demung as pitch levels 2, 3, 2, 1. The presence of a dot below each cipher in the four-note phrase 6 5 3 5 indicates that this phrase should be played in the next lower octave. Some instruments in the gamelan manifest more than one octave, but as the saron demung does not, the musician transposes the phrase up one octave and plays 6 5 3 5. The arch over the 5 indicates that the kenong plays simultaneously with the last note of the saron phrase. The circle around the last cipher in the notation, 6, indicates that the large gong and kenong play simultaneously with the saron note. The two dots in the first four-note phrase of the third line indicate that the previous pitch level played, pitch level 2, is sustained without damping throughout those two beats.

Other refinements not shown in figure 5 include a dot above the cipher to indicate the upper octave, horizontal lines above the ciphers to indicate rhythm, and a small zero after a cipher to indicate a damped rest. The basis and refinements of this system were derived from a nineteenth-century European system, the Solfege system, the creation of Galin, Paris, and Chevé.[9] (See figure 6.) All the Javanese sources on notation acknowledge the European basis of their most popular notation system, the *Kepatihan* system.[10] Thus the notation systems developed in Central Java in the late 1900s were based upon previously existing European models.

The use of *Kepatihan* notation for the saron part is now well established in central and eastern Java. Notation is considered to be progressive and modern, and is highly valued if not always practiced. Increasingly, teachers who themselves learned gamelan without benefit of notation are now using notation to teach their pupils. The musicians of the court centers of Yogyakarta and Surakarta have proceeded further in the refinement of the notation system and can now use notation as a pedagogical aid to teach any instrument of the gamelan. (See figures 7, 8, and 9.) Since the highly trained

Ladrang Gléyong
Pélog Pathet Nem

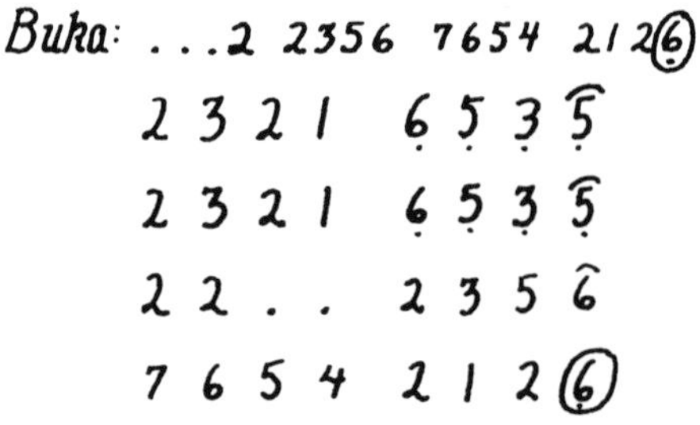

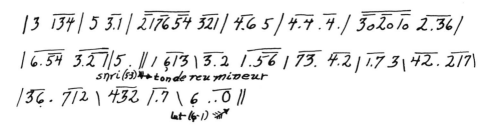

FIG. 5. *Titilaras Kepatihan*, Kepatihan notation, developed about 1890. The composition is *Ladrang Gléyong*, Pélog Pathet Nem. The numbers read across the page from left to right. A circled note indicates gong; an arch indicates kenong. (From Soetandija, p. 26.)

FIG. 6. Galin-Paris-Chevé. Vocal notation. Developed in France, about 1884. (From *Méthode Galin-Paris-Chevé: Méthode Elémentaire de Musique Vocale*, p. 176.)

and accomplished musicians of Yogyakarta and Surakarta are the models for musicians of all central and eastern Java, it is probably only a matter of time before the use of notation for all gamelan parts will become widespread. What, then, are the broader implications and subtle effects of this innovation?

In the towns of central and eastern Java, it is possible to observe a gradual shifting from an oral tradition to a written tradition. In the villages, the use of notation is sporadic. In the cities, notation is more widely used but does not yet dominate the oral tradition. But clearly an important trend is taking place.

The term *oral tradition* has a much wider meaning than simply the absence of an elaborate notation system, just as the term *written tradition* implies more than just the use of notation.[11] Too often, oral tradition is equated with oral performance, that is, playing without written music, or with aural learning of a composition, that is, memorization through

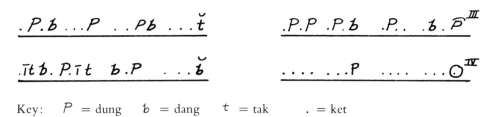

Key: *P* = dung   *b* = dang   *t* = tak   . = ket

FIG. 7. *Titilaras kendhang.* Drum notation for the *suwuk*, or closing phrase, for *Kendhangan Kalih Ladrangan.* Superscript III and IV indicate the third and fourth kenong tones. (From a book of kendhang parts compiled by Sulaiman Gitosaprodjo, Malang.)

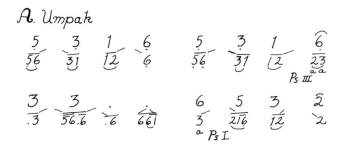

FIG. 8. *Titilaras rebab.* Rebab notation for the composition *Ketawang Laras Maya,* Pélog Pathet Barang. The numbers above the line represent the saron part, the numbers below represent the rebab part. Diagonal lines indicate bowing. "Ps I" and "Ps III" indicate finger positions. (From a book of rebab parts compiled by Sulaiman Gitosaprodjo, Malang.)

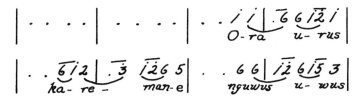

FIG. 9. *Titilaras gérong.* Gérong notation for the composition *Ketawang Pucung,* Sléndro Pathet Manyura. The numbers correspond to pitch levels on the saron, the text is beneath. (From *Peladjaran Bawa Gérong,* compiled by Soewardi, Direktorat Djenderal Kebudajaan, Djawa Timur, Surabaja, 1967.)

repeated hearings. Or, the term oral tradition may be equated with im-provization on a theme or motif as practiced by some jazz musicians. None of these interpretations describes the practice of the musician in an oral tradition. The musician in an oral tradition, rather, has mastered a *technique* of composition, based upon the manipulation of formulas, which allows him to perform and compose at the same moment. For this musician, the moment of performance is the moment of creation. The group per-formance in Java puts many restrictions on the freedom of the musician, but still the music must be re-created, not reproduced, in any given per-formance.

The training of the musician in Java can be described as encompassing several stages. The initial stage is the slow process of absorption of the tradition which begins in earliest childhood. A great many facets of the tradition are unconsciously internalized such as the formal structures, density ratios of different instruments, appropriate styles for given occasions, and elemental stylistic traits such as how hard to hit a given instrument. At some time, perhaps at adolescence or earlier, the Javanese musician begins to learn a specific instrument. He may have one predominant model, his father or teacher, or he may have several models, all the skilled performers on the instrument in his village. He begins to learn the formulas which he will imitate, vary, expand, and rearrange for the rest of his life. The formulas are melodic contours for arriving at a certain pitch level. The formulas do not cover a whole piece, or even a whole gong unit, but only a small section of it. From the lower density parts of the slènthem, to the melodic patterns that combine to create the saron barung part, to the high density parts of the gendèr or celempung, every aspect of gamelan music is for-mulaic. The same formulas may occur in many different pieces. The formulas are not fixed and will be altered to suit the demands of tempo (*irama*), mode (*pathet*), and position within a piece.

It is important to stress that at this stage, the musician is not learning pieces, but ways of realizing pieces; he is learning process, not fixed content.

The final stage in the development of a musician comes when he has internalized the underlying forms of his formulas and their proper places within a composition. From then on, he is free to use them creatively within a performance. The best musicians rarely repeat themselves precisely, but constantly create new patterns while conforming to the restrictions of contour, pitch level, length, pattern placement, and style.

In his book *The Singer of Tales*, Albert Lord delineates in detail the technique of oral composition. Although speaking of the formulaic com-position of epics in Yugoslavia, his description aptly applies to the Javanese musician as well.

We shall see that the formulas are not the ossified clichés which they have the reputation of being, but that they are capable of change and are indeed frequently highly productive of other and new formulas. We shall come to realize the way in which themes can be expanded and contracted, and the manner in which they are joined together to form the final product which is the song. . . . The singer of tales is at once the tradition and an individual creator. His manner of composition differs from that used by a writer in that the oral poet makes no conscious effort to break the traditional phrases; he is forced by the rapidity of composition in performance to use these traditional elements. To him they are not merely necessary, however, they are also right. He seeks no others, and yet he practices great freedom in his use of them because they are themselves flexible. His art consists not so much in learning through repetition the time-worn formulas as in the ability to compose and recompose the phrases for the idea of the moment on the pattern established by the basic formulas. He is not a conscious iconoclast, but a traditional creative artist. His traditional style also has individuality, and it is possible to distinguish the songs of one singer from those of another.[12]

The introduction of notation into an oral tradition brings with it the concept of a fixed formula that is to be repeated exactly.

Notation systems are not new to Asia and do not necessarily replace oral traditions. Traditionally, Asian notation systems have been mnemonic devices. It was assumed that the musician consulting the notation already knew the composition in question and needed only to be reminded of certain passages. Thus, Asian notation systems were never devised or used to teach a composition. In the past, systems of notation were nearly always semisecret and used within the confines of a court, and thus were very limited in their impact. It was never possible to re-create the sound of the full ensemble solely from a notation system that gave only rudimentary melodic progressions. Asian notation systems cannot be compared to a Western score. Learning the musical tradition has always been an aural, never a visual, process. What is new in Java is not so much the fact of a notation system, but the attitude toward notation and the reliance placed on it.

An increasing number of students, particularly, but not exclusively, those who study at the Akademi Seni Karawitan Indonesia in Surakarta, are becoming familiar with and skilled in the use of Kepatihan notation. On the blackboards in classrooms the melodic formulas for the saron, the gendèr, the rebab, and so forth, of a given teacher are written out in full and copied in notebooks by the students. These formulas are then memorized and repeated exactly by each student. Before notation, precise repetition of the performance of a teacher was not only difficult, but not considered a thing of any value. A student learned method or process from a teacher, not full content. The emphasis has now changed, and the student memorizes formulas, or the content of the piece. The student has in his notebook—fully notated and precisely repeatable—the melodic formulas of his teacher. In a culture which places great importance on and reverence toward the role of the guru, these written formulas assume a greater significance and aura of sanctity than the classroom notes of a Western student. It seems inevitable that the written parts of the venerated teacher will assume such authority as to stifle the student's own impulses toward the re-creation of formulas. It is likely that what is now intended as suggestions for variation possibilities will in time, because of the repeatability of written formulas, become prescribed methods of procedure. The graduates of the Akademi Seni Karawitan Indonesia in Surakarta become gamelan teachers in all urban areas of central and eastern Java. Because of their credentials, and because they control the technology of writing gamelan parts, they often become the foremost gurus in the area, regardless of ability or experience.

The court areas of Yogyakarta and Surakarta have been models for artistic activity of large areas of central and eastern Java for a long time. With a medieval communication system, it was largely impossible for people in outlying areas to copy with accuracy the musical styles of those centers. Within the last twenty years, however, cheaply produced books containing the saron parts for hundreds of traditional pieces have become available. Nearly all these books represent the Yogyakarta or Surakarta version of these pieces. The availability of a printed book, with a prestigious version of a piece slightly different from that used by a local gamelan group, is enough to induce that group to change its version. Printed books with court-city versions of pieces, plus the presence of Surakarta-trained, notebook-toting teachers, has already produced a great deal of homogenization of gamelan style in the urban areas.[13]

The city of Malang, a large commercial town in East Java, is a case in point. Thirty years ago, specifically East Javanese gamelan style flourished along with other East Javanese art forms such as *wayang klithik* (wooden *wayang kulit*), and *wayang topèng* (masked dance-drama). Now, *wayang klithik* and *wayang topèng* have disappeared, and East Javanese gamelan style is in full retreat. Nearly every gamelan in the town plays Surakarta style and those that are not yet restructured are apologetic.[14] All this is justified in terms of improving the rougher, more dynamic gamelan style of East Java. The resultant performances conform more closely to the high prestige, Central Javanese gamelan style than before, but at the high cost of loss of regional style, diversity, and variety.

Besides the easily observable effects of the introduction of notation, there are other, subtler implications. Print technology, in this case musical notation, teaches that parts can be separated from their total environment and broken up into smaller units. On the printed page one letter follows another, one word follows another word.[15] The unity of experience is broken up into bits, all in linear sequence. The synthesis, if it happens, must occur in the mind of the reader. In musical terms, this means that a young pianist trying to learn a Beethoven sonata will work on one section at a time, even breaking the section into smaller bits and working on one phrase at a time. Only after weeks of detailed, phrase-oriented practice will he attempt to synthesize the whole piece. For the student of Western classical music, the totality of a musical composition may be the last thing he learns.

The early training and subsequent predilection of the gamelan musician is quite otherwise. The totality, the experience of the whole piece is learned first, and only slowly and gradually does he learn to fill in the component parts. A child begins his gamelan performance experience as young as five or six, at rehearsals in his neighborhood gamelan, by playing the gong which marks the largest formal unit of the piece. He thus learns to experience a complete musical section. Later, he may be entrusted to play a smaller gong, which subdivides the largest formal unit. At this point in his training he is still far from playing anything close to a "melody." What he is learning is the overall structure of a composition by first experiencing the largest units of the structure. As a result, the particular melodic content of a composition never becomes more important than the formal structure. Later in his career he will learn that a misplaced tone on a gendèr (high density instrument) is scarcely noticeable, a wrong note on a saron (medium density instrument) can be overlooked, but to omit or misplace one of the main structural markers such as the kenong, or especially the gong, is almost unforgivable. In gamelan music, the slower the instrument, the lower its density, the greater its importance. The early training emphasizing structural form remains with the musician throughout his career.[16]

Related to learning the totality of the composition first is the concept that parts of the composition are not isolable or separable. An oral tradition of ensemble performance, based as it is upon the use of formulas, has an upper limit of complexity for any one instrument that a system using notation does not have. Therefore it is possible and usual for the gamelan musician to have much greater familiarity with all the gamelan instruments than the Western musician in a symphony can possibly have. Even though a man may be considered a specialist on one instrument, he will certainly be able to substitute on many other instruments to an extent not common in the West. This kind of flexibility produces great awareness of, and sensitivity to, other members of the gamelan. One gets the distinct impression that the total sound of the gamelan is passing through the mind of the musician even if he is playing alone, in the privacy of his home. Never does one hear a musician playing alone without his singing or humming or speaking some other part simultaneously. There is no solo tradition in gamelan. Each part is totally integrated into, and conceptually indivisible from, the whole.

The dependence upon written music trains the musician to grasp one musical line at a time. In a symphony orchestra a musician is required to play only his own part and follow sensitively the indications of the conductor. In Western classical music the parts are isolated both physically and psychologically. Only the conductor is required to make the synthesis that Javanese musicians make unconsciously. Traditional gamelan music is, to the highest degree, integrative and communal. Individualism or pyrotechnic display have no place.

It is possible that widespread use of notation can change the communal and integrative aspects of gamelan playing, and therefore change the essential ethos of the music. Notation works hand in hand with new lifestyles to alter old teaching methods. More and more Javanese are living in cities and are no longer tied to an agricultural cycle. Increasingly, they have jobs in offices or schools with regular working hours. The changing lifestyle affects gamelan pedagogy. Traditionally, learning is totally informal. The teacher does not "teach" in the Western sense of the word. The student spends days and weeks observing the teacher, the model, and imitates to the best of his ability. This is a very slow process, but it produces musicians with profound intuitive understanding of their music system. Today's urban gamelan teachers cannot spend infinite hours demonstrating for students. The teacher may have a job that requires him to be in an office for most of the daytime hours and therefore he cannot teach long hours at night. Notation gives this teacher an easy answer to his problem. He need only write out the parts for the instruments and the student can practice them privately. It therefore becomes possible for the student to conceive of one part as separable from the total gamelan sound. Formerly, all learning was within the context of the whole gamelan, now it is not necessarily so. A student may learn a part without hearing the sound of the total gamelan simultaneously. With notation, it is possible to break through the confines of a formulaic system and create high-density parts of great complexity. This in turn leads to greater specialization in the gamelan, and concomitantly, greater reliance on a leader who has to assume the integrative role of the Western conductor. Already, it is possible to see the seeds of such a development in the new compositions for gamelan written by Java's innovative composers.

The movement toward a notation-based music system is today only a trend. Its effects are most evident in the cities. The rural areas seem relatively unaffected. But since the cities or court centers are the models for rural behavior, it seems likely that city styles will in time be disseminated to the villages.

There is an important factor not yet mentioned that could reverse the whole process. Notation and its concomitant implications are accepted because they are believed to be modern. Many Javanese musicians are convinced that standardization and permanence are positive values in music. The attitude that the multiformity of the old oral tradition is backward and that progress lies in establishing fixed standards is widely prevalent and illustrated by the quotation below taken from a master's thesis by a student from the Akademi Seni Karawitan Indonesia in Surakarta.

> In former times when someone wanted to study music, it was considered enough to feel, to listen, to see and to practice, without thought or understanding. Indeed, some people said that music was based upon feeling only, without understanding or thought.
>
> However, in this time of reality and facts, problems like this must be solved by methodology based upon fixed norms.[17]

The need for notation, based upon European musical developments, has been accepted by the Javanese musician for his own system, which has a very different structural basis and a different history. Notation systems were developed in response to Dutch concepts that pieces would be lost if not notated. That era has now passed in the West. In a sense, Western musicians and composers are now looking eastward as well as back into their own past. Things written down, or notated works, in all the arts no longer have the authority they once had. Simultaneously, scholars are becoming increasingly aware of the modus operandi of oral traditions, and nineteenth-century biases toward fixed texts are now questioned. It may be that Javanese musicians will come to realize that their traditional oral system is actually the more modern, and notation may once again be relegated to libraries, of interest to scholars and historians but not of any particular use to a practicing musician.

3

Traditional Kingship, Nationalism, and the Gamelan

The crisis forced upon gamelan traditions by the adoption of notation is intensified by the difficulties of adjustment to the new values of Indonesian nationalism.

Nationalism has been and still is one of the most potent forces promoting change in the twentieth century. Indonesian nationalism has colored Javanese artistic activity since at least the early 1940s. Although its roots go back much further, Indonesian nationalism as a widespread motivating force in Javanese society can be viewed as dating from March 1942, when the Japanese invaded Indonesia, then called the Dutch East Indies. The quick collapse of the colonial government proved to be a watershed in the long, sustained efforts of those men who had been striving for many years to free their country from Dutch domination. From that moment on, the Dutch were discredited in the minds of many Javanese who formerly might have continued to accept their colonial status as inevitable. Although seven long years of occupation and revolution were to pass before the dream of independence became an actuality, the changed climate of opinion preordained the final outcome.[1]

Colonial occupation had scarcely disturbed traditional sources of power and authority or tarnished the luster of their supporting artistic institutions. The Dutch had supported the traditional rulers of Java, the *priyayi*, or aristocracy, and in part had ruled through them. The role of the gamelan under the Dutch colonial government was essentially the same as in the times of the Javanese kingdoms. In a subtle way, gamelan ensembles and gamelan music played in the palaces were a legitimizing force for the authority and power of the nobility. Closely mirrored in the music of the palace gamelan ensembles was the psychological set or the state of mind of the ideal monarch. The rule of cyclic order was felt to be the law of the universe. Intimately connected to the concept of endlessly recurring cycles in time was the value put upon an accepting, tranquil, almost impassive state of mind. The closer one came to this calm, serene state of mind, the higher one's inner state of being. The nobility, by virtue of being born into an honored position, ought to be more ordered and serene than ordinary men. In his monograph on statecraft in Java from the sixteenth through the nineteenth centuries, Soemarsaid Moertono discusses at length the philosophical and psychological framework of the Javanese monarchy.

> In attuning himself to the Great Order man is led to accept the concept of *Harmony*, a cosmic harmony, in which everyone and everything has its ascribed place. . . . It is a harmony not only of man's world, the micro-cosmos, with the greater macro-cosmos, but also a harmony within his own sphere of life. . . . The Javanese . . . would not consider the state to have fulfilled its obligations if it did not encourage an inner psychological order (*tentrem*, peace and tranquility of heart) as well as enforcing the formal order (*tata*). Only then is the state of perfect balance, of perfect harmony, achieved. . . . It is not surprising, therefore, that the state should have been seen as an image of the Great Cosmic Order, in which the gods maintain absolute dominion. This schematic similarity between cosmic order and the state is seen as identity, and this serves a double purpose. First, . . . the safety of one assures the safety of the other. Second, and politically the most important, it serves to establish the king's power over his subjects. . . . Thus, the state as a replica of the cosmic order must also have the propensities and capacities of that higher order, a power which, as a part of the Great Order, no subject people dare restrict or disturb. This belief accounts for the absolute character of the old kingdoms.[2]

The importance of the "Great Cosmic Order" to concepts of state and statecraft in ancient and medieval Java finds a remarkable parallel in the development, within the palace, of extraordinarily elongated formal gamelan structures. The extreme length of the gong phrases in these compositions can hardly be understood if purely musical considerations are the only basis. (See Appendix 1, *gongan* forms Mérong kethuk 8 kerep, Mérong kethuk 8 awis, or Minggah kethuk 16.)

A Javanese musician must at all times know exactly where he is in relation to the approaching gong. It is the focal point toward which he consciously and deliberately moves. Within a hierarchical musical structure —a gong section subdivided by kenong sections, kenong sections subdivided by kethuk, and so forth—it is possible for the musician to comprehend very large time units as one musical phrase, but it is difficult to understand the necessity for it. Why not two shorter gong units? But if the long unit is a musical portrayal of a cosmic cycle, the great length immediately makes sense. Greatly elongated musical forms are a palace development and have never been popular outside of those circles.

There is another way in which gamelan music, all gamelan music, subtly reinforces Javanese concepts of cosmology and by implication, kingship. The important structural points in gamelan music are those points at which several horizontal lines come together on the same note. The greater the number of horizontal lines which coincide at one point, the more important is that point in the formal structure. (See Appendix 1, diagram 2.) The gong is the most important point of coincidence, where the greatest number of parts coincide. The kenong marks the point of next importance where many parts coincide, the kempul the next, and so on. In like manner, time in Java is reckoned by the distance between points of coincidence of two calendrical cycles.[3]

> The Javanese combine their own five-day market week (Legi, Paing, Pon, Wagé, Kliwon) with the Western-Moslem seven-day week (Minggu, Senèn, Selasa, Rebo, Kemis, Djumuwat, Setu).... As seven times five is thirty-five, there are thirty-five possible separate days (Minggu-Legi . . . Senèn-Paing . . . Djumuwat-Legi . . . Setu-Paing . . . etc.), and this cycle forms the "month." Actually, however, these "months" are not fixed and absolute units as ours but merely the length of time between any one singled-out day and its next occurrence thirty-five days later.... Javanese calendrical time is pulsative, not spatial like ours. When the cogs of the calendar click together in a certain combination, it is time for a certain ceremony to be held, a journey to be begun, or a medicine to be taken.[4]

The calculation of time by the distance between points of coincidence of different cycles is pan-Indonesian. Sometimes the parallel between cycle coincidence and melodic coincidence in gamelan music even extends to terminology. "The Achenese seasons [Northwest Sumatra] are regulated by the conjunctions of Kala (the Scorpion) with the moon. These conjunctions they call *keunong* (Indonesian: *kena* = to hit, come into contact with)."[5]

The similarity of morphology between Achenese *keunong* and Javanese *kenong* (*kena*, pronounced kenaw, to hit + *ng*, a bright, metallic sound) suggests that the term as used in the gamelan also refers to cyclic coincidences.

The repetition of large cyclic forms, the coincidence of smaller cyclic forms within the large forms, cycles within cycles, points to the philosophical basis for the ostinato, or infinitely recursive, formal structures of gamelan music. In this suggestive, subliminal yet penetrative way gamelan music supported ancient and medieval Javanese concepts of the cosmos and of kingship.

A cosmology, reflected in a theory of kingship, reflected again in a music system cannot help but result in political and musical conservatism. Referring to the consequences of Javanese kingship theory, Moertono says: "This leads to an attitude of conservative traditionalism, a clinging to established customs and so to a distaste for change or for whatever may disturb the regular and predictable flow of events."[6]

The religious basis for conservatism is intensified for the Javanese musician by the intrinsically conservative nature of oral traditions. The musician does not think of himself as a creator, but as a preserver. Through his musicmaking, he carries forward a treasured inheritance from his honored ancestors. Albert Lord states well the attitude of the musician in a traditional culture. "What is of importance here is not the fact of exactness or lack of exactness, but the constant emphasis by the singer on his role in the tradition. It is not the creative role that we have stressed for the purpose of clarifying a misunderstanding about oral style, but the role of conserver of the tradition. . . . the picture that emerges is not really one of conflict between preserver of tradition and creative artist; it is rather one of preservation of tradition by the constant re-creation of it."[7]

The court musician in Central Java was not only a conserver of a musical tradition but a supporter of a monarchical and cosmological tradition as well. Even the instruments that he played served to legitimize the role of the king. Several of the gamelan, or gongs within a particular gamelan, found within Central Javanese palaces are *pusaka*, magically charged items, usually of considerable age. As the wealthiest and most powerful man in the kingdom, it was easy for a monarch to acquire the finest and/or the oldest gamelan in the area. As all gamelan are to some degree sacred, very old or very fine gamelan are more so. Possessing such fine sets of instruments both enhanced the prestige and power of the monarch and established his right to that power. ". . . certain pusakas in the palace of the Sultan ([gamelan], spears, swords, flags), have magical powers which support any Sultan who is legally and cosmologically entitled to rule over the country. . . . These pusakas are an essential part of the Sultan's authority; without them, it is believed, a Sultan cannot enjoy the faith and loyalty of the people and thus he cannot rule over the state."[8]

One of the duties of a king was to put on the best, the most magnificent performances of the traditional arts, *wayang kulit*, *wayang orang*, and so forth. If some other nobleman staged more grand performances than he (hardly likely in view of his tremendous financial advantage), there might be doubts as to his right to be the monarch. It has been suggested by several Javanese scholars that the great flowering of artistic activity at the two major courts of Surakarta and Yogyakarta from the mid-nineteenth through the mid-twentieth centuries was because both courts were rendered politically impotent by the Dutch and therefore transferred their innate hostility and competition from the political to the artistic sphere. In any event, the finest performances were given by the princes, who although largely neutralized politically, still kept and maintained the trappings of power.

> In these ceremonies the Sultan used to display much pomp and splendor according to the ancient traditional rules, in order to maintain his dignity and esteem in the eyes of the nobility and the priyayis. It was essential in the setting of the Javanese belief system regarding the Sultan that the traditional ceremonies and rituals in the kraton [palace] be observed. If they were ever neglected, the royal ancestors, the goddess of the Indian Ocean, the heavenly guardians of the mountains and the state pusakas might feel offended and evil would befall the state and its people.
>
> The court ceremonies and rituals were certainly an effective means of preserving unity between the Sultan, the nobility, and top-ranking officials of the state including the grand vizier. These occasions functioned as a social prestige building and maintaining system for those who had the privilege of attending them, and this privilege tended to strengthen loyalty to the Sultan.[9]

The power of the princes ended abruptly and finally with the arrival of the Japanese. Japanese sanction and support were not given to the nobility, the *priyayi*, but to two groups with quite different motivations, backgrounds, and aspirations: the nationalists (including Communists), and the *santri*, those Javanese with strong loyalties to Islamic traditions and aspirations.

The primary aim of the nationalists was to overthrow the Dutch and their allies the Javanese nobility and to establish an independent Indonesia. The *santri* were also nationalists, but primarily they were orthodox Moslems with considerable antagonism toward the Javanese nobility.[10] As orthodox Moslems, the *santri* were offended by the religious syncretism of the princes. Although nominally Islamic, the *priyayi*, by their behavior patterns, their world views, and their support of the traditional arts, were potent forces in sustaining animism, ancestor worship, and Hindu-Buddhist beliefs in Java.[11] Thus the *santri* were hostile not only to the political position of the *priyayi*, but also to their social behavior and religious orientation.

The changing attitudes toward traditional rulers that had been spreading throughout the world came belatedly to Java. All the spirituality and mystical power of the *priyayi* had been unable to prevent colonial occupation by the Dutch or military occupation by Japan. The best hope for the future lay in the hearts and minds of a small group of men who, for the most part, did not share either the ascribed status of the *priyayi* or their interest in the mysticism and symbolic function of traditional Javanese arts. Although Sukarno in his later years became kinglike and used the traditional arts in their old legitimizing role, between 1942 and the present there has been a gradual but continuing trend toward secularization of Javanese arts.

The loss of their role in legitimizing kingship, the secularization of society, and the rise to prominence of men from outside the Javanese *priyayi* constituted a serious and continuing challenge to the traditional arts.

The intellectual climate that prepared acceptance of the political changes described above had been developing in Java for some years prior to World War II. In the 1930s a group of artists, writers, and poets explored the role of the arts and emerging nationalism, and began the search for a national, as opposed to a Javanese, culture. The establishment of the literary magazine, *Pudjangga Baru*, in July 1933, proved to be the gentle herald of a momentous upheaval in the attitudes and directions of those involved in Javanese arts.

The title of the magazine deserves attention. *Pudjangga Baru* means simply "New Poets," but implies a good deal more. *Pujangga* is the Old Javanese word for poet, also meaning one who can foresee the future, a prophet.[12] The term was used for either poet or musician, both often the same person. Generally, a *pujangga* was associated with a particular king or realm, and his works usually were dedicated to his king. Sometimes he would sign his king's name to his own works. The *pujangga* were important sources of legitimizing power for the ancient Javanese kings. They could rewrite history as well as create proper genealogies for a usurper of the throne: "Each time the center of power shifted to a new place, the claim to legitimacy was sanctioned by the new king's *pudjangga*, the poet of the court, who wrote the miraculous tale of the king's descent from mighty rulers eminent in their magic power."[13] The *Pudjangga Baru*, however, had quite different sources of inspiration and allegiance. In its third year, the magazine was given the subtitle "Bearer of a new spirit in literature, art, culture, and general social problems." Later still the subtitle became "Conveyer of a new, dynamic spirit for the formation of a new culture, a culture of Indonesian unity."[14]

The question of a national language was the most burning issue. Language was the central problem in forging a meaningful unity in the heterogeneous area that was Indonesia. A form of Malay language, Bahasa Indonesia, had already been decreed the national language in 1928,[15] but was far from being universally understood. Along with their interest in a national language, the contributors to the magazine were concerned with the creation of a national culture. Thus began a great debate concerning methods to attain a national culture which continues only slightly abated into the present.

All of the men involved in the magazine were nationalists, and many of them were non-Javanese. The non-Javanese among them, joined by a number of Javanese intellectuals, feared Javanese domination of a unified republic, were suspicious of traditional Javanese conservatism, and resented the assumed superiority of many Javanese toward the peoples of the outer islands. The desire to break the power of traditional Javanese attitudes and loyalties is forcefully expressed in a poem by one of the leading proponents of Indonesian nationalism, Sutan Takdir Alisjahbana. The poem was written about the Central Javanese Shaivite temple, Candi Prambanan (Loro Janggrang). This is the last stanza of the poem.

> My heart does not yearn for your era,
> When the priest announced the presence of Shiva,
> when the object of worship becomes incarnate
>   in a temple statue,
>   No, no! No, no!
> Yes God, Yes Divine, make sincerity and
> integrity of the soul return to your
> religious order
> and I will give birth to a new art, not in
>   this shape or form . . .
> But eternally in accordance with the impassioned
>   spirit of my time.[16]

Takdir Alisjahbana went further than most nationalists in his advocacy of the use of models from the West for the new nationalism. A brief summary of the views of Alisjahbana is quoted below:

Time and again . . . he [Alisjahbana] depicts the development of the West since the Middle Ages, the change from a static to a dynamic society, the freeing of the individual from traditional fetters, the expansion of Western man in all fields of life, which finally gave the West the hegemony in the world, culturally, politically, economically. This freedom may have its dangers, it may lead to extreme individualism, licentiousness, even chaos, but that is not relevant in the case of Indonesia. Takdir is convinced that only by following in the steps of the West will Indonesia by able to play an adequate role in the modern world. And with special vehemence he rejects the idea, so dear to many of his countrymen, that the West leads only in matters of technical skill, and that spiritually and culturally Indonesia, and the East in general, is much richer than the so-called materialistic West, and that therefore Indonesia should remain its own old self. People fostering such illusions are wont to recall Indonesia's glorious past, famous kings and poets, Gadjah Mada and Borobodur. But to Takdir all this is irrelevant. First of all, he points out, everything that these modern leaders are, and all that they know, came to them from the West, which revealed to them the treasures of Indonesia's past by the work of scholars and scientists. Even the name and concept of Indonesia is a Western one. There had been no Indonesia before the twentieth century, and the glorification of heroes and achievements of the past actually introduces a degree of provincialism and regionalism which is dangerous to the unity of modern Indonesia. Moreover, he argues, a temple like Borobodur, beautiful as it may be, could only be built in a society where 90% of the people lived in slavery or great poverty, and worked for the convenience of the lofty, spiritual civilization of a small court clique.[17]

Alisjahbana links modernization and Westernization, a connection most Indonesians would also make.

Where is the place and what is the role of the gamelan in this new world proclaimed by Alisjahbana? The argument summarized above is still used against those committed to Javanese arts. Many of the compositions of Java's modern composers can be interpreted as an attempt to answer the charges above.

The pro-Western, antitraditional attitude of many of the "New Poets" was opposed by a number of the same group who felt that the past glories of Java should be the foundation of the new nationalism, that Indonesia should affirm its ancient traditions, maintain its individuality, and seek a synthesis with the West rather than imitate it. A Javanese physician and psychiatrist expressed these views:

> I myself was a student of a Western school . . . from the first to the last grade. I was able to study Western society not only in our country but also, for many years, in Europe. No one could accuse me of despising Western science, art, and culture. Yet I am convinced that the spiritual development of our people—though our minds be sharpened in laboratories, in the Western manner—will progress along its own lines as in Japan, China, and India. There, though Western-oriented, the culture in essence certainly retained its own Eastern base. Once more, it does not matter if we use spoons and forks, machines and tools from the West. It's no mistake to read Shakespeare, Dante, and Goethe. It's very beneficial to admire the figures of Rembrandt and Da Vinci. We are delighted to hear the music of Beethoven and Wagner. Yet, we must seek an art of our own, a culture of our own, a literature of our own.[18]

One of the most famous supporters of Javanese cultural traditions as a foundation for a new culture was Ki Hadjar Dewantara. He established a widespread school system, the Taman Siswa (garden of pupils), in which gamelan, Javanese dancing, Javanese language, history, and literature formed the core of the curriculum.[19] Though thoroughly traditional in outlook, Ki Hadjar Dewantara did not remain passive in the face of change. "The late Ki Hadjar Dewantara believed that human desires are but cogs in the Universal Machine. The individual's will is subject to 'the laws of cause and effect', which he identified with the Indian conception of Karma. Change is inevitable and, confronted with it, people are always ambivalent —deploring loss of the old, yet welcoming the new as a liberation. Though man is only a small part of the universal will, he still can give direction to the era, participate in shaping his world."[20]

One of the consistent themes of the *Pudjangga Baru* was the necessity for the artist to take an active role in the formulation of new attitudes. The artist had a responsibility directly to society that replaced the traditional personal responsibility of the poet to his ruler. ". . . it is the artist who must lead the way and pass on whatever he has found to be of value for himself. His art should be in the service of the people.[21]

The establishment in December 1949 of an independent Indonesia with Sukarno as its first president had immediate and lasting repercussions for the Javanese artistic world. It is not surprising in a country where artistic activity has had so much symbolic meaning that very early the newly independent government turned its interest to the gamelan. It was decided to establish a school of music. The idea of a school of music, clearly based on Western models, is a radical development within an oral tradition. Perhaps there was a recognition by those in the new government that the arts, particularly the gamelan, must change their focus, their orientation, their very meaning, and come to terms with a new world. Or perhaps the motivation was more simple and self-interested. Like the traditional kingdoms, the new government may have wanted to enlist the help of the arts in legitimizing the regime. Whatever the underlying motives for the building of a conservatory may have been, the declared purposes are fascinating in themselves.

One repeatedly articulated aim was that within the confines of the conservatory an attempt should be made to synthesize Indonesian musical arts and create an artistic expression that would be representative of the whole republic. "Thus, later will come to pass results from all the Indonesian artists of the new generation, because there (at the conservatory) all the abovementioned artists have the opportunity to organize a thousand and one varieties, experiments, until finally, with contented hearts, they will meet that which they are always seeking, that is Indonesian music that is truly based upon the foundation of national culture."[22]

Twenty-five years later, this high hope must be termed a failure. The closest thing to a pan-Indonesian musical expression is *kroncong*, popular songs accompanied by Western stringed instruments, which flourishes outside of the confines of any conservatory.[23] Still, the ideal of a pan-Indonesian musical expression continues to be an important source of inspiration for Java's gamelan composers.

The choice of Surakarta in Central Java as the seat of the first music conservatory is interesting. On the surface, it would appear that Jakarta, in West Java and the new capital, should be given preference. Jakarta does not have the strong regional character of Central Java. Its population represents peoples from all over Indonesia. As a government sponsored and supported institution, the conservatory might better be near the source of its support. If, however, the government hoped to tap some of the legitimizing power of the gamelan tradition, then the school had to be placed close to the sources of that power, the courts of Central Java.

The school was opened officially on 27 August 1950, in Surakarta, with an evening of artistic entertainment at a *pendhopo*, a large, opensided, square veranda especially for artistic performances. The curriculum from that day until now looks astonishingly broad, including in addition to gamelan performance, dancing, singing, acoustics, Western music, Indonesian language, English, sociology, history of art and culture, and research into the music of non-Javanese areas of Indonesia.[24] In fact, most of the non-music subjects are neither taught regularly nor taught well. The strength of the school is the strength of its faculty. They are superb performers of Surakarta-style traditional gamelan music. Also, they are for the most part intellectually committed to modernizing gamelan traditions while at the same time emotionally attached to the old traditions.[25] This curious ambivalence leads to conservative, traditional gamelan style that is taught in a radical nontraditional way. Old court gamelan compositions are taught with notation. A thin, delicate old man in traditional dress may be found presiding over a class of rebab players, all playing in unison. Because of the background of its teachers, the Surakarta conservatory, far from becoming the fountainhead of experimentation and synthesis as was originally hoped, is now one of the few viable institutions sustaining court traditions.

Against the music conservatory and the traditions it upholds are the *santri* (orthodox Moslems) and certain sections of the intelligentsia. Independence and the search for new goals, new symbols, gave moral and intellectual support to those forces within Java that were traditionally hostile to Javanese arts, such as the *santri*, as well as many high-minded, intellectual Javanese who felt gamelan to be a conservative force, binding the people to their old habits and patterns of thought, and contrary to the spirit of discovery, ferment, and democratic idealism in which they lived.

The Indonesia-wide interest in the problem of a national music brought to the surface a good deal of outright resentment and disparagement of the gamelan and its associated lifestyle and thought patterns. In a book about national music, published in 1952, is the following passage:

> Even though difficulties and psychological problems appear before us, we are carrying out our intentions. Not only modern musical forms and note arrangements have already entered deep in our souls, but also all our conscious thoughts have become *modern*, contemporary. And even our feelings are different, not because we have already come face to face with the international world, outside countries, but also from the influence of

our revolution. We have studied how to think quickly and how to feel no fear, as is demanded by our situation and the world nowadays, which is full of dynamism, turbulence, and conflict. We are at once already familiar with the problems of life and their solutions, familiar with technical progress and scientific knowledge. We are no longer tied to provincial music, whether Javanese gamelan, Sumatran music, or to the music of our other islands. Our new soul prefers music that can portray the turbulence of the soul, the contrasts of life and thought, feelings of ecstasy, not merely relaxation entertainment while chatting and eating fried peanuts as is usual with our indigenous music. If Jaap Kunst . . . says that most of our music which is loved and praised has a magico-religious quality, then we say we no longer enjoy music which is magical and primitive, and our religious feelings have changed.

A good example of the change in our souls could be seen when the film "Six Hours to Jogdja" by Usmar Ismail was first shown in Djakarta. It began with a battle scene accompanied by gamelan. Spontaneously came the response from the audience, "Why, it's a gamelan! Why not a stirring march?"[26]

The traditional Javanese foes of gamelan, the *santri*, were joined by fervent nationalists from all parts of Indonesia who felt gamelan traditions were an obstacle to democracy and a hindrance in the path of a nation trying to modernize. Non-Javanese in the new government had no emotional attachment to gamelan traditions and a good deal of distaste for all manifestations of purely Javanese cultural traditions. On the side of the gamelan were those who felt that the cultural past should not be overthrown in a senseless, headlong rush toward modernization, that to lose one's cultural heritage is to lose one's soul. Also on the side of the gamelan were the great majority of the Javanese people not deeply involved in the polemics of the day; ordinary people for whom gamelan had been an integral part of their whole life and who, in all innocence, loved it.

Caught between these two opposing forces, modern gamelan composers have sought, sometimes tentatively, sometimes forthrightly, and with varying degrees of success, a way to make gamelan traditions meaningful, relevant, and contemporary.

4

Music and Politics: Ki Wasitodipuro as a Modern-Day Pujangga

The musical responses of modern gamelan composers to the new cultural and political environment in Java have been highly varied, but all share at least one element. In their innovative compositions, modern composers have attempted to reach a compromise between the ethos and structure of traditional gamelan music and the changing tastes and attitudes of the present. During the period from Indonesian independence in 1949 until the fall of Sukarno in 1965 Ki Wasitodipuro was actively involved in writing political and propaganda songs in support of the national government. By transferring the *pujangga* role of the artist in support of his king to the modern concept of the artist in support of a national state, Ki Wasitodipuro has tried to adjust his traditional role to one compatible with contemporary Indonesian needs.

Music has played a role in strengthening and propagating the symbolic formulations of the national government. The importance of symbols in Indonesian political life can scarcely be exaggerated. Often, the formulation and proclamation of a new policy in itself is sufficient to maintain the interest and trust of the people in their government. Sloganizing reached almost unbelievable proportions under Sukarno, largely replacing other types of political activity. In his book, *Indonesia in Travail*, Herbert Luethy describes the formulation of slogans by the national government, and the magical quality of these slogans.

The *Pantja Sila* of the national coat of arms and the hastily drafted presidential unitary constitution of 1945, which was put into force again by the *coup d'etat* of 1959, became transformed, under Sukarno's personal rule, by the *Manipol* (Manifesto politik) of 1959, into a national catechism known under the initials of USDEK. Its study serves as the obligatory initiation into Indonesian politics ... fundamental law of 1945, Indonesian socialism, guided democracy, guided economy, Indonesian national identity. More frequent still are the Tri Sila or synthetic trinities such as R.I.L. (Revolusi-Ideologi-Leadership) ... or Re-So-Pim (Revolusi-Socialisme-Leadership), the title and credo of the Presidential speech of August 17th, 1961. Finally, the cornerstone, which is the magical threefold formula of the *Nasakom* launched by the *Manipol* of 1959 and elevated into a slogan for the fundamental integration of the regime: Nasionalisme-Agama-Komunisme (Nationalism-Religion-Communism) a synthesis of the national spiritual forces and of three "major" parties united in the National Front.

It would be impossible to exaggerate the spiritual and magical efficacy attributed to these formulas, the constant renewal and exegesis of which are regarded as essential contributions to the national wealth and power.[1]

Symbolic political activity has a very long history in Indonesia. Kertanagara, the last king of the thirteenth-century East Java kingdom of Singosari, feared the expansionist tendencies and great power of the Chinese empire under Kubla Khan. Kertanagara sought to counter this strength by the development of his own magic power, which was symbolized by the erection of a statue of himself upon the spot where a great wizard is believed to have lived. A similar statue was sent to Sumatra in an attempt to widen the spiritual shield of safety against the Mongols. Symbolic magic was used in the same way that the Western world uses military treaties and armaments.

Ever since, a great deal of Indonesian political activity has had this same symbolic quality. It has been argued that the national elections of July 1969 were a ritual act rather than an empirical test of political support for the present government.[2] The government needed to stage an election and win it in order to fulfill the ritual requirements of a modern democracy.

The great output of political propaganda songs by Ki Wasitodipuro during the Sukarno era can be seen as part of his role as a modern day *pujangga* for a new-style government. The songs supported and publicized the slogans, giving the people the feeling the government was actively concerned with them. It would be a mistake to interpret this activity cynically. Symbolic political activity takes place in a nation where ritual is often considered more real, more potent than everyday activity, where words still possess magic power, where the spirit behind an act is often more valued than the deed. Also, traditionally the prosperity and happiness of the people were directly in proportion to the strength and spirituality of their ruler. "The old Javanese writers had a worthier task to fulfill than merely to satisfy the curiosity of posterity, it was their duty to strengthen the king whose inner power was the main pillar upon which his kingdom and the well being of his people rested."[3] Therefore, it was in the self-interest of the artist to aid, in any way possible, the acquisition and maintenance of power by his ruler. The government of a newly independent state, recovering from three hundred years of colonial domination, is a fragile thing. Surely, Ki Wasitodipuro was sincerely motivated in his desire to lend whatever support he could, to volunteer whatever talents he had to strengthen his fledgling government.

The work by Ki Wasitodipuro that most clearly links him to the role of the *pujangga* is a composition in the form of an hour-long suite with gamelan, chorus, and soloists called *Jaya Manggala Gita*, or "Song to the Victory of Happiness and Welfare."[4] The composer attempts to portray musically the history of Java from the eleventh century up to the moment of the proclamation of independence in 1945. Fittingly, it was first performed on 17 August 1952, the seventh anniversary of *Proklamasi*, Proclamation of Independence. The performance was held in Yogyakarta at a *pendhopo*, a square, opensided, royal-audience hall, and was simultaneously broadcast from the national radio stations in Yogyakarta, Surakarta, Semarang, and Jakarta. *Jaya Manggala Gita* is a strong affirmation of Javanese identity, emphasizing Java's role in the history of Indonesia, glorifying Javanese heroes, and idealizing the Javanese people. The patriotic fervor and high hopes expressed in the composition are a perfect reflection of the state of mind of Wasitodipuro's compatriots at that time. The work also signals the willingness of a court musician to use his powers to serve and support the republican government. *Jaya Manggala Gita* can be viewed as a ritual evocation of all Java's past in order to link it with the present, an establishment of sequence, an ordering of credentials necessary in traditional terms to legitimize the new regime.

The work is subtitled "History illustrated with gamelan pieces from the time of Erlangga (eleventh century) until the time of the Proclamation of 1945." The sources of inspiration and the aura the suite seeks to convey are revealed in the texts and the gamelan used.[5] The texts, dating mostly from the fourteenth century, are associated with Javanese history and evoke regional pride and loyalty. The three special gamelan types used in the performance, Gamelan Corobalèn, Gamelan Kodok-Ngorek, and Gamelan Monggang are very old forms of gamelan, the extant examples probably dating from the Majapahit era (A.D. 1100–1300) of East Java. These gamelan are found only in the palaces of Surakarta and Yogyakarta, where they are accorded the highest respect and are believed to be magically powerful. The instrumentation for these ancient ensembles is much simpler than that for present-day gamelan, and the instruments themselves tend to be larger than their present-day counterparts. All these ensembles contain approximately the same instruments and all shared the same functions in the days of the Javanese kings. They were used to welcome important guests at the palace; to celebrate royal weddings, rites of circumcision, and religious festivals; to accompany tiger-buffalo fights and the drills of the soldiers; or to play at any other time the king commanded.[6]

The composition begins with three slow strokes on the suwuk hanging gong followed by a Hindu-Buddhist mantra:

> Aummmmmmmmmm
> We give praise to the most merciful spirit as
>   is our duty.
> May we encounter no obstacles,
> Making every effort to reach long life,
>   loyalty and perfection.
> Aummmmmmmmmm[7]

As an ancient-style gamelan with only four tones plays in the background, the narrator speaks the following lines: "It is written in Old Javanese classical poetry [kakawin] the story of a former time, called the age of Kretoyoga, the great king Erlangga, ruler of the world, the island of Java, in the kingdom of Kahuripan, in the year A.D. 1028."[8] A flute (suling) joins the ensemble and the narrator continues. "Counting from the time of Singosari,[9] for one-hundred-thirty years the island of Java had no enemies, the time was peaceful, the kingdom always victorious, the jewel age arose on the island of Java. The most excellent ruler, the world famous King Hayam Wuruk, deified king, the second ruler of Majapahit, with his advisor, the most extraordinary minister, Prince Gajah Mada, spread the fame of the kingdom of Majapahit throughout Nusantara [Indonesia] as well as to foreign countries."[10]

While a few gamelan instruments play in the background a man sings a poem in Kawi, the classical literary language of Java. The text can be translated as follows:

> When the great king Kertanagara,
> Remembered the perfected world [the realm
>   of religion]
> Throughout the world the news was spread.
> He returned again, with a calm heart,
> To the religion of Shiva.[11]

The gamelan changes from the old four-toned Corobalèn Gamelan to a modern *sléndro* gamelan and the narrator continues: "One hundred and eight years later, the times were changing ... changing ... changing ... finally, corrupt and immoral! [in Arabic] Peace be with you, May God bless you."[12]

At this point, another old gamelan style is introduced. Using a modern *pélog* gamelan the ensemble plays in the style of the Sekatèn Gamelan. Sekatèn Gamelan are played just outside the largest mosque in either Yogyakarta or Surakarta, exclusively for the Islamic festival, Garebeg Mulud.[13] While the gamelan plays softly the narrator says: "There was a strong wind, blowing from the north port, from Demak it came, bringing the thunderous sound, [in Arabic] 'I acknowledge, there is no God but Allah, and Mohammad is his prophet'.[14] Praise the Lord, Praise the Lord."[15] This leads into a song of praise in Arabic accompanied by the gamelan. The translation of the Arabic is as follows: "May God bless you. The most honorable Mohammad has come to us as our Prophet. And God has sent him to us as our leader."[16]

The narrator continues: "The holiness of the Wali spread far, everywhere entering deep into the hearts of men, everywhere can be heard the songs of praise."[17]

The song of praise is repeated again, and afterward the gamelan changes to a piece associated with Yogyakarta known as *gangsaran*, leading into a loud-style form called *lancaran*. This sequence on the gamelan creates an aural image of the Central Javanese kingdom of Mataram.

While the gamelan plays, the narrator reads: "After the time of the Wali, in the south, divine revelation came to the country of Pajang in the form of the venerated Sultan Hadiwijoyo, in the year A.D. 1594."[18] Then there is a transition to the archaic Gamelan Kodok-Ngorek, playing an archaic piece of the same name while the narrator continues: "Kingdom of Pajang, again passed westward the path of inspiration. Truly, it was the son of Sultan Hadiwijoyo who received grace, Prince Sutowijoyo who ruled in Mataram. He was called Prince Senopati, in the year A.D. 1614."[19]

Following this the gamelan plays the traditional piece *Gendhing Gambir Sawit*,[20] often attributed to Prince Senopati, and the narrator continues:

> Mataram, Mataram which had its capital three times at Plèrèt. It was the year 1613 according to the Christian system, that the great Sultan Hanyo-Krokusimo, the famous prince shared alike the joys and sorrows of his people. Since then, Java has not known such a golden age as the age of Kawijayan.
>
> Aummmm   Aummmm   Peace

> However, nothing in the world remains constant. What trouble came to the land of Java? The Dutch trading company seeking the produce of Indonesia such as cloves, pepper, and nutmeg; allowing a lustful atmosphere

and intending to take all. The V.O.C. was established at Betawi![21] It was said to be a business cooperative venture, but after a time forts were built, then came cannons.

Why?—What kind of businessmen bring cannons; they meant otherwise, it was not the way of a trader, but the way of an imperialist, the wider their control, the more cruelly it was/applied. The tactics of Kancil were used;[22] without gentleness, the strategy could not have been more low, flattery, without considering the misery of the people, only thinking of their own happiness. Consequently, several times they were at war with Mataram but without success.[23]

From *Gendhing Gambir Sawit*, the composition continues with another popular traditional piece *Ladrang Gonjang-Ganjing*.[24] Throughout the playing of *Gambir Sawit* and *Gonjang-Ganjing* the simple, archaic *Kodok-Ngorek* piece is played in the background.

The elaborately contrapuntal style of *Gambir Sawit* and *Gonjang-Ganjing* superimposed upon the archaic *Kodok-Ngorek* gives a striking effect, like that of the ghost of past gamelan style walking softly beside its more beautiful, more sophisticated descendant. Simultaneous or superimposed images fit Javanese conceptual patterns better than do temporal, linear, sequential images. The feeling that the history of Mataram exists in the present Mataram is effectively expressed by this musical device.

While *Gonjang-Ganjing* (*Kodok-Ngorek*) are heard faintly, the narrator recites:

> The company pressed forward more and more, taking over the power of the Javanese rulers. Beginning with Sultan Agung Sinuhun Amangkurat the First, Sinuhun Amangkurat the second, the third who was called the "golden" Sunan, until Sunan Pakubuwono the First in Kartasura, continuing with Pakubuwono the Second, until the third who became ruler in Surakarta.
>
> The kingdom of Mataram was divided in two, Surakarta and Yogyakarta. The prince Mangkubumi was named Sinuwun Hamangkubuwono the First, followed by the second and the third. . . . Meanwhile, Prince Diponegoro could not stand hearing the suffering of the people, and finally it was as if the buffalo had run amuck and broken down the stable.[25]

The narrator says: "The people rallied, following their Prince in 1825."

While the gamelan plays a simple form, *Kebogiro*, loudly and fast, voices are heard shouting: "Don't retreat a single step, friends! Let's go, like the moth[26] irresistibly drawn into the flame. The bamboo curtain[27] is broken and the barricades are smashed! Amuuuuuuuuuukkk!"[28]

Then the gamelan suddenly drops in volume and a female soloist sings a song of grief over the fate of Diponegoro.

> Who would have supposed, who would have guessed
> The Dutch would deceive in such a smooth manner
> The way without simplicity
> The consequence, Diponegoro came to grief.
>
> From ignorance and greed
> All the people have suffered greatly.
> They fervently request
> Reason and Order be granted to them.[29]

After one time through the song, the narrator says: "Ah, Prince Diponegoro, the jewel of the nation, the champion of Java, you were tricked and trapped by the oppressors."[30]

The gamelan plays *Kodok-Ngorek* while the narrator speaks the following: "Comrades, comrades! Over and over again you endure misery! Hey! Go to the limits! Drown your grief in pleasure."[31]

After this, the gamelan plays a Ladrang form, while the narrator continues: "Must we accept this state of affairs? Oh no, surely not! The nation feels the beginnings of a will to reach a goal, many people are increasingly aware. The movement for nationhood arises! A strong unity, all working together. Yes, remember the advice of our ancestors, as is written in the prophetic writings, that help will come to abolish the trials of Indonesia. When? Oh when will it happen?"[32] As the gamelan switches to a more forceful, louder form, shouts are heard in the background: "Banzai!"[33]

Then begins one of the most curious musical sections of the whole composition. While most of the instruments drop out and the remaining ones play in *sléndro*, the gendèr panerus plays in *pélog* a piece entitled *Lagu Mars Jepang*, which means a Japanese march tune and is based on a Japanese marching song that the Javanese learned during the Japanese occupation.[34] The gamelan plays *Lancaran Panggugah* in typical quadratic rhythm while the gendèr panerus plays a triple rhythm consisting of a quarter note and an eighth note. (See figure 10.) The effect is polymetric, two against three or six against four, as well as polytonal, *sléndro* plus *pélog*. This piece changes to a transition on the saron which in turn leads into a piece called *Gendhing Sakura* in three-four meter. (See figure 11.) The words of *Gendhing Sakura* are translated as follows:

> Great Japan, my friends,
> Ambassador of God,
> Bringing happiness to our country.
> Within the realm of Greater Asia
> They are prepared to help in
>   all kinds of undertakings.

Lagu Mars Jepang/Lancaran Panggugah

FIG. 10.

Simultaneously, the narrator states: "Ah, now the meaning of the prediction is clear. . . . Prosperity and happiness together within Greater Asia. We trust the guidance of our elder brothers. Hopefully, He Who is All Powerful will permit this great idea to be fulfilled."[35]

Then the gamelan accompanies a female soloist singing a *welasan*, a song of compassion or grief. "More and more oppressive becomes the guidance."[36] At the same time the narrator says:

Oh! Oh! Where is the evidence? They say prosperity together, they say happiness together. Why? It turns out like this! The longer the time, the longer the . . . Oh, my people![37]

Is there no end to the sufferings we must endure? My God, we got rid
of the colonialists only to get another oppressor. Forced labor! Burlap bags
for trousers! Rattan to make shawls! Rotten sweet potatoes to eat! Snails.
Finally, beriberi. Fearful, sad, cold, hot, stinging! Many of our cleverest
people are destroyed.[38]

The gamelan changes to a livelier style as the narrator continues with
the following: "Because of the stress of suffering, the people emerge
courageous. But because they are always pushed this way and that, they
are confused, in doubt, they do not yet see the way. Everywhere are under-
ground movements. The Supriyadi rebellion breaks out in Blitar! Japan
becomes nervous, seeing the clear signs of the future."[39]

The previous piece fades into the background while a running passage
up and down the row of small gongs on the bonang comes to the fore-
ground. This passage is described by the composer as the portrayal of the
sound of water, *damel swanten toja* or *manggambarkan suara air*. The narrator
continues: "Finally . . . [loud beat on large bedhug drum]. The atomic
bomb at Hiroshima. Japan surrenders to the Allies. The people of Indonesia
are more and more determined and will not be denied their future."

The gamelan becomes loud again briefly, then stops abruptly as the
narrator says *Proklamasi*, introducing the Indonesian Proclamation of
Independence. (After the narrator says *Proklamasi*, there are three slow
strokes on the bedhug drum. Then the Gamelan Monggang begins playing
the archaic piece *Monggang* while the *Proklamasi* is being read.)

We, the people of Indonesia, hereby declare the independence of Indonesia. The transfer of power and other matters will be carried out carefully
and as quickly as possible.

> Jakarta, 17 August 1945
> In the name of the people
> of Indonesia
> Sukarno/Hatta

As a coda, the rebab, gendèr, gambang, and suling play a soft postlude,
Pathetan Pélog Lima, while the narrator concludes with the following:
"This musical presentation ends with the blessing: May the Republic of
Indonesia be forever victorious, peaceful, mighty, long lived and free from
all danger."[40]

The fervor and idealism of a newly independent state radiate throughout *Jaya Manggala Gita*. The establishment of the Republic of Indonesia
is portrayed as an extension of the kingdoms of Mataram and Majapahit.
Undoubtedly it still remains so in the eyes of many Javanese, much to the
discomfort and dismay of the Sumatrans, Balinese, Makassarese, Banjarese,
and others. *Jaya Manggala Gita* is a summation of the past history of the

Gendhing Sakura

Fig. 11.

association of gamelan and monarchies, and relates that past to the present. While the semantic content of the composition is heavy with Javanese values and traditional attitudes, structurally it is very untraditional. From the perspective of an oral tradition, the work is quite radical. At certain points one feels the firm structural rules of the Javanese oral tradition breaking apart. For untold centuries the absolute tyranny of the quadratic, or multiples of four-beat, structural units has gone unchallenged. Yet in this composition there are two pieces, *Gendhing Sakura* in three-four meter and *Lagu Mars Jepang* in six-eight meter, which break this unwritten law. The attempt at imitation of Japanese music in these examples might be considered as a kind of parody and therefore not relevant to the tradition

```
                          P                    N
slènthem:   .  5  3  2  3  2  5  i̇  6  .  3  5
                          ─────────────────────────

                          P                    N
            .  5  3  2  3  2  .  1  1  .  2  1
                          ─────────────────────────

                          P                    N
            .  2  2  1  6  5  6  5  i̇  6  5  2
song:       .  .  2  .  2  5  .  6  i̇  .  5  2
               Dai Nippon,      iku kanca,

                          P
            1  3  2  1  3  2  .  5  i̇  .  6  ⑤
            .  3  2  .  .  5  .  5  i̇  .  6  5
               kanca,    Du-taning    suksma,

                          P                    N
            .  1  1  .  2  1  6  5  3  .  1  2
            .  .  1  .  1  1  .  1  1  6̣  3  2
               Ga-wé    ra-ha-yu      ning Nusa

                          P                    N
            6  6  .  i̇  5  6  i̇  5  2  5  i̇  6
            .  .  6  .  6  6  i̇  5  2  5  i̇  6
               Sa' ja-gad    Asia    Raya

                          P                    N
            i̇  .  5  .  6  i̇  2  5  3  2  3  2
            .  .  6  .  6  i̇  .  5  3  2  3  2
               Mar-ma  a-yo    si-ya-ga

                          P
            .  .  5  5  1  3  2  1  6  5  3  ⑤
            .  5  5  .  3  2  3  1  6̣  1  6̣  5̣
               Amban-tu  sa'  liring    karyo.
```

as a whole. However, other compositions by the same composer that contain triple meters demonstrate that the innovation is not used only as an imitative device. Triple meters break one of the most elemental structural rules of gamelan music, the rule of subdividing the gong cycle binarily.

The same could be said of the overall form of the composition. *Jaya Manggala Gita* is a series of small compositions that are presented as a whole, a unit, which has a definite beginning and which progresses until the conclusion is reached. Traditional dramatic and musical arts are cyclic. A gamelan piece can be repeated any number of times and need not always end with the last gong section. Traditional dramatic forms using the Javanese/Hindu epics as basic story material may pick up the tale at any point and drop it again at any other point.[41] Music, like literature, follows endless cycles, having no clear beginnings or endings.

Jaya Manggala Gita could not conceivably begin or end anywhere else than it does, and to repeat it several times would be quite meaningless. It is presented as a work of art composed before, not during, the performance, demanding the close attention of the listener and heard only once. It compels the focus of the listener in a way traditional Javanese music never does.[42] Normally, long programs are assembled as beads are strung, by adding one item to another. Good taste will produce a more pleasing string than insensitivity to mood and mode but, nevertheless, it is always possible to remove from, or add to, or substitute within the string. In *Jaya Manggala Gita*, however, each piece has its place in a fixed temporal sequence aimed toward a specific goal. This is a Western use of time in the arts rather than a Javanese one.

Another innovation is the self-conscious use of archaic gamelan styles for mood and effect. Within a purely oral tradition, all music is contemporary. While the roots of any piece may be ancient, all compositions are contemporary in style and in meaning. The archaic gamelan, Monggang, Corobalèn, and Kodok-Ngorek, do not represent musical styles familiar to those outside the court cities of Surakarta and Yogyakarta. They are played only rarely, at fixed ritual occasions. The resurrection and use of these sounds in a contemporary composition are another example of the kind of tampering with the tradition typical of modern gamelan composers. It is clear that Ki Wasitodipuro, while remaining one of Java's finest traditional musicians, thinks like a Western composer. The gamelan, the musical structure, the texture of the individual instruments are all tools for him to manipulate in a new way. He rearranges the framework, the syntax of the Javanese oral tradition, and creates something new and original. The striving toward originality, toward uniqueness, is one of the distinguishing marks of a Western composer. Were it not for the momentum of the oral tradition in Java, the tendency toward the emergence of the composer as distinct from the performer would be more pronounced. As it is, a new idea such as the use of archaic styles in modern compositions rather quickly becomes part of the public domain, and soon shows up in the works of other composers.

Jaya Manggala Gita is a very personal statement as well as a national one, and one that would not likely have been written by any other Javanese composer. It presupposes deep roots in the court traditions as well as an intellectual commitment to a modern state. On the most personal level, it can be viewed as a transfer of allegiance. *Jaya Manggala Gita* can be seen as a public pronouncement of a shift of loyalty by Ki Wasitodipuro from the dedication of his ancestors to the Javanese princes to his own service to the independent Republic of Indonesia. Any declaration of loyalty involves risk; this one perhaps no less than his ancestors' fidelity to a king who might be overthrown. Governments change too, and persons in favor with one are likely to be out of favor with another. *Jaya Manggala Gita* is the impressive herald of a great number of songs by Ki Wasitodipuro written in support of the various programs and slogans of the free Indonesian state. It also vividly illustrates the beginnings of a new approach toward gamelan composition, with the composer/performer no longer only a medium of transmission of traditional materials, but a self-conscious creator who organizes and focuses the musical materials of his tradition and expresses, if not uniquely himself, at least his interpretation of the events about him.

Of the many short political songs written by Ki Wasitodipuro since independence, most were forgotten as quickly as they were written. He was the principal songwriter for the Sukarno era, producing a song for every slogan. Most of them are undistinguished, written in the style of *dolanan*, children's songs. Some must even cause him acute embarrassment such as the song *Nekolim* (figure 12) written during the time of Sukarno's agitation against Malaysia known as "Confrontation." The English translation is as follows:

> Neocolonialism, obstructor of freedom,
> Your suspicious ways are many.
> We who experienced colonialism,
> Still our slavery goes on.
> Let's go, let's go, smash them all.
> Let's go, let's go, smash them all.
> Kill neocolonialism, attack imperialism.
> Crush to bits, the English project Malaysia.

One political commentator has indicated that the verbal attacks on Malaysia may have served to distract attention from economic distress at home as well as providing an outside enemy to promote inside unity. "Sukarno's fight against Malaysia was actually a fight against the 'imperialist devil' and equally a fight for forging the unity of the country. . . . The cry of Ganjang Malaysia fulfills the crying need of a people for whom independence has not meant material welfare, and who must therefore seek its meaning elsewhere."[43]

The verbal violence of *Nekolim* gives way to gentle teaching in *USDEK* (figure 13). This song refers to the program put forward in President Sukarno's Independence Day speech, his political manifesto (*Manipol-Manifesto Politik*), of 17 August 1959.[44] The English translation of *USDEK* is as follows:

> USDEK, USDEK, USDEK
> We all must be happy taking the road in building
>   our country.
> Older sister, U, what does it mean, older sister?

Nekolim
Sléndro Pathet Sanga

Buka celuk (vocal introduction)

. 5 5 5 . 6 1̇ 2̇ . 1̇ 6 5 . 3 6 5̂
Nekolim penghalang tujuan merdika,

. . . . 1 1 2 3 . 5 3 2 . 1 3 2̂
aneka warna carané curiga.

. . . . 5 5 6 1̇ . 2̇ 1̇ 6 2̇ 2̇ 2̇ 2̂̇
Kita kabeh ngalami penjajahan,

. . . . 5 5 6 1̇ . 2̇ 1̇ 6 2̇ 1̇ 6 5̂
nerusaké anané perbudakan.

. . 5 5 . . 5 5 . . 5 5 2̇ 1̇ 6 5̂
Ayo, ayo, ayo da diganyang.

. . 6 6 . . 6 6 . . 6 6 2̇ 2̇ 2̂̇
Ayo, ayo, ayo da diganyang.

1 2 3 5 5 5 5 . 1̇ 2̇ 6 5 5 5 5 ⌒
Kita ganyang nekolim, kita serang imperialis.

. . . . 5 6 1̇ 2̇ . 6 2̇ 1̇ 6 5 3 5̂
Hancur lebur proyèk Malésia Inggris.

SOURCE: Soeranto, *Lelagon Dolanan Populér* (Kediri: Toku Buku Marhaen, 1965), p. 31.

FIG. 12.

> Oh, little brother, it is a call to return to the
>   spirit of 1945.
> Older sister, S, what does it mean, older sister?
> It means we must possess a Socialist spirit.
> Older sister, D, what does it mean, older sister?
> Older sister, E, what does it mean, older sister?
> Older sister, K, what does it mean, older sister?
> I must understand, I must understand.
> Not like that, not like this.
> The heart is content when one understands.
> Let's go, let's go.
> Let's go to where?
> Let's take the path, under the guidance that we all
>   understand.

The examples so far give the impression that all songs of this genre are pure sloganizing with very little reference outside of themselves. The next two songs reflect the more humanitarian concerns of the composer. *Kuwi Apa Kuwi* (figure 14) refers to corruption. Initiated by economic need and sanctified by tradition, corruption is an aspect of life in Java that darkens the spirit of all Javanese. The English translation of *Kuwi Apa Kuwi* is as follows:

> That thing, what's that, a jasmine flower?
> Not, I pray, corruption.
> Because if we have corruption
>   it is our country that loses.
> What is that thing?
> Surely not, no, not that.
>
> That thing, what's that, a new flowering tree?
> I pray the people become united
> Because if they are united,
>   the country can go forward.
> What's that thing?
> Surely, no, not corruption.

The song *Lancaran Keluarga Berencana*, "Family Planning," (figure 15) addresses itself to the most serious, perhaps insoluble, of Java's problems, overpopulation. The English translation of *Lancaran Keluarga Berencana* is as follows:

> Remember, please remember, friends who are living now,
> So that we don't make difficulties for our descendants,
> Society must be ordered and in harmony,
> Also, the many children of our era, it is best, it is necessary,
>   must be limited according to one's salary.

USDEK
Sléndro Pathet Manyura

Ki Wasitodipuro

Us-dek Us-dek Us-dek Ki-ta ka-beh kudu gelem anglako-ni sa-ka-běhing tindak kang wus kapacak nagari. Yu mbak-yu, "U", a-pa te-ge-sé mbak-yu? o Da-di, un-dang undang da-sar ba-li ma-rang em-pat li-ma. Yu mbakyu, "S", a-pa te-ge-sé mbakyu? Ki-ta ku-du an-dar be-ni sosialis jiwa. Yu mbakyu, "D", a-pa te-ge-sé mbakyu? Yu mbakyu, "E", a-pa te-ge-sé mbakyu? Yu mbakyu, "K", a-pa te-ge-sé mbakyu? A-ku ku-du nger-ti, a-ku ku-du nger-ti. Ho-rak ho-rak ngo-no ho-rak ho-rak ngené. Yen wis nger-ti bisa ma-remaké a-ti. A-yo yo, A-yo, A-yo yo, A-yo, A-yo menyang endi? A-yo menyang endi anglakoni dawuhé kang pada ngerti.

FIG. 13.

Buka celuk: (vocal introduction)

i 2̇ i 6 i 2̇ i 6 . . i 3̇ . . . .
  Usdek   Usdek   Usdek

. . . . 3 5 6 i 6 2̇ 6 5 3 5 6 i
          Kita kabeh kudu gelem anglakoni

. . 3̇ 2̇ 6 5 3 6 2̇ i 2̇ 3̇ 2̇ i 2̇i̅ 6
      sakabèhing tindak kang wus kapacak nagari.

3̇ 2̇ 3̇ . 6 . 6 i 2̇ i 2̇ 6 i . . .
Yu mbakyu, "U", apa tegesé mbakyu?

. . . . . 6 5 3 . . 3 5 3 5 6 i
          Dadi,   undang undang dasar

. 6 . 2̇ . 6 . 3̇ . . 2̇ 2̇ 3̇ 2̇ i 2̇
  bali   marang   empat lima.

3̇ 2̇ 3̇ . 6 . . 6 i 2̇ i 2̇ 6 i . .
Yu mbakyu, "S",   apa tegesé mbakyu?

6 6 6 6 6 6 3 5 6 2̇ i 2̇ 3̇ 5 23̅ 16̅
Kita kudu andar beni sosialis   jiwa.

3̇ 2̇ 3̇ . 6 . . 6 i 2̇ i 2̇ 6 i . .
Yu mbakyu, "D",   apa tegesé mbakyu?

3̇ 2̇ 3̇ . 6 . . 6 i 2̇ i 2̇ 6 i . .
Yu mbakyu "E",   apa tegesé mbakyu?

3̇ 2̇ 3̇ . 6 . . 6 i 2̇ i 2̇ 6 i . .
Yu mbakyu, "K",   apa tegesé mbakyu?

. . 3̇ 2̇ 6 5 3 6 . . 2 3 2 1 3 6̣
    Aku kudu ngerti,   aku kudu ngerti.

. . 6̣ 1 6̣ 1 3 2 . . 6 i 6 i 3̇ 2̇
    Horak horak ngono,   horak horak ngené.

. 3̇ . 3̇ . i . 2̇ 6 2̇ 6 3 6 5 3 2
  Yen wis ngerti   bisa maremaké ati.

. . 6̣ 1 2 . 1 2 . . 6 i 2̇ . i 2̇
    Ayo yo, Ayo,   Ayo yo,   Ayo,

. . 6̣ 1 2 3 5 3 . . 6 i 2̇ 3̇ 5̇ 3̇
    Ayo menyang endi?   Ayo menyang endi

. 3̇ . 3̇ . i . 2̇ 6 2̇ 6 3̇ 2̇ 3̇ i 2̇
  anglakoni   dawuhé kang pada ngerti.

SOURCE: Soeranto, *Lelagon Dolanan Populér*, p. 10.

Kuwi Apa Kuwi
Pélog Pathet Barang

Fig. 14.

> In order that stability be reached, each family must be thankful and
>   feel content with two, at the very most, three.
> We must be steadfast, all the people believing in God and
>   abiding by Pancasila.
> So that it may be realized, the happiness and prosperity of
>   the Indonesian people.

The message of these songs—nationalism, modernization, social welfare—is a new message. Often, the musical form which conveys this message contains new elements, indirectly reinforcing and reflecting the semantic content of the songs.

The trend toward incorporating other gamelan styles into Central Javanese gamelan composition is one of the most prominent traits found

                                                                    G
Buka: 3 . 2 . 3 . 2 . 7 . 6
Irama lancar   N   P   N   P   N   P
                   . 2 . 3 . 2 . 3 . 2 . 3 . 6 . 7
                   . 3 . 2 . 3 . 2 . 3 . 2 . 7 . 6

Irama tanggung   . 2 . 3 . 2 . 3 . 6 . 3 . 2 . 7
Gérong   ⎰   . . 2̇ 3̇ .6̅ 7 2̇ 3̇ 2̇ 3̇ 7 .6̅ .7̅ 3 2 7̣
            ⎱   Kuwi, apa   kuwi é   kembang   melati?

                   . 5 . 6 . 7 . 5 . 2 . 7 . 5 . 6
                   . . 5 6 6 6 7 5 6 . 2 7̣ .3̅ 2 7̣ 6̣
                      Ya, tak puja puji.   Aja da   korupsi.

                   . 2 . 3 . 2 . 3 . 6 . 3 . 2 . 7
                   . . 2 3 .2̅ 6 5 3 . . 6 7 .6̅ 5̅6̅ 3̅2̅ 7̣
                      Marga yèn korupsi negarané rugi.

                   . 5 . 6 . 7 . 5 . 2 . 7 . 5 . 6
                   . . 5 6 6 . 7 5 6 .6̣̅ 7̅2̣̇ 3 .3̅ 2̅3̅ 2̅7̣̅ 6̣
                      Pripun kang niku iyak ora, ora, ora ngono.

              Kuwi, apa kuwi
              E kembangé waru?
              Ya, tak puja puji.
              Rakyaté bersatu.
              Marga yèn bersatu,
              Negarané maju.
              Pripun kang niku
              Iyak ora, ora, ora ngono.

SOURCE: Sukanto Sastrodarsono, *Tuntunan Nabuh Gamelan* (Surakarta: Yayasan Lektur Kesenian/Kebudayaan Nasional "Kemudawati," 1960), p. 34.

in modern compositions. This is part of a general tendency toward expanding the musical language of the gamelan and is related to the ideal of finding or developing a pan-Indonesian music. The syncretized elements are limited. Almost all are either Sundanese or Balinese. Cumulatively they represent a significant amount of new material absorbed into Central Javanese gamelan style.

The song *Modernisasi Désa*, "Village Modernization," (figure 16) illustrates the incorporation of Balinese elements into a Javanese song. *Modernisasi Désa*, unlike many of the propaganda songs, is widely known and has maintained its popularity over a number of years. It is frequently heard on the radio and often sung by the clowns in the various Javanese theatrical forms. Underlining and underlying the musical structure is a drum rhythm based on Balinese-style drumming: a nervous, driving counterpoint adding great dynamism to the overall effect of the piece. The English translation of *Modernisasi Désa* is as follows:

Lancaran Keluarga Berencana
Pélog Pathet Barang

Fig. 15.

Hey, friends, listen to me.
Look now, friends,
Work quickly.
For a long time our villages have been studied.
    [The implication is that they were studied by scholars interested in
        their backwardness.]
Now that is all changed.
Village modernization, village development.
That means, my friends, we must all take part
    in matters of politics, economics, society and culture, making them our
    own concerns, until finally unemployment is abolished.
Village modernization!
Mental modernization!
Village modernization all over Indonesia.

The frenetic Balinese drumming as a backdrop for the whole piece forces the song into a very fast tempo. The generally slower tempos of Javanese pieces and the generally faster tempos of Balinese pieces constitute one of the most obvious differences between the two gamelan styles, well known to the Javanese and Balinese musicians themselves. Tempo differences are usually the first to be parodied when Javanese or Balinese musicians make fun of each other.

Another innovation in this composition is a new-style kempul part. One of the traditional functions of the kempul is to subdivide the kenong phrase, as shown in the following diagram:

Buka bonang: .   6   .   7   .   6   .   7   2   6   3   2   6   .   6   ⊙
                 N   P   N   P   N   P

Umpak: .   2   .   7   6   7   6   7   .   .   3   5   6   7   6 $\widehat{7}$
          .   3   .   2   3   2   3   2   .   .   5   6   7   5   7 $\widehat{6}$
          .   2   .   7   2   7   2   7   6   5   6   5   6   2   5 $\widehat{3}$
          .   2   .   3   2   3   5   6   .   .   2   7   3   2   7 $\widehat{6}$
                   Wirama tamban setitik diterusaké swara bebarengan

Balungan: .   2   .   3   .   2   .   3   .   6   .   5   .   6   . $\widehat{7}$
Gérong   .   . $\dot{2}$ $\dot{3}$ $\dot{2}$ 7   6 $\dot{3}$ 6   6   3   5   6 $\dot{3}$ $\dot{2}$ 7
          Éling dipun éling   kanca wong urip puniki,

          .   3   .   2   .   5   .   3   .   7   .   2   .   7   . $\widehat{6}$
          .   . $\dot{3}$ $\dot{2}$ 6   5   2   3   5   6   7 $\dot{2}$ $\dot{3}$ 5   7   6
          mrih tan   répot pemburiné, bebrayan diatur,

          .   7   .   5   .   2   .   3   .   2   .   3   .   2   . $\widehat{7}$
          .   .   7   5   6   2   5   3   2   3   6   7   6 $\dot{3}$ $\dot{2}$ 7
          rukun   sakaroné   kehing putra   neki,

          .   5   .   3   .   5   .   3   .   2   .   3   .   5   . $\widehat{6}$
          .   7   2   3 $\overline{.6}$ 6 $\overline{75}$ 3   .   . $\dot{3}$ $\dot{2}$ $\overline{.3}$ $\dot{2}$ $\overline{\dot{2}3}$ 6
          beciké,   mestiné,   kudu   diwatesi.

          .   2   .   7   .   6   .   7   .   3   .   5   .   6   . $\widehat{7}$
          .   .   7   7   .   .   6   7   .   . $\dot{2}$ $\dot{3}$ 5   6   7
          Manut   kehing   pengasilané

          .   3   .   5   .   7   .   6   .   7   .   5   .   2   . $\widehat{3}$
          .   .   3   5   6   7 $\overline{\dot{2}3}$ 6   .   .   7   5   6   2   5   3
          mrih tentrem   pinanggin,   sakula wargané,

          .   5   .   5   .   3   .   5   .   6   .   7   .   6   . $\widehat{5}$
          .   5   5   . $\dot{2}$ 7   6   5   .   . $\dot{2}$ $\dot{3}$ $\dot{2}$ 7 $\overline{6\dot{3}}$ 5
          sukur cukup   loro,   keh akehé   telu,

          .   2   .   3   .   5   .   3   .   5   .   6   .   7   . $\widehat{6}$
   $\overline{.\dot{2}}$ $\dot{2}$ $\dot{2}$ $\dot{2}$ $\dot{2}$ $\dot{2}$ $\dot{5}$ $\dot{3}$ $\dot{2}$ 7   3   5   6   7   5   6
          netepi anggoné   dadi,   anggotaning masyarakat

          .   3   .   2   .   3   .   2   .   3   .   5   .   6   . $\widehat{5}$
   $\overline{.\dot{2}}$ $\dot{2}$ $\dot{2}$.   5   6   7 $\dot{2}$ 7 $\dot{3}$ 7 $\dot{2}$ 7   6   7   5
          bertuhan lan bermoral   pancasila,   mahanani

          .   7   .   5   .   6   .   7   .   6   .   5   .   3   .   ②
          .   6   6   .   7   5   6   7   6   5   3   2   1 $\overline{23}$ $\overline{53}$ 2
          kerta raharjaning bangsa   kita   Indonesia.

SOURCE: From the magazine *Mekar Sari*. vol. 14, no. 7 (July 1970), p. 20.

Modernisasi Désa
Pélog Pathet Nem

FIG. 16.

Modernisasi Désa
Pélog Pathet Nem

Buka kendhang: . . 6 . . . . . 5 . . . $\overline{55}$ $\overline{65}$ $\overline{42}$ ①

	.P	N	P	N	.P	N	P	N	.P	N	P	N	.P	N	P	N
Umpak: ⎡ .Ṭ	.	1	6	$\overline{.6}$	.	.	6	1	.Ṭ	.	1	6	$\overline{.6}$	.	6	②
.2	.	2	6	$\overline{.6}$	.	6	4	$\overline{.4}$	.	4	6	$\overline{55}$	$\overline{65}$	$\overline{42}$	① ⎤

.P N P N .P N P ⁿS .P N P N .P N P N etc.

saron: . 5 . 6 . 1 . 2 . 3 . 1 . 2 . ⑥
gérong ⎰   5 6 5 2̇ . . 3 1̇ 2̇ 5 1̇ 6
       ⎱   Ayo, ayo   kanca   tilingena.

       . 5 . 4 . 6 . 5 . 3 . 1 . 2 . ③
              5 4 2 4 6 5 . . 3 6 5 1 2 3
              Kanca   piyarsakna,   enggal katindakna.

       . 6 . 5 . 6 . 1 . 3 . 1 . 2 . ⑥
              3 5 6 1̇ . . 6 2̇ 1̇ 5 1̇ 6
              desaku   wiwit kuna   wis   mesti

       . 5 . 4 . 6 . 5 . 6 . 3 . 2 . ①
              5 4 2 4 6 5 . 1̇ . 5 6 3 2 1
              tansah   dadi obyèk, ning   saiki   ganti.

       . . . $\overline{.6}$ $\overline{.5}$ $\overline{.4}$ $\overline{56}$ 1̇ . 5 . 3 . 2 . ①
                        1̇ . . 2̇ 3 5 3 2̇ 1̇
                        Modernisasi   désa,

       . 3 . 5 . 7 . 6 . 5 . 4 . 6 . ⑤
              2 6 5 3 5 7 6 . . 5 4 2 4 6 5
              pembangunan   désa.   Ya, tegesé kuwi,

       . 3 . 6 . 3 . 5 . 3 . 5 . 6 . ①
              3 . . 3 6 3 5 3 6 3 5 3 5 6 1̇
              ca,   kudu   dadi   subyèk mèlu   nemtokaké

       . 2 . 3 . 2 . 1 . 2 . 6 . 4 . ⑤
              2̇ . . 2̇ 3 2̇ 1̇ 6 5 7 6 5 4 6 5
              ing bab   politik,   ékonomi   lan   sosial,

       . 3 . 2 . 1 . 6 . 5 . 6 . 1 . ②
              3 . . 3 2 1 6̣ 3 2 1 6̣ 6̣ 1 3 2
              lan   kabudayan,   duwé   oto aktivitas,

       . 4 . 5 . 6 . 1 . 6 . 3 . 2 . ①
              4 . . 4 5 6 1̇ 2̇ 1̇ 6 5 $\overline{65}$ 3 2 1
              mrih   kang   tundoné   kanggo brantas   pengangguran.

       . 1 . $\underline{1}$. 1 . 3 . 1 . $\underline{1}$. 1 . ③
       . 1̇ .1̇ 1̇ 1̇ . 3̇ 3̇ . 1̇ .1̇ 1̇ 1̇ 1̇ 3̇ 3̇
       Modernisasi   désa,   modernisasi   mental,

       . 2 . 2 . 2 . 6 . 5 . 3 . 2 . ①
       2̇ .2̇ 2̇ 2̇ 3̇ 2̇ 1̇ 6 . 5 6 5 3̇ 2̇ 1̇
       Modernisasi   désa   sa' Indonesia.

SOURCE: From the book *Gérong* compiled by Ki Wasitodipuro for teaching at RRI, Radio Republic Indonesia, Yogyakarta.

```
(P)   N   P   N   P   N   P   N
_____   _____   _____   _____
  .   .   .   .   .   .   .   .   .
```

N = kenong   —— = kenong phrase
P = kempul   . = regular pulse

The relationship of the kempul to the kenong phrase in *Modernisasi Désa* is:

```
      N         N         N         N
   P      P          P         P
_____ _____ _____ _____
   .   .   .   .   .   .   .   .   .
```

The traditional relationship of the kempul to the gong phrase is:

```
          P         P         P    G
   .   .   .   .   .   .   .   .
_____
```

G = gong   —— = gong phrase

In this composition, the relationship of kempul to gong phrase (siyem gong in this case) is:

```
          P                   P         G
   .   .   .   .   .   .   .   .
_____   _____   _____
   3    +    3    +    2
```

or if gong is interpreted as beat one:

```
                              3    +
            3    +    2
```

The additive three + three + two rhythm is not typically Javanese. India might be a possible source for this borrowing. However, Indian music has had little impact on Java. The only Javanese who listen frequently to Indian popular music are the *santri* who feel that it is more religious than is gamelan music because it is closer to Arabic (Islamic) music. Certain Near Eastern/Indian musical styles are heard at Moslem religious festivals. Even though the gulf between the *santri* and those involved in gamelan traditions is great, Indian/Arabic rhythmic patterns occasionally occur in other modern gamelan compositions.[45] There is the possibility that this innovation is based upon Indian/Arabic rhythms.

A more likely alternative is that this kempul pattern is based on rhythmic patterns of South American dance forms. These are among the few Western musical styles that are at all well known in Java. The rumba, the samba, and the tango enjoyed a long period of popularity. They were played by dance orchestras during colonial times and continue to be heard today on the radio. In a composition by Ki Nartosabdho, *Ayo Praon*, the composer indicates that the kempul and kenong should be played as in a samba (kempul-kenong gantos, samba).[46] Another composition by Ki Nartosabdho employs maracas.[47]

More interesting than the ancestry of this rhythmic pattern is the assignment of a new function to the kempul, that of providing rhythmic contrast to the basic four-square rhythms of the gamelan. Transforming the kempul into a rhythmic instrument obliterates one of the traditional roles of the kempul as a primary subdivider of the gong phrase and as a marker of an important point of convergence of different melodic lines.[48] The additive three + three + two pattern cannot possibly mark regular points of coincidences. In a traditional piece the points of convergence or coincidence are derived by *division* of the unit: one (gong phrase) becomes two (kenong phrase) becomes four (kempul phrase) becomes eight (kethuk phrase), and so on. This regularity and order in turn reflects the orderly universe. Traditional gamelan music both sanctioned and was sanctioned by heaven, resulting in a musical conservatism manifested by the rigid adherence to four-beat units, which may be either multiplied or subdivided. The introduction of an additive rhythm on an instrument of high structural importance in gamelan music is more than just an interesting oddity. It is a musical statement that the old sanctions are no longer in operation, that gamelan music is just like any other music of the world, that it expresses men, not gods, and that one man may alter a musical relationship that has remained fixed for a thousand years or more.

The rhythmic kempul part in *Modernisasi Désa* is previewed in the *umpak* section of the piece by the saron (figure 16, measure 16).

kempul/siyem: P   P   S   P   P   S
saron: 1   1   6   6   6   1

$$\overline{(3 \; + \; 3 \; + \; 2)} \; + \; (\; 3 \; + \; 3 \; + \; 2)$$

Syncopated figures such as this are common in the works of Ki Wasito-dipuro and other composers as well. The concept of syncopation is new in Java and represents another break with traditional modes of musical expression. There is a great deal of "off-beat" playing in traditional Javanese music, but it is of a special kind. The "off-beat" pattern is regular and consistent and played on one instrument.

Thus a bonang panerus part might look like this:

bonang panerus: 5   5   6   6   5   5   3   3
basic pulse:

At the same time, the bonang barung, whose rhythm coincides with the regular points of convergence of the formal structure, plays the following:

bonang barung: 5   5   6   6   5   5   3   3
basic pulse: .   .   .   .

Put together, the parts look like this:

bonang panerus: 5   5   6   6   5   5   3   3
bonang barung: 5   5   6   6   5   5   3   3
basic pulse: .   .   .   .

The end result does not sound "off-beat," but is perceived as a division of the basic pulse into four equal units, divided between two instruments playing interlocking parts.

The syncopations in *Modernisasi Désa* do not follow the traditional pattern. Most important is the fact that the "on-beats" and "off-beats" are not divided between two instruments. Within the part of a single instrument, rests may occur at points where a stress is expected, and a stressed note may be placed where a rest is expected. The music is in effect syncopated in a way that traditional gamelan music is not.

The rapid tempo, syncopation, the element of dynamism and restlessness in *Modernisasi Désa* can be found in many of the politically motivated songs of Ki Wasitodipuro. The whole musical structure of *Modernisasi Désa* underscores the fervent cry of the singers, "Village Modernization, Mental Modernization!"

The modern intellectual resistance to gamelan traditions, as distinct from the *santri* religious objections, is based on the feeling that gamelan music is "old-fashioned" and "feudal" and prevents the populace from developing new attitudes and progressing in the modern world. It is not hard to understand why traditional gamelan music conveys this impression, this ethos of acceptance, to members of the society. Ki Wasitodipuro understands too, and it is no surprise that young gamelan musicians are eager to play the fast-tempo, syncopated, new gamelan pieces, often to the disapproving grumbles of their elders. Somehow the faster tempos, the syncopations, better reflect the world of the young Javanese, who have lost their anchorage in the ancient Javanese mysticism and Hindu-Buddhist philosophy that sustained traditional gamelan forms.

Songwriting for political purposes did not end with the termination of the Sukarno era. Sukarno's government fell with the attempted Communist coup in 1965, and the army took over power under the leadership of General Suharto. While not so involved with symbol making as was Sukarno, the new government still needs the validation and legitimizing

Orde Baru
Pélog Pathet Barang

Fig. 17.

power that is to be derived from slogans. One of the new slogans is *Orde Baru*, "The New Order." There is also a song *Orde Baru* (figure 17).

The words, like those of *Modernisasi Désa*, are suitably vague for a song intended to arouse the emotions and to instill allegiance, and not to propagate specific actions.

> Go forward, go forward, go straight forward!
> Hey, young people, step forward!
> Move at a trot, fan enthusiasm,
> Attack all obstacles and obstructions to the New Order,
> Smash them to bits,
> Go forward for the sake of victory.

This song, unlike those previously discussed, does not use Javanese, the regional language of Java, but the national language, Bahasa Indonesia.

The saron part in this composition, unlike in *Modernisasi Désa*, is not in itself distinctive. The melodic contours and sequences are all possible within the traditional rules of *pathet*. (See Appendix 4.) Only the tempo is extra-ordinary, as the piece is played much faster than is usual in Javanese

```
                     N            N            N            N
        saron:   .  2  2  2  .  .  .  .  6  5  6  7  6  5  3  2̲
               ⎧ I  .  .  2̇  2̇  .  .  2̇  2̇  .  .  3̇  2̇  7  6  7  5
suara bersama  ⎨ II           5  5  .  .  5  5  .  6  5  2̇  3̇  2̇
               ⎩      Maju,  maju,  maju,  maju,  maju  terus  maju.

                 .  .  .  .  5  5  5  5  7  5  6  7  .  .  6  5̲
            I                7  2  3  5  6  7  .  6  2̇  7  6  5
            II  .  3̇  2̇  7  .  .  .  .  2̇  3  2̇  7  3  5  6  7
                     Hai para,  Hai para pemuda  melangkah  maju.

                 .  7  7  7  .  .  .  .  3  5  3  5  6  7  6  7̲
            I    .  .  7  6  5  .  7  6  5  .  3  5  6  7  2̇  7
            II  2̇  3̇  2̇  7  6  5  7  6  .  .  3  5  6  7  6  5
                     Ayo bergerak    berderap,   kobarkan  semangat.

                 7  7  .  .  7  7  .  .  7  7  .  .  6  5  7  6̲
            I                3  5  6  7  .  3̇  .  2̇  .  7  .  6
            II  6  7  .  2̇  7  6  5  6  .  .  7  5  6  5  3  2
                     gempur      segala      rintangan

                 .  .  2  2  .  .  2  2  .  .  7  5  6  5  3  5̲
            I    .  6  7  5  6  5  3  2  .  .  2̇  3̇  2̇  7  6  5
            II  .  2  2  2  3  5  6  5  .  .  6  7  6  5  3  6
                     Penghalang orde baru      hancur habis musna.

                 .  2  3  5  .  2  3  5  .  2  3  5  .  .  .  ②
            I    .  .  6  7  .  .  2̇  7  .  .  2̇  7  6  5  4  5
            II  7  6  5  .  2  3  5  .  7  7  .  5  6  5  3  2
                     Maju, maju, terus demi      kejajaan.
```

gamelan pieces. The gendèr, playing the vocal melody with a hard mallet, is one of the innovations found repeatedly in modern compositions. Initially, this is a Balinese borrowing and gives some of the metallic percussive flavor of the Balinese gamelan to the Javanese gamelan. More important is the fact that this use of the gendèr stresses *one* line of the whole polyphonic structure out of proportion to any other. By eliminating one of the contrapuntal lines and reinforcing one of the others, the texture comes close to a Western melody and accompaniment. Thus, while the texture suggests the Balinese gamelan, structurally the innovation reflects Western influence. As such it is part of a generalized trend toward adoption of some of the techniques of Western music, examined in the next chapter.

All of the songs discussed above and the many more like them indicate an attitude of social responsibility on the part of their composer, Ki Wasitodipuro. The traditional *pujangga* had a deep moral/religious obligation to support his overlord. The transference of this concept to the state of Indonesia was facilitated by the fact that Sukarno often acted in the manner of a traditional Javanese king. Old Javanese traditions informed the thought and behavior of both Sukarno and Ki Wasitodipuro and forged the link between them.

5
Western Influence in Gamelan Music

Western ideas and Western technology have become influential in Java over the last three hundred years. As a nation, Indonesia is fully committed to the ideals of modern agriculture, improved harbors, railroads, trucking and bus systems, European governmental bureaucracy, a large standing army, and general elections. Most Javanese will say that advancement and status should be the result of talent and effort, not birth. Most of them articulate a desire for social mobility and hope that their children will be better educated than they are. Being progressive and modern, being concerned with the development and improvement of the country, being involved in the political concerns of the day are inextricably linked with an image of Western man. Nationalism itself is, in some respects, a Western concept.

> Many Indonesian students associated readily with their Dutch co-students in Holland ... they were strengthened in their nationalist convictions by their European experience. In those days (before 1941) Europe was the scene of national revivals in many countries. The liberation of Poland by Pilsudski and others, of Czechoslovakia by Masaryk, of Finland and the Baltic states, and the war waged by the Irish Sinn Fein against British rule, stirred the feelings of the younger generation in nearly every country of Europe as well as the colonial areas.[1]

Underlying all conscious innovation, in music or any other area, is the unspoken assumption that experimentation is legitimate, even praiseworthy. In contradiction to the expressed desire for modernization, traditional Javanese society, and to some extent present-day Javanese society, does not value experimentation. Any new program in Java will encounter opposition, or, rather, passive resistance. The disappointing results of high-minded programs such as the miracle-rice program only tend to confirm the deep-seated feeling that any new program will not be better than the old way and will very likely be worse. The reluctance to attempt innovation, specifically musical innovation, is illustrated by the results of a contest held in the 1930s to judge new gamelan compositions. The criterion of originality had to be abandoned as all the compositions submitted seemed based on traditional pieces.[2] For certain segments of the population, this traditionally conservative position is changing. Large numbers of Western-trained Javanese in high-level positions in government, education, business, communications, and the arts have lent a certain authority to the concept of experimentation.

While Ki Wasitodipuro and Ki Nartosabdho are in background and behavior traditional Javanese, both of them have frequent and sometimes intensive contact with the "new Indonesian," the Western-influenced elite in government, education, the army, and business. They have had ample opportunity to observe and absorb the new approaches and attitudes of this prestigious group. While not abandoning traditional Javanese values, a new set of motives and aspirations has been added to old values. These new values find reflections in their new music.

The profound impact of Western-derived musical notation on gamelan traditions was examined in chapter 2. Less ubiquitous, less radical, but more obvious influences are also to be found. These include purely musical influences whose sources are easy to identify, and the influence of Western attitudes, less easy to pinpoint.

Of the innumerable styles of Western music of the past and present, only a few have influenced gamelan music, and those few come from rather unexpected sources. One might assume that Western popular music, particularly rock, as it is the most widespread of Western styles, would have left its imprint on the music of the gamelan. Western popular music can be heard anywhere, anytime, mostly on the radio. However, there has been no assimilation of contemporary Western popular music with gamelan music. Perhaps the fact that Western popular music appeals to a select group within the society—upper-class urban youth who are largely divorced from old Javanese associations—has prevented any assimilation of Western rock styles to gamelan traditions. The Western styles that have been imitated and fairly successfully assimilated into gamelan traditions are what might be called light classical show tunes and Catholic liturgical styles. These styles appear in gamelan music only in vocal parts.

Gamelan music and gamelan formal structures are based on cyclic forms, subdivided in a mathematical way by many different instruments of fixed pitch. The vocal elements found in the gamelan include, in addition to actual voices, instruments that closely follow the vocal lines and, like voices, do not have fixed pitch and do not mathematically subdivide the musical phrases, that is, the fiddle (*rebab*) and the flute (*suling*). These "vocal" instruments and the parts for voices are additions to the gamelan and are of no structural importance. They may be eliminated without affecting the formal structure, unlike, for example, the kenong which can never be eliminated. With no prior evidence, it would be possible to predict that innovation would be most extensive in those aspects of gamelan music that are least important. Compared to the structural changes discussed in the previous chapter, changes in vocal style, while very noticeable, are relatively innocuous. However, what may develop as a significant innovation is the increased importance of the vocal element of the gamelan. Mere imitation of Western vocal style does not change anything fundamental in gamelan music. But to give the importance and primacy of a Western melody to the vocal part, and thereby reduce the gamelan to the role of an accompanying ensemble, would be a major innovation. There are certain indications that this is happening.

One of the most frequently encountered forms of vocal innovation is a technique called *suara bersama*. The term simply means "singing together" and is used to describe nontraditional styles of two- or three-part singing. Traditional Javanese two-part singing includes a male chorus, *gérong*, and a female soloist, *pesindhèn*, that sing with the gamelan. The differences between traditional Javanese two-part singing and *suara bersama* are illustrated in figures 17 through 20. *Ladrang Sri Rejeki* (figure 18) illustrates a Javanese way to create vocal polyphony, while *Aku Ngimpi* (figure 19), *Orde Baru* (figure 17), and *Kawiwitan Meditasi/Konsentrasi* (figure 20) represent Western ways of combining vocal lines. What are the conceptual differences between such different-looking notations?

In *Ladrang Sri Rejeki* the melodic line of the male chorus is a rather simple elaboration, basically syllabic, of the saron line. The melodic line of the female soloist appears unrelated to the tones of the saron or the male chorus. The apparent freedom of the female soloist is deceiving since she operates within rather rigid melodic and syntactic rules. Her phrase must end on the same pitch level as the kenong. She is always aiming toward the kenong tone, but in order to be stylistically correct she must arrive late. (See arrows on figure 18.) Thus the phrase of the female soloist overlaps with the next kenong phrase. Her phrases are based on a limited number of melodic formulas and consist of fixed poetic verses. If her poetic line consists of twelve syllables, she must begin her phrase after the fourth saron stroke of the kenong phrase. If her poetic line consists of eight syllables, as in *Ladrang Sri Rejeki*, she must begin after the fifth saron stroke of the kenong phrase (third measure of the Western notation, or as indicated by the underlining in the Kepatihan notation).

The third line of *Ladrang Sri Rejeki* contains an irregular *pesindhèn* phrase, the declaimed "hijo." A simple phrase or a single word is substituted for a poetic line when the saron line is "queer" or "uneven," *padang*,

Ladrang Sri Rejeki
Pélog Pathet Nem
Traditional

Fig. 18.

									N
(1st gongan only)	1	6	1	2	1	6	3	5
	1	6	1	2	1	6	3	5
	2	1	2	.	2	1	2	.
	2	3	2	1	6	5	6	1

ganjil,[3] containing rests at important structural points within the whole gong phrase. The irregular third line is underlined below:

Saron: 1 6 1 2   1 6 3 5
         1 6 1 2   1 6 3 5
         2 1 2 .   2 1 2 .
         2 3 2 1   6 5 6 1

"Hijo" is one of a number of words and phrases, called *isèn-isèn* or *abon-abon*, that may be used by the female vocalist when the saron line is irregular. The melodic lines of the male chorus and the female soloist are not closely related at all. The style of the female soloist is often florid and melismatic, like the first phrase in the example, in contrast to the more regular, syllabic melody of the male chorus. Both the soloist and the chorus are singing formulaic melodies whose contours and positioning are part of the rules of the vocal tradition. The melodic contours of the male chorus are different from those of the female soloist and are not directly related to hers. The instrument of the gamelan that is of structural importance and is most closely related to the female soloist is the kenong. The instrument of the gamelan that is of structural importance and is most closely related to the male chorus is the saron. The concept of two simultaneous vocal lines related not to each other, but rather to two different instruments in the ensemble, is in striking contrast to Western practice.

The vocal style of *Aku Ngimpi* (figure 19), by Ki Nartosabdho, is based upon a different conceptual framework from that of *Ladrang Sri Rejeki*. Here the parts are not equally independent or equally melodic. The "tune" is the melodic line of the female soloist with the two choral parts in supportive roles. This example comes close to a melody with a harmonic structure beneath. The vocal parts are more closely related to each other than to any musical line outside of themselves and both are syllabic. The voice quality and vocal style of this song as sung under the direction of the composer has a hauntingly familiar quality. One hears the shade of Gertrude Lawrence in the light, girlish voice and the lilting phrases.[4] It is one of the accidents of history that recordings of European and American show tunes of the 1930s were popular in Central Java during the youth of the composer Ki Nartosabdho. This source of new material, however, is only one of many sources for an eclectic man like Ki Nartosabdho and should not be overstressed.[5] The English translation of *Aku Ngimpi* follows:

> What's that? Who's that?
> For a long time,—I'm surprised,
> —slender—yellow—
> waving—beckoning
> The door moves, the door creaks,
> Someone sweet comes near.
> The dream is broken.
> Ah, my disappointment subsides.

The use of a three-four meter (see also *Gendhing Sakura*, figure 11), while structurally a radical innovation, cannot be equated with a Western three-four meter. Even though this meter is a direct borrowing from the West, as it is notated by the composer, a gamelan-type formal structure has been superimposed on the foreign meter (see diagram below). The stress is placed at the end of the unit rather than at the beginning of the measure, as in Western music. Also, the three-beat groupings are arranged into larger units of four groups of three (P, N, P, N), and this larger unit is again grouped by fours into the whole gong unit. In addition, the gong unit is divided in a regular way by the kempul, P, and the kenong, N, as common in several gamelan gong structures. This superimposition of an indigenous metric structure on a foreign one attests to the power and viability of traditional musical concepts.[6]

kaé a-pa kuwi sapa, suwé su-wé, gawé ga-mun etc.

The song *Orde Baru* (figure 17) includes a contrapuntal vocal section. The two lines are conceived as two equal melodies, and follow Javanese tradition in this respect at least. But both lines relate more closely to each other, melodically and rhythmically, than do the melodies of the Javanese female soloist and male chorus.

Thematic development as practiced in Western classical traditions is not a Javanese way of handling musical materials. Gamelan music is based upon many sets of melodic formulas, which can be contracted, expanded, reordered, or varied, but not, as the term is used in Western music, developed. Gamelan compositions are not built upon the principle of taking one small amount of musical material and expressing it any number of different ways as in many Western compositions. Oral traditions cannot easily encompass this kind of fragmental thematic development, especially with two voices, because the technique presumes a sophisticated notational system.

In embryonic form, one finds this kind of treatment in *Orde Baru*. A small musical phrase forms the basis of the whole composition. (See the bracketed phrase in figure 17.) Sometimes inverted (measure nine, Voice II), sometimes fragmented (measure five, Voice I), sometimes augmented (measures seven and eight, Voice I), often repeated and tossed between the voices—the kernel melody is musically "played with" in a way that is uncharacteristic of traditional gamelan pieces.

Also unlike gamelan practice is the irregular rhythmic displacement of the kernel melody. In chapter 5, in connection with the song *Modernisasi Désa*, the gamelan technique of rigidly regular rhythmic displacement was described. In contrast, the rhythmic placement of the appearances of the kernel melody in *Orde Baru* is unpredictable. Within the measure it may appear in any position.

The treatment of melodic pattern found in *Orde Baru* does not illustrate

Aku Ngimpi
Pélog Pathet Nem

Fig. 19.

a Javanese use of pattern. However, it does illustrate a long established European way of handling melodic pattern, which was especially popular in the Middle Ages from the tenth through the fifteenth centuries.

The question arises, How is it that a medieval European compositional technique suddenly appears in the works of a twentieth-century Javanese composer?

The connecting link in this case is the Catholic Church. The fragmentation of basic melodic pattern and the rhythmic displacement of that pattern found in *Orde Baru* are consonant with the kind of counterpoint employed in the early history of liturgical counterpoint in the West and in the rhythmic patterns of Gregorian chant.

```
    Buka:  6   6 5 4 2     6 6 4 5   2 3 2 ①
                           N
  Irama I  2 1 2 3   5 3 2 1
           2 3 5 6   3 5 3 2
           1 2 4 5   1 6 4 5
           1 6 4 2   6 5 4̄2̄ ①
```

```
                Irama II                                          N
  slènthem:     .   1   5   6   5   3   .   1   5   6   2   1
  pesindhèn:    0̄1̄  2̄3̄  5  .5̄1̄  6̄5̄  3  .̄0  2̄3̄  5  .̄6  5̄6̄  i
  gérong I:     0   6   5   .   6   3   0   5   3   .   2̲   i
  gérong II:    .̄5  6̄5̄  5  .̄6  5   6  .̄6  5̄6̄  i  .̄6  1̄2̄  i
  (words of pesindhèn) Kaé apa    kuwi sapa   suwé suwé   gawé gumun

  slènthem:     .   6   5   6   3   2   .   2   2   3   1   2
  pesindhèn:    0̄2̄  i̲6̄  5  .̄3  5   6   0   2   2   3   1   2
  gérong I:     0   6   5   .   3   6   0   5   6   5   3   2
  gérong II:    .̄6  5   i  .̄6  3   2   .   6   6   i   6   6
                Lencir kuning narintingan ga-wé a-wé

  slènthem:     1   6   5   .   3   5   .̲  6̄5̄  6   .   5̄4̄  5
  pesindhèn:    0̄1̄  6   5̲  .̄1  2̄3̄  5  0̄2̄  i   6  .̄5  4̄6̄  5
  gérong I:     0   2   2   .   3   5   0   6   4   .   6   5
  gérong II:    .̄5  3   2  .̄2  3   5  .̄2  6   4  .̄6  4̄2̄  5
                Wong manis          tika        mréné

  slènthem:     .   1   6   .   4   2   .   6   5   4   2   ①
  pesindhèn:    0   1   6   .   4   2   .   6̄4̄  5  .̄3  2̄3̄  1
  gérong I:     .   5   6   .   4   2   5̲   6   1   2   3   1
  gérong II:    .   1   6   .   4   2   .   2̄2̄  3  .̄5  2̄3̄  1
                jebul      ngimpi    gelaku     kepati
```

The Catholic Mass would seem to be an unlikely source of inspiration for a court musician unless one is aware of the special role of the Catholic Church in Yogyakarta. In the heartland of traditional Java, the Catholic Church has provided a catalyst for change and innovation and produced writers and artists far out of proportion to its representation in the whole society. The Catholic Church in Yogyakarta and in Semarang has held gamelan masses long enough for there to have developed a body of gamelan pieces in traditional style for church use.[7] While Ki Wasito-dipuro is not Catholic, he has written many compositions on a Christian theme, including the music for two Christian dance-dramas, *Aleluyah* and *Kelahiran Kristus*, "The Birth of Christ."

The strict parallelism found in *Kawiwitan Meditasi/Konsentrasi*, (figure 20) also derives its inspiration from liturgical sources. *Kawiwitan Meditasi/ Konsentrasi* is the most radical of the three examples showing Western influence in gamelan music because it is conceived harmonically. The three parts are locked together rhythmically, moving as a block. The predominance of parallel fourths gives this piece a medieval, organum-like quality.

Kawiwitan Meditasi/Konsentrasi
Pélog Pathet Nem

gérong I:	5 .6̄ 1 .2̄ 6 5 . . . . .1̄ 3 .1̄ 2 .1̄ 3 .1̄ 2 . 3 . .
gérong II:	3 .5̄ 6 .1̄ 6̄5̄3̄ . . . . .3̄ 6 .3̄ 5 .3̄ 6 .3̄ 5 . 6 . .
gérong III:	1̇ .2̇̄ 3̇ .2̇̄ 2̇ 1̇ . . . . .6̄ 2̇ .6̄ 1̇ .6̄ 2̇ .6̄ 1̇ . 2̇ . .

Aum   Hong I la hing a wig na mas,

5 .3̄ 2 1 6 5 .6̄ 1 1 . . . .1̄ 3 .1̄ 2 .1̄ 3 .1̄ 2 . 3 . .
1 .6̄ 5 3 2 1 .2̄ 3 3 . . . .3̄ 6 .3̄ 5 .3̄ 6 .3̄ 5 . 6 . .
3 .2̄ 1 6 5 3 .5̄ 6 6 . . . .6̄ 2̇ .6̄ 1̇ .6̄ 2̇ .6̄ 1̇ . 2̇ . .

Tu na ma si dam,   muga mu ga raha yu wa,

.1̄ 6 .1̄ 2 .3̄ 5 3 2 .1̄ 3 2 . . . 1 3 2 .1̄ 2 .1̄ 2 .1̄ 2 3 .5̄ 5
.4̄ 2 .4̄ 5 .6̄ 1 6 5 .3̄ 6 5 . . . 3 6 5 .3̄ 5 .3̄ 5 .3̄ 5 6 .1̇ 1̇
.6̄ 5 .6̄ 1̇ .2̄ 3̇ 2̇ 1̇ .6̄ 2̇ 1̇ . . . 6 2 1 .6̄ 1̇ .6̄ 1̇ .6̄ 1̇ 2̇ .3̇̄ 3̇

Negarané, Bangsané   Rakyaté, Alam kalatida swasti

FIG. 20.

In addition to the parallel motion, the voice quality on the taped performance of *Kawiwitan Meditasi/Konsentrasi* given the author by Ki Wasitodipuro suggests Western influence.[8] Under the direction of the composer, the vocal quality of the singers is not the rather tense, nasalized quality of a Javanese chorus, but a more relaxed quality associated with Western choruses. The text of the composition, however, unites these Western elements with Javanese mystical traditions:

> In the name of God the merciful and powerful,
> Bless our country, our land, our people,
> Even in this difficult era.

This Old Javanese invocation to the gods is still used in Hindu Bali, in Java as a solo sung by the puppeteer in a shadow-puppet-play, and in rituals of the mystic sects combining elements of animism, Hinduism, Buddhism, Islam, and ancestor worship known as *kejawèn*, "Javaneseness," or *ilmu Jawi*, "Javanese science."[9]

The concert of new compositions, which opens with *Kawiwitan Meditasi/Konsentrasi*, continues with a gamelan piece called *Kagok Pangrawit* (figure 21). *Kagok* in the title of the composition means "deviating" or "strange." *Pangrawit* means "gamelan playing." Thus at one level of meaning the title refers to the nontraditional style of this composition. The title is open to another interpretation. It can also mean a deviant version of *Gendhing Pangrawit*, a very long traditional piece.[10] Many pieces in the gamelan repertoire have titles such as *Kagok x* or *Kagok y*, meaning that they are similar to some other piece of the same title. For example, there is a piece *Ladrang Sumingin* and another piece which is in some respects strikingly similar to it called *Ladrang Kagok Sumingin*.[11] Often, the model has disappeared and there is only a *kagok* version extant, such as *Ladrang Kagok Madura*.[12]

Those readers familiar with Javanese cipher notation will see that there is no structural or melodic relationship between *Gendhing Pangrawit* and *Kagok Pangrawit*, other than the fact that they are both in the same mode, Pélog Pathet Lima. It would be possible to say that no connection between the two was intended were it not for the fact that Ki Wasitodipuro is deeply rooted in old court traditions and is aware of the inevitable association of *Kagok Pangrawit* with *Gendhing Pangrawit*. By giving *Kagok Pangrawit* the same name as the *gendhing* the two pieces are juxtaposed in the mind of the listener, and a comparison of them becomes inevitable. *Kagok Pangrawit* is short, fast, and syncopated. *Gendhing Pangrawit* is long, slow, and rhythmically regular. *Kagok Pangrawit* is startling to hear, while *Gendhing Pangrawit* produces in the listener the state of mental repose called *iklas*, so valued in traditional Java. The driving drum rhythms that underlie *Kagok Pangrawit* and the syncopated saron line suggest a

Kagok Pangrawit
Pélog Pathet Lima

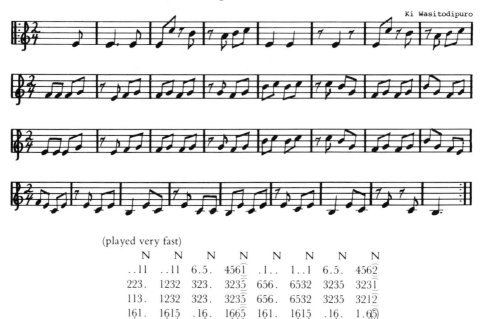

Ki Wasitodipuro

(played very fast)

	N	N	N	N	N	N	N	N
	..11	..11	6.5.	4561	.1..	1..1	6.5.	4562
	223.	1232	323.	3235	656.	6532	3235	3231
	113.	1232	323.	3235	656.	6532	3235	3212
	161.	1615	.16.	1665	161.	1615	.16.	1.65

Fig. 21.

nervous dynamism which, for good or ill, is in keeping with the values of modern Indonesia. It seems likely that this mental contrast was intentional on the part of the composer, and that in this way he has underlined the changing attitudes of Javanese society and the changing ethos of Javanese gamelan music.

On the taped version directed by the composer, nearly all the melodic instruments drop out the second time through, leaving the two gendèr playing alone with wooden mallets, Balinese style. The third time through, all the instruments join in again. This did not occur spontaneously; it was planned that way. The manipulation of orchestral sound, found again and again in new-style gamelan music, is a feature of Western music. In traditional gamelan music, the *way* an instrument is played depends on tradition; *when* it is played depends on the style of the piece and the *irama*, never on the whim of one man. No traditional gamelan director has the power of a Western composer or conductor. Likewise, the autonomy of any gamelan musician far exceeds that of his Western orchestral counterpart. A knowing smile is practically the strongest expression of disapproval one musician can direct toward another. The fact that Ki Wasitodipuro can silence half the gamelan at his will is the assumption of a kind of control common in Western traditions, but unknown in traditional Java.

The emergence of the composer, as one who creates a composition in full detail, directs the composition, and whose name is attached to the composition, is an innovation in Java leading away from an oral tradition. Both Ki Wasitodipuro and Ki Nartosabdho sometimes actually conduct the gamelan during rehearsals. Traditionally, musical direction is always covert, never overt. The leader gives aural signals with the rebab or the drum, with no accompanying physical gestures. The sight of a composer waving his hands over the heads of the gamelan players, albeit gently, presages a new relationship between the members of the gamelan. Some of the old communality has gone; a certain amount of individual autonomy has been surrendered.

6

Old Modes and New Music

Traditional Javanese musicians frequently charge modern composers with "destroying" *pathet*. *Pathet* is the Javanese system of classifying gamelan pieces, usually translated as "mode." In Central Java each scale system has three modes, as follows:

Sléndro	*Pélog*
Pathet Nem	Pathet Lima
Pathet Sanga	Pathet Nem
Pathet Manyura	Pathet Barang

The six modes differentiate compositions musically[1] and have different associations of mood and time of performance. *Wayang kulit*, shadow-puppet, performances are divided into three sections according to time and mode: 9:00 P.M. to 12:00 midnight, Sléndro Pathet Nem; 12:00 midnight to 3:00 A.M., Sléndro Pathet Sanga; 3:00 A.M. to 6:00 A.M., Sléndro Pathet Manyura. Pathet Nem is associated with youth, Pathet Sanga with maturity, and Pathet Manyura with old age. The temporal associations of the *pélog pathet* are: Pélog Pathet Lima, 8:00 A.M. to 12:00 noon; Pélog Pathet Nem, 12:00 noon to 3:00 P.M., and Pélog Pathet Barang, 3:00 P.M. to 8:00 P.M.[2] As the *pélog pathet* do not have strong associations with wayang performances as do the *sléndro pathet*, they likewise do not carry as strong temporal or sequential associations of progression from youth to old age. Pathet Lima, the first *pélog pathet*, is felt to be rather melancholy, very serious, and suitable for feelings of religious devotion. Pathet Lima has become the favored *pathet* for Christian gamelan pieces, perhaps because church services are held between 8:00 A.M. and 12:00 noon. The related aspects of time and mood are known in Java as the *rasa*, the "feeling" of a given *pathet*.

In addition to the associative meaning of time and mood, the various *pathet* also imply a range or a register. It is this aspect of *pathet* which links it to the *dhalang*, the puppeteer. The aspect of *pathet* as register is also the

meaning of many of the rather nebulous definitions of *pathet* given by
Javanese musicians such as "*pathet* is the place of a certain piece" or "*pathet*
is used to give place to a piece."[3] When accompanying the *dhalang* in a
shadow-puppet-play, the gamelan must accommodate itself to the voice
range of the *dhalang*. If the *dhalang* cannot sing a high pitch comfortably
the gamelan will shift down one note and go on as before. When a piece
is transposed in this way to accommodate a *dhalang*'s voice, some musicians
will say the *pathet* has changed, some will say it has not. As the all-night-
long *wayang kulit* performance progresses, the *dhalang*'s general pitch
range rises. This is most noticeable when the *dhalang* sings *suluk*, passages
of classical poetry, and when a few of the gamelan members play *pathetan*
(a brief free-rhythm interlude). The general register of the *pathetan* rises
from Pathetan Sléndro Nem to Pathetan Sléndro Sanga to Pathetan
Sléndro Manyura. The same is true of the *pathetan* in *pélog*. Pathetan Pélog
Lima rises to Pathetan Pélog Nem which rises to Pathetan Pélog Barang.
Another Javanese definition is based on this aspect of *pathet*, playing of
the *pathetan* and singing by the *dhalang*. "*Pathet* is the singing of the *dhalang*
accompanied by rebab, gendèr, gambang, suling, kendhang, and sometimes gong."[4] In instrumental pieces, the range aspect of *pathet* as associated with the temporal aspect of *pathet* is followed only loosely. Pieces
in Sléndro Pathet Manyura (theoretically high range) are often played in
the first section of the wayang night (Sléndro Pathet Nem, theoretically
low range). The emphasis on the range aspect of *pathet* is thus a singer's
definition and probably has its origin with the *dhalang*—singer, actor,
and priest of Javanese theater. The ranges of the *pathet* are variously given.
Pathet range according to Sulaiman Gitosaprodjo, is as follows:[5]

Sléndro Nem	2 3 5 6 1 2 3 5 6 1 2 3
Sléndro Sanga	5 6 1 2 3 5 6 1 2
Sléndro Manyura	3 5 6 1 2 3 5 6 1 2 3
Pélog Lima	1 2 3 4 5 6 1 2 3 4 5 6
Pélog Nem	3 4 5 6 1 2 3 4 5 6 1 2 3
Pélog Barang	2 3 4 5 6 7 2 3 4 5 6 7 2 3

Sléndro pathet range, according to Ki Hadjar Dewantara, is as follows:[6]

Sléndro Nem:	2 3 5 6 1
Sléndro Sanga:	5 6 1 2 3
Sléndro Manyura:	6 1 2 3 5

The explanations given above do not define *pathet*, but only describe
some of the associative meanings of the word.

Pathet has a musical meaning as well. Every music system has a formal syntax, a grammar, a means of restricting the musical material in order to give meaning to particular shapes, contours, and configurations. The *pathet* categories are the Javanese way of giving their music system structure, order, or grammar. This limitation of musical materials and the ordering of their use makes possible all the extramusical meanings, which have through time attached themselves to certain musical configurations. For all of these reasons, Javanese musicians feel that the *pathet* system is the very essence of Javanese music. Therefore, the charge that modern composers violate *pathet* is a serious one.

In order to examine this charge and determine its meaning, one must first establish a definition of *pathet*. This necessitates a rather long digression since *pathet* is not a simple, easily defined concept.

The most important aspect of *pathet* is melodic pattern, or melodic formula. There are many words in Javanese which indicate melodic formulas. Their difference in meaning lies in their different positions relative to a continuum from formulas at one end to loosely restricted formulaic melodies at the other. Included are such words as *rumus*, melodic formulas for gendèr, pesindhèn, rebab, and so forth; *cèngkok*, formulaic melodies for saron, gendèr, bonang, gambang, and so forth; *wilet*, formulaic melodies more free than *cèngkok* for rebab, pesindhèn, suling, and others. All these formulas or formulaic melodies have *pathet* or modal restrictions, final pitch level restrictions, and syntactic, or placement restrictions.

According to R. M. Sarwoko, "the difference between one *pathet* and another is based upon a certain difference in the formulaic melodies (*cèngkok*).[7]

Ki Sindoesawarno states: "Actually, *cèngkok* have personal characteristics, according to the individual and also according to their locality. Theoretically, the number of *cèngkok* is unlimited. But as everyone knows, *cèngkok* are restricted by the characteristics of the instrument, by the laws of the tuning system and by *pathet*, and certainly by aesthetics."[8]

Jaap Kunst, although subscribing to another theory than the one presented here, had similar thoughts about *pathet*.[9] With disarming honesty he lists some of the unsolved problems of his analysis as well as those elements he feels have been slighted. "As a matter of fact there are certain indications that the essential being of the pathets is not exclusively determined by the gong-tones and the pitch, but that other elements may possibly play some part. Thus it is not quite impossible that . . . there is a difference in the turn of the melody, especially in the manner in which the kern [kernel?] melody reaches the finish of the gong phrases."[10]

Mantle Hood, even more than Jaap Kunst, recognized the importance of melodic formulas when he wrote the following: "I believe the preference for a one-octave saron as the instrument to be entrusted with the nuclear theme is directly attributable to a desire, conscious or otherwise, to preserve the melodic contour or *shape*, if you will, of the principal melody—the melodic *shape*, I repeat, of the all-important cadential formula which closes the three critical sections, which serves as the framework of the whole gendịng, which, in short, is one of the strongest features in the identification and, consequently, the very preservation of the paṭet concept itself."[11]

It is not only cadences that are formulas. Gamelan *gendhing* (pieces) are formulaic from beginning to end, from the *buka* (introduction) to the final gong, and in all the musical lines whether played by saron, bonang, gendèr, rebab, suling, kendhang, or any other instrument.

The analysis presented in this chapter and in Appendix IV was prompted by the author's belief that *pathet* recognition was based upon three interlocking factors: (1) melodic pattern, formula or contour, (2) the pitch level of that pattern, and (3) the position of the pattern within the formal structure of the piece. Given the necessity for a vast amount of data to establish the theory, it was useful and convenient to use the saron line in the analysis since the saron part is found most extensively in notation.[12] No repetitions of gong sections are included in the data.

The basic unit of the analysis is the four-note saron unit called *gatra*. "The smallest part of a composition which still has meaning is called *gatra*, or unit."[13]

The *gatra*, like all Javanese musical units, is weighted at the end. Each successive note becomes more important as the final note is approached. The fourth position note is the most important, the third next, the second next, and the first position note the least.[14] Thus in the analysis in Appendix IV the *gatra* are grouped first according to their final note. Different tables separate different final notes. Within one table, the *gatra* are grouped first according to their last two notes, and second, according to their last three notes.

The saron lines of the *gendhing* in the data were divided into *gatra* in the following way:

If the piece is in Ladrang form:

Ladrang Remeng, Sléndro Pathet Nem

			N
. 6 6 .	6 6 5 6	1 6 5 3	2 2 3 2
gatra	gatra	gatra	gatra

N = kenong

If the piece is in Ketawang form:

Ketawang Martapuran, Sléndro Pathet Manyura

                                             G

| . . 2 3 | 2 1 2 6 | 3 5 6 5 | 2 1 3 2 |
| gatra | gatra | gatra | gatra |

G = gong

If the piece is in Gendhing form:

Gendhing Tejo Sari, kethuk 2 kerep, Pélog Pathet Lima

| . 1 1 . | 1 1 2 3 | 5 3 2 3 | 2 1 2 1 |
| gatra | gatra | gatra | gatra |

Within Javanese formal structures the primary subdividers mark points of great structural importance, that is, important points of convergence of various lines. The finer the subdivision, the less important it is structurally. The *gatra* in the corpus are ranked according to their structural importance. The *gatra* whose last note falls on a gong is in a very strong position, the *gatra* whose last note falls on a kenong is in a strong position, and the *gatra* whose last note falls on a kempul is in a position of lesser strength. For the sake of simplicity the third-ranked position of lesser strength is called "weak" position. However, it is "weak" only in relation to the two stronger positions, and is "strong" in relation to lesser subdivisions.

In one *gongan* (section marked at the end by the large gong) of Ladrang form there are one very strong position (gong), three strong positions (kenong), and four weak positions (kempul).

                (kem)P(ul) (ke)N(ong)

	(kem)P(ul)	(ke)N(ong)	
4 weak gatra	. 6 6 .	6 6 5 6	3 strong gatra
	1 6 5 3	2 2 3 2	
	. . 6 1	2 2 3 2	
	3 2 1 6	5 6 1 2	G(ong) very strong gatra

In the analysis, the occurrence of given patterns is recorded according to position as follows: G(gong = very strong), N(kenong = strong), P(kempul = weak).

In one gong section of Ketawang form there are one very strong position (gong position), one strong position (kenong position), and two weak positions (kempul position).

	(kem)P(ul)	(ke)N(ong)	
2 weak gatra	. . 2 3	2 1 2 6	1 strong gatra
	3 5 6 5	2 1 3 2	G(ong) 1 very strong gatra

(The weak position is not always marked by a kempul, as in the first *gatra* of a Ketawang form or in the first three *gatra* of a Gendhing form. Regardless, the position is weak and is marked as P in the analysis.)

In Gendhing form, for every *gongan* there are one very strong position, three strong positions, and twelve weak positions. Originally, the three weak *gatra* of each line in Gendhing form were separated into three categories. As no significant grouping of patterns resulted, all three were subsequently grouped together.

```
                    (kem) P (ul)              (ke) N (ong)
            ⎡ . 6 5 .  5 6 1 2  1 3 1 2 ‖ . 1 6 5         ⎤
12 weak   ⎧ ⎢ 2 2 . .  2 2 . 3  5 6 5 3 ‖ 2 1 2 6         ⎥ ⎫ 3 strong
gatra     ⎨ ⎢ . . 2 1  . 6 5 3  2 2 . 3 ‖ 5 6 3 5         ⎥ ⎬ gatra
            ⎣ . 6 5 .  5 6 1 2  1 3 1 2 ‖ . 1 6 5  G(ong) ⎦ ⎭ 1 very
                                                              strong
                                                              gatra
```

According to the analysis presented here, contour is the underlying formula of the patterns. The realization of a given contour at a given pitch level results in a pattern. Each *gatra* is given a number indicating its contour. The same number indicates the same contour regardless of the pitch level on which the patterns begin or end. For example, No. 1 is the same contour on the table of patterns ending on 1, the table of patterns ending on 2, et cetera. Or,

```
2 3 2 1                                    —
3 5 3 2         Contour 1. ⎯   ⎯
5 6 5 3                                         —
6 1 6 5 (played 6 1̇ 6 5)
1 2 1 6
```

are all the same contour, No. 1, although the starting (and ending) pitches differ.

Figure 22 is a diagram of all the contours frequently found in gamelan compositions. As they are generally played on a one–octave saron, at some point every contour becomes distorted by transposition to the adjoining octave. For example, on an instrument whose keys are numbered

contour No. 2, ending on pitch level 2, maintains itself as four descending steps. Ending on pitch level 5, however, it becomes 2 1 6 5. The fact of disjunction through transposition does not appear to be a factor which influences frequency of use. Contour No. 16, in the conjunct form 1 2 3 5

Contours of Saron Gatra

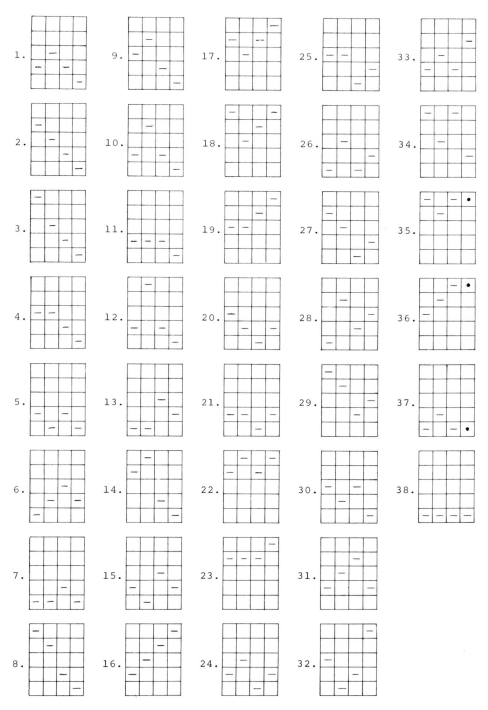

F<small>IG</small>. 22.

does not occur in the data. In the conjunct forms 2 3 5 6 and 3 5 6 1̇ it is common. It is also common in the disjunct forms 5 6 1 2 and 6 1̇ 2 3 or 6 1 2 3.

The contours are numbered for two reasons: first, to indicate how restricted is the total number of contours used and, second, to facilitate the comparison of the use of a given contour on different pitch levels. Given a four-note unit with the final note fixed, there are 125 combinations possible, or 125 possible contours. Actually, fewer than thirty-eight contours occur five or more times in this collection of data.[15] In *sléndro*, a total of either thirty-one or thirty-three contours occur regularly on any given pitch, in *pélog* even fewer, averaging only a total of twenty-six of the possible 125 contours. Contour Nos. 1 and 2 are the highest frequency contours, occurring on every pitch level in nearly every position (G, N, P), therefore giving little information about pathet identification. Other contours give strong pathet clues. For example, contour No. 20 ending on pitch level 6 (1̇ 6 5 6) is most likely to be a Sléndro Pathet Sanga pattern in weak position (P) (Appendix 4, table 5). The same contour ending on pitch 1 (2 1̇ 6̣ 1) is rarely to be found at all. The preferred contours are those which end on a descending step (Nos. 1–15) _ _ 1 6, _ _ 6 5, or _ _ 3 2, et cetera, or those ending on an ascending step (Nos. 16–29) _ _ 5 6, _ _ 3 5, or _ _ 1 2, et cetera. Of a total of twenty-five possible contours ending on a descending step, only fifteen occur regularly. Of a total of twenty-five possible contours ending on an ascending step only fourteen occur regularly. Thereafter the percentage of contours that occur compared to the number of possibilities drops off sharply. Of the remaining seventy-five possibilities (3 × 25) only nine occur regularly.

In Javanese notation a dot, . , means that the previous note is sustained and not damped. Thus the previous note continues sounding through the symbol . . Therefore all patterns (and there are many) including the symbol . are recorded as though . were a repetition of the previous tone. For example 5 5 . 6, or 5 . 5 6, or (last note of previous *gatra*) 5 . . 5 6 are all considered variants of 5 5 5 6 and are recorded under that contour. One of the most common examples is the pattern in gong position (last note of previous *gatra*) 2 . 1 6 5, which is classified as the pattern 2 1 6 5. Another common use of the dot symbol occurs in contour No. 38, where 6 6 6 6 (or the same contour on any pitch level) may occur as 6 . 6 6, or . 6 . ., or . . 6 6, or 6 6 . ., or . 6 6 ., and so forth. (I hope the reader will accept a straight line as a contour). The exceptions to this general practice in the analysis are contour Nos. 35, 36, and 37, which rarely occur with the sustained last note filled in. Therefore, they are left in the data as they generally occur in a composition.

Spaced patterns such as . 2 . 3 . 2 . 1 with only four saron strokes per kenong are treated the same as 2 3 2 1. Formal expansion and compression are common in gamelan music (see Appendix I) and do not affect characteristic contours of the saron.

Pitch level 4 occurs in Pathet Pélog Lima and Pathet Pélog Nem, where it is in variation with pitch level 3. (Pitch level 4 occurs less frequently in Pélog Pathet Barang, where it is in variation with pitch level 5.) Pitch level 4 is called *sorogan*, or alternative, to pitch level 3 in Pathet Pélog Lima and Nem, or alternative to pitch level 5 in Pathet Pélog Barang.

Pitch levels 1 and 7 are (with rare exceptions) mutually exclusive, or in complementary distribution. This makes it possible for them to be treated as variants of each other, that is, structurally the same.[16] Within their respective scale systems, pitch levels 2 and 7 (Pathet Barang) and pitch levels 2 and 1 (Pathet Lima and Nem) are adjacent tones. Thus both the patterns 2 3 2 7 and 2 3 2 1 are classified as contour No. 1. The possible interchange of pitch levels 3 and 4 and pitch levels 1 and 7 within the same contour with the same final pitch level necessitated the assignment of a letter, a, b, c, or d, to each of the contours in *pélog*.

Tables 1 through 12 of Appendix 4 record the frequency of occurrence within the corpus of a given contour, on a particular note or pitch level (pattern), in a specific position (G, N, P). Melodic patterns do not appear with random frequency within every *pathet* or in every position. The occurrences tend to cluster. It is the clustering of occurrences of a particular melodic pattern in a specific position that gives the profile of each *pathet*.

No Javanese musician needs any table of occurrences. The information is already cataloged in his brain, already internalized. He need not wait for the final gong to identify the *pathet*. His clues begin with the very first *gatra*.

Tables 13 through 18 of Appendix 4 give a profile of pattern use for each *pathet*. Each table focuses on one *pathet*. The significant patterns of the *pathet* are listed by the order of the pitch level of their final digit. The patterns are ranked according to their frequency of occurrence as follows:

    * = important pattern = ten or more occurrences in that position
    × = frequent pattern = five or more occurrences in that position

The relative frequency of the same pattern in other *pathet* is also given in each table. This is to allow the reader to discriminate between frequent patterns which are *pathet*/position specific and those which are not. At the left of each table, the information is summarized again according to position (G, N, P).

Sléndro Pathet Nem

The profile of pattern use for Sléndro Pathet Nem is given in Appendix 4, table 14. Of a total of 625 possible patterns (125 contours × five pitch levels), only forty-nine are frequently used in Sléndro Pathet Nem. Of a total of 125 possible contours, only twenty-five frequently occur in Sléndro Pathet Nem.

Sléndro Pathet Nem avoids patterns ending on pitch level 1 in gong position and stresses patterns ending on pitch levels 2 and 6 in gong position.

The overall profile of pattern use in Sléndro Pathet Nem is similar to the profile of pattern use of Sléndro Pathet Manyura. Patterns ending in the configuration _ 1 3 2, _ 1 2 3, and _ 5 2 3 are frequently heard in both Sléndro Pathet Nem and Sléndro Pathet Manyura, rarely in Sléndro Pathet Sanga. Also, patterns ending on pitch level 6 in gong position are shared between Sléndro Pathet Nem and Sléndro Pathet Manyura.

The most significant difference between the two *pathet* is that contours ending on pitch level 5 in strong position are frequent in Sléndro Pathet Nem (and Sléndro Pathet Sanga) and rare in Sléndro Pathet Manyura. Also, patterns ending in the configuration _ 6 5 6 are common in kenong and kempul position in Pathet Nem and Pathet Sanga and are rare in Sléndro Pathet Manyura.

Sléndro Pathet Sanga

The profile of pattern use for Sléndro Pathet Sanga is given in Appendix 4, table 15. Of a total of 625 possible patterns only forty-five are frequently used in Sléndro Pathet Sanga. Of a total of 125 possible contours, only twenty-one occur frequently.

Sléndro Pathet Sanga avoids patterns ending on pitch level 3 in strong positions and stresses patterns ending on pitch level 5 in gong position.

Patterns ending in the contour _ 6 1 5 are exclusive to Pathet Sanga, occurring in all Sanga positions. These patterns, together with the other three exclusive Sanga patterns and the strong emphasis on patterns ending on pitch level 5 in kenong and gong position, make Sanga the easiest of *sléndro pathet* to identify.

Sléndro Pathet Manyura

The profile of pattern use for Sléndro Pathet Manyura is given in Appendix 4, table 13. Of a total of 625 possible patterns only forty occur frequently in Sléndro Pathet Manyura. Of a total of 125 possible contours only nineteen occur regularly.

Patterns ending on pitch level 5 in strong positions are avoided in Pathet Manyura and patterns ending on pitch level 6 in strong position are stressed. The only important pattern ending on pitch level 5 frequently found in Pathet Manyura is 3 2 6 5 in weak position. Patterns ending in the contour _ 2 5 3 are most likely to be Manyura patterns. Also, the "hanging" (*gantung*) pattern 3 3 3 3 is most likely to occur in Manyura.

Pélog Pathet Lima

The profile of pattern use for Pélog Pathet Lima is given in Appendix 4, table 16. Of a total of 625 possible patterns only twenty-four occur frequently. Of a total of 125 contours only thirteen occur regularly.

Pélog Pathet Lima stresses patterns ending on pitch level 1 or 5 in strong position. *Gatra* that begin with pitch level 4 strongly suggest Pathet Lima and occur only rarely in Pathet Nem or Barang. Patterns including *sorogan*, pitch level 4, are much more frequent in Lima than in Nem. (See Appendix 4, table 7, contour 26, and table 10, contour 6d.) Patterns ending in the contour _ _ 4 2 are exclusively Pélog Pathet Lima kempul patterns.

Pélog Pathet Nem

The profile of pattern use for Pélog Pathet Nem is given in Appendix 4, table 17. Of a total of 625 possible patterns only thirty-six occur frequently. Of a total of 125 possible contours only fourteen occur regularly.

In Pathet Nem, patterns ending on pitch levels 5 and 6 are stressed in strong position. Patterns ending in the contours _ 1 2 6 or _ _ 3 6 are usually Pélog Nem. Pattern 2 3 2 1 also is usually Pélog Nem. Pélog Nem shares with Pélog Lima the heavy use of pattern 2 1 6 5. Patterns ending in the contour _ _ 1 2 in gong or kenong position are almost always Pélog Pathet Nem.

Pélog Pathet Barang

The profile of pattern use for Pélog Pathet Barang is given in Appendix 4, table 18. Of a possible 625 patterns only thirty-two occur frequently. Of a possible 125 contours only fourteen occur frequently.

Patterns ending on pitch levels 2 and 6 are stressed in strong position in Pélog Barang.[17] Because of the use of pitch level 7, Pélog Pathet Barang is the easiest of all *pathet* to identify visually and aurally. In addition, some patterns not involving pitch level 7 are indications of Pélog Barang, such as those ending on the contour _ 6 3 2.

To summarize, *pathet* is the profile of the use of characteristic contours on particular pitch levels (patterns) in particular positions within a composition.[18]

It is now possible to return to the original problem posed at the beginning of this chapter. Are the modern composers Ki Wasitodipuro and Ki Nartosabdho, as their critics charge, destroying *pathet*? The quest for a reasoned answer to the question will begin by examining the attitudes of the composers themselves and continue by looking at their works.

First of all, both men would object to the accusation. They are first and foremost traditional musicians, closely tied to traditional forms of artistic expression. Ki Wasitodipuro, as the leader of one of the finest court gamelan, the Pakualaman gamelan, and the descendant of a long line of court musicians, would be among the first to protest if he felt honored traditions were being violated. Ki Nartosabdho is best known as a *dhalang*, shadow-play puppeteer, and is thereby immersed in the most traditional and most philosophic of forms, *wayang kulit*. The years of his early manhood were spent as the drummer for the *wayang orang* company Ngesti Pandowo, and thus he absorbed the traditional epics, the Hindu philosophy, the ethical codes and behavior patterns manifested in the *wayang orang* and *wayang kulit* stories. There is nothing in the background of either man to lead one to expect to find an avant-garde composer.

The basic musical conservatism of both men must be understood in order to appreciate the full import and impact of their innovations. The majority of the new compositions by Ki Wasitodipuro and Ki Nartosabdho are traditional in style, do not violate the rules of *pathet* structure, and, in time, will blend into the traditional repertoire. One of the common types of musical creation of both composers is the writing of a new vocal part for a traditional composition. These modern-style vocal parts for traditional pieces abandon traditional poetic forms, are written in modern Javanese, and are musically less formulaic than traditional *gérong* (choral) parts. (See figures 23 and 24.) This is the kind of gradual change that goes on in all oral traditions. It is not the kind of change that alters attitudes about music or threatens the basic structural relationships of the music.

A different type of change can be seen in the composition *Kagok Pangrawit* (figure 21), discussed in chapter 5, which presents some problems of *pathet* identification. According to the composer, the piece is in Pélog Pathet Lima. The gong patterns (G, very strong position) are the fourth and eighth *gatra* of each line and are as follows:

contour No.	pattern	relation to chart of traditional gong patterns
16	4 5 6 1	
	(variant of 3 5 6 1)	possible in Pélog Lima
?	4 5 6 2	not in data
17	3 2 3 5	possible in Pélog Lima
30	3 2 3 1	possible in Pélog Lima although variant 4 2 4 1 is more common
20	3 2 1 2	strong in Pélog Lima
?	1 1 6 5	not in data

Ketawang Suba Kastawa
Pélog Pathet Nem
Traditional

Vocal part by Ki Nartosabdho

Ngelik: N
saron: . 2 . 1 . 6 . 5
voice: . . . 5 5 6i 2̇ i 2̇ i 6i2̇ii655

Angripta   reng ganing gunung Im-

 . 2 . 1 . 6 . ⑤
42.456. 6 5 421 . . . . 6i2̇i2̇i65
bangé juangé yen kadulu saking tebih

 . 2 . 1 . 6 . 5
 5 5 .6i 2̇ i 2̇ i 6i2̇ii655
Warna biru maya maya wa-

 . 2 . 1 . 6 . ⑤
42.456 6 5 421 . . 6i212165̣
tuné alasé   kang jenar   sinawul wiwilis

 . 2 . 1 . 2 . 6
1 1 . 4565421 2 1 2   1 5̣ .16̣
É É gawé lamlam ing paningal

 . 2 . 1 . 6 . ⑤
2 2 . 2 4 .21 .21 .21 6̣1212165̣
Lho lho suwé suwé nandoki rasa ngrespati.

SOURCE: *Gending Djawi saha Dolanan gagrak enggal,* by Ki Nartosabdho, p. 18)

FIG. 23.

Ladrang Ayun–Ayun
Pélog Pathet Nem (Ir. III)
Traditional

Vocal part by Ki Wasitodipuro

nDawah:																N
saron:	5̣	6̣	.	.	2	3	2	1	2	1	.	.	3	5	3	2

1 2 . . 2 3 2 1 2 1 . . 3 5 3 2
voice   2 3 .235566 .56 2̇ 3̇ 2̇ 1̇2̇6̇2̇1̇ 2̇1̇1̇ 2̇ 1̇ 6 5 3 5 . 6 2 1 6̣ 3 132
Mèh rahina semu agang ing wetan pernahé é mratandani wiwit bangun esuk

1 2 . . 2 3 5 6 2 3 2 1 6 5 4 5
32.12 35 .62 . 2 3 5 6 5̇1̇6 56.5̇1̇6 2̇ 3̇ 2̇ 1̇ 3̇ 2̇ 6 5 4 2 465
Para tani ama karya anggarap sawahé manggul pacul garu luku sinambi nggerak
keboné
. 3 5 6 3 5 3 2 5 3 1 6̣ 1 2 1 ⑥
. 2 35566 3 6 5 3 2 312 1 2 132 3 56216̣ 2 231 32312̇1̇6̣
Anggaliyak tansah ramé ing gawé Paedahé wanci ngunduh tikel
ing pametuné

SOURCE: *Gérong*, a book compiled by Ki Wasitodipuro for teaching purposes.

FIG. 24.

The second subdivision, or the strong patterns (N) in this piece are the second and sixth *gatra* of each line and are as follows:

contour No.	pattern	relation to chart of traditional kenong patterns
38	1 1 1 1	frequent in Pélog Lima
6	1 2 3 2	possible in Pélog Lima
2	6 5 3 2	frequent in Pélog Lima
30	1 6 1 5	not found in the data in Pélog Lima

The third subdivision of the gong unit, yielding a position of lesser strength (P), includes the first, third, fifth, and seventh *gatra* of each line and they are as follows:

contour No.	pattern	relation to chart of traditional kempul patterns
38	1 1 1 1	frequent in Pélog Lima
?	6 6 5 4	not in data
?	2 2 3 2	not in data
35	3 2 3 3	not found in data in Pélog Lima
35	6 5 6 6	not found in data in Pélog Lima
17	3 2 3 5	frequent in Pélog Lima
?	1 1 3 3	not in data
35	1 6 1 1	not in data on that pitch level
?	5 1 6 6	not in data

The overall profile of *Kagok Pangrawit* reveals a piece inclining toward Pélog Lima with a number of nontraditional contours introduced, particularly in the kempul position, although the final gong is also a nontraditional contour. A piece such as *Kagok Pangrawit* cannot be said to "destroy" the *pathet* concept, yet it seems to be pushing rather hard at the constraint of contour use in Pathet Lima.

A similar phenomenon can be found in many of the compositions of Ki Nartosabdho. They represent not so much an annihilation of *pathet* structures as a slight deviation from them.

The composition *Ketawang Mèh Rahina* (figure 25) is offered as an illustration.

The gong patterns of *Ketawang Mèh Rahina* are:

contour No.	pattern	relation to chart of traditional gong patterns
1	2 4 2 1	possible in Pélog Nem, usually in variant form 2 3 2 1
20	6 5 4 5	possible in Pélog Nem, but usually found in variant form 6 5 3 5
8	6 5 2 1	possible, but rare in all *pathet*
16	2 4 5 6	possible, but much more common in variant form 2 3 5 6

The kenong patterns of *Ketawang Mèh Rahina* are:

contour No.	pattern	relation to chart of traditional kenong patterns
17	6 5 6 1	not found in data except in variant form 6 5 6 7 (Pélog Barang)
6	6 1 2 1	not found in data for Pélog Nem, frequent in Pathet Lima
27	6 5 2 3	strong pattern in Pélog Nem although more frequent in Pélog Barang
?	6 1 3 1	not in data

The kempul patterns are:

contour No.	pattern	relation to chart of traditional kempul patterns
38	1 1 1 1	frequent in Pélog Nem
6	2 4 5 4	specific Pélog Nem kempul pattern
14	2 4 6 5	possible Pélog Nem, more usual in Pélog Lima; variant 2 3 6 5 more common in Pélog Nem
2	1 6 5 3	possible in Pélog Nem
?	3 6 5 4	not in data
10	6 2 6 5	not in data on that pitch level

Ketawang Mèh Rahina
Pélog Pathet Nem

<pre>
                                      G
        Buka: 6   6 6 5 3   . 6 . 5   . 2 . 1

                          N   G
        . . 1 .   6 5 6 1   2 4 5 4   2 4 2 1
        . . 1 .   6 5 6 1   2 4 5 4   2 4 2 1
        2 4 6 5   6 1 2 1   . 6 5 3   6 5 4 5
        2 4 6 5   6 1 2 1   . 6 5 3   6 5 2 1
        . 1 1 1   6 5 2 3   . 6 5 4   2 4 5 6
        . 2 6 5   6 1 3 1   . 6 5 3   6 5 2 1
</pre>

Fig. 25.

Ketawang Mèh Rahina inclines toward the *pathet* of its designation but again stretches the *pathet* limits somewhat. Not one of the gong *gatra* is strongly indicative of Pélog Nem. Had the digit 4 been replaced by digit 3 in the gong *gatra*, it would have given a stronger feeling of Pélog Nem. One kempul and one kenong *gatra* represent contours not commonly found in traditional pieces.

It may well be that this type of change, like rearranging an old composition, is also traditional. Perhaps the *pathet* boundaries have expanded or shifted or even become blurred from what they were one hundred or two hundred years ago. Over time, new *pathet* patterns and configurations may become fashionable and form the nucleus around which *pathet* practices cluster. In fifty or one hundred years a given *pathet* name may indicate a different set of melodic patterns and related positions than it does today. This is the kind of change that does not really change anything. It represents an artistic stasis, or steady state. While a traditional music system may not be static or immutable, the changing of its surface features does not demand a readjustment of musical values and orientation.

I do not believe it is the kinds of change described above that disturb a certain segment of the Javanese musical public. Rather, it is the introduction of phrases based upon diatonic scales, and the writing of pieces com-

Suara Suling
Pélog Pathet Nem

	N	N	N	N
Buka kendhang:	. . . 2	. . . 1	. . . 2	. . . 1
Saron:	. . . . 5 6 5 1	. . 5 $\widehat{6\ 5\ 4\ 3\ 2}$

Buka kendhang: . . . 2 . . . 1 . . . 2 . . . 1
Saron: . . . . 5 6 5 1 . . 5 ⏜(6 5 4 3 2)
. . . . 1 3 1 2 . . 5 6 5 3 2 1
. . . .6545 6 1 . . 3 2 . 1 6 5
$\overline{424}$ . . 4 5 ⏜(6 5 543). . 3 5 3 2
$\overline{2424}$ . . 4 5 6 5 . . 1 6 5 3 2 ①
Umpak: . 1 . 1 . 1 . 5 . 5 . 5 . 5 . 2
. 2 . 2 . 4 . 4 . . 1 6 5 3 2 ①

FIG. 26.

posed mostly of nontraditional contours that seem to pose a threat to the *pathet* system.

In the *pélog pathet* system, pitch level 4 is always used as an alternative to pitch level 3 (Pathet Lima and Nem) or pitch level 5 (Pathet Barang). The scale system for Pélog Lima and Pélog Nem is 1 2 3 5 6 or 1 2 4 5 6. Pitch level 4 changes the intervallic relationships of the scale by changing the position of the large interval, but it never adds another tone. Pitch level 4 is strictly *sorogan*, or substitute, tone. Occasionally, modern composers will treat the seven pitch levels of the *pélog* system as though they comprise a diatonic scale. By using pitch level 3 and 4 together within a single *gatra*, a single saron unit, the scale becomes 1 2 3 4 5 6 . The song *Suara Suling* is among the most popular tunes in Java and illustrates the use of pitch levels 6 5 4 3 2 in sequence, as if they were a scale (figure 26). The passages using pitch levels 3 and 4 in sequence are encircled.

Even more objectionable to conservative musicians is the vocal use of the *pélog* system as if it were a diatonic scale. The female singer often uses tones outside of the regular *pathet* structures, but only for special

Aja Ngono

```
. . . . 6 5 6 1 1 1 2 3 3̄4̄3̄ 2 1̂
. . . . 6 5 6 2 1 2 3 5 5̄6̄3̄ 2 1̂
. 7 7 . 7̄ 6̄ 5̄ 4̄ . 4 4 . 4̄5̄3̄ 2 1̂
. . . . 7̄ 6̄ 7̄ 1̄ 1 3 1 2 2̄4̄3̄ 2 1̂
. 1 1 . 5̄ 6̄ 1̄ 5 5 5 6 5 3 3̄5̄3̄ 2 ①
```

FIG. 27.

Lagu Gerilya

```
. . . . 6  1 6 4 1 . 1 . 1 6 1 4̂
1 . 1 . 6  1 6 4 . 4 4 4 5 6 4 5̂
. . 3  3 3̄2̄ 1 1 1 3̄2̄ 1 1 1 3̄2̄ 1 3̄2̄ 1̂
3 3 . . 3̄2̄ 1 1 1 3̄2̄ 1 1 1 3̄2̄ 1 2 4̂
. . 4  4 6̄5̄ 4 4 4 6̄5̄ 4 4 4 6̄5̄ 4 6̄5̄ 4̂
4 4 . . 6̄5̄ 4 4 4 6̄5̄ 4 4 4 6̄5̄ 4 2 1̂
4̄2̄.4̄ 1 4̄2̄ .4̄ 1 4 5 4̄6̄.4̄ 5 4̄6̄ .4̄ 2 4 1̂
4̄2̄.4̄ 1 4̄2̄ .4̄ 1 4 5 3̄1̄.3̄ 1 5 5̄6̄ 5̄4̄ 3̄2̄ ①
```

FIG. 28.

effect, to give color and feeling to the regular pitch levels, and never in strong final positions or in syllabic singing—one note, one syllable.[19] The song *Aku Ngimpi*, discussed in chapter 5 (figure 19), illustrates the Western and un-Javanese use of the *pélog* system. (See the last line in particular.) The listener is given the impression that the piece is written in the *Phrygian* mode. The *pélog* pitch levels used in the vocal part are 1 2 3 4 5 and 6. Only pitch level 7 is omitted.

A song which makes use of all seven *pélog* pitch levels is *Aja Ngono* (figure 27), by Ki Wasitodipuro. The resulting tonality is not really diatonic as the intervals do not correspond to the diatonic scale, yet the *gatra* of the piece are not in any *pélog pathet* either. All the underlined *gatra* in figure 27 do not occur in the data in those positions and some do not occur at all. The harmonic structure of the three vocal parts of this piece is also an example of the influence of Western vocal techniques on modern composers. (See chapter 5.) Because the tonality and the three-part singing style of *Aja Ngono* are foreign to most Javanese, this piece could be learned within a pure oral tradition only with great difficulty. Notation has made it possible for such deviations from tradition to appear. The title of the piece is "Don't Do Like That." The English translation of the words is as follows:

> The horse runs back and forth making funny faces and
>   teasing,
> The pony trots back and forth,
> In spite of that, the horse teases with funny movements.
> Much later, competition.
> The horse is cornered,
> The pony becomes courageous.

It may be that the introduction of all seven pitch levels in this piece is a deliberate musical reflection of the teasing, uncomely horse, a musical portrait of unseemly behavior.

Another composition by Ki Wasitodipuro that illustrates the instrumental use of melodic patterns that never appear within traditional pieces is *Lagu Gerilya* (figure 28). *Lagu Gerilya* was composed for a modern dance-drama, a *sendratari*, depicting the revolt of Prince Diponegoro against the Dutch in 1825. The title means "Song of the Guerilla Fighters."

None of the *gatra* listed below from *Lagu Gerilya* has a contour number. In other words they are nontraditional and have no place in the *pathet* system.

6 1 6 4	1st line, 2nd gatra
1 6 1 4	1st line, 4th gatra
$\overline{32}1$ 1 1	3rd line, 2nd gatra

$\overline{321}$ $\overline{321}$	3rd line, 4th gatra
$\overline{321}$ 2 4	4th line, 4th gatra
$\overline{654}$ 4 4	5th line, 2nd gatra
$\overline{654}$ $\overline{654}$	5th line, 4th gatra
$\overline{42.41}$ $\overline{42}$	7th line, 1st gatra
$\overline{.41}$ 4 5	7th line, 2nd gatra
$\overline{31.3}$ 1 5	8th line, 3rd gatra

No one could accuse Ki Wasitodipuro of not understanding *pathet*. The unusual contours and scale found in *Lagu Gerilya* are deliberately introduced. This is an example of the conscious introduction of alien elements into the musical structure.

Another exception to the usage of patterns in traditional *pathet* in *Lagu Gerilya* occurs in the prominent use of pitch level 4 in strong position. If one refers to the chart for pitch level 4 (Appendix 4, table 9), it can be seen that relatively few patterns end on pitch level 4 and fewer still in any strong position. In *Lagu Gerilya* pitch level 4 occurs often in strong kenong position and three times in gong position. The liberal use of pitch level 4 in strong position in this composition gives it a different mood or feeling than would be possible with any of the traditional modes.

The fact that *Lagu Gerilya* first appeared in the context of a modernized dance-drama, the genre *sendratari* that violates many of the rules of traditional dance-drama, may have allowed the composer to feel enough freedom from traditional *pathet* constraints to write such a piece. Ki Wasitodipuro intended that the piece should be striking and dramatic. By introducing many alien contours, he assured that the piece would induce some degree of shock. A piece written to surprise and stimulate the listener illustrates again the new Javanese concept of manipulating the sound of the instruments and the structure of the music to create special effects.

It is difficult to evaluate the overall impact on gamelan music of innovations in the use of a diatonic scale structure and in the introduction of melodic patterns outside of the traditional modes. The examples cited above form only a small fraction of the musical output of these composers, and only the tiniest part of the total quantity of gamelan music heard on the island. Still, these men are musical leaders, trendsetters. Conversely, it is they who reflect in their music the changing moods and musical tastes of Java. The pieces that most blatantly violate *pathet* grammar seem to be in a category apart from the usual kinds of compositions by Ki Wasitodipuro and Ki Nartosabdho. They usually occur in *pélog* and usually reveal influence from Western musical styles (*Aku Ngimpi*, figure 19, and *Aja Ngono*, figure 27). It must be very awkward for the composers of these compositions to try and assign to them a traditional *pathet*, and equally awkward for the listener to accept them as belonging to a traditional *pathet*. Through years of playing or listening the gamelan audience in Java has come to associate certain melodic patterns, certain sequences of sound, with particular *pathet*. The fulfillment of those expectations is part of the pleasure of listening to the music. A slight deviation from expectations may actually enhance the pleasure, but a radical departure from the norms of *pathet* will be likely to annoy the listener and interfere with his enjoyment.

It is clear that some of the compositions of Ki Wasitodipuro and Ki Nartosabdho *do* fall outside of the traditional *pathet* structure, and that there is some substance to the charges made by their critics. If these pieces and others like them are, in time, accepted as belonging to the *pathet* system, then the modal structures will have been redefined. Alternatively, if these pieces are rejected and forgotten, the *pathet* system as it is practiced now will continue in effect.

7
Conclusion

The focus of this study has been on musical innovation and change. Musical change, like any other, is not of one kind. All music systems are in flux, and only the most detailed notation can momentarily hold time still. Often it is only ignorance of detailed histories that gives the outsider (in space or in time) the illusion of stability. However, the changes occurring in Javanese arts today are quantitatively more than, and of a different nature from, the usual accumulative changes of an oral tradition, and these changes are directly linked to changes occurring in the society and in the philosophic beliefs that support and sustain the society.

Medieval Java was an agrarian-based society headed by a god-king, who was the link between heaven and earth. Although there was much surface turmoil, Java apparently had a relatively integrated social structure. All of the arts of that society presented subliminal but substantive support for the world view, the philosophies of the ruler and ruled. *Wayang kulit*, *wayang orang*, gamelan, *tembang* (singing and poetry)—all combined to enhance and reflect the traditional values of Old Java. The hierarchical structure of society with the king at the top, the mirroring of the cosmos in the microcosmos of the kingdom, the high value placed on the search for inner harmony and perfection, the striving for emotional detachment from the events of the world (*iklas*), the inevitability of one's destiny fixed by birth—each is reiterated time and time again in a thousand covert and overt ways by the traditional arts.

The system was maintained, albeit somewhat crippled, by the Dutch occupation. There is ample evidence of musical change during the centuries of Dutch occupation, from the seventeenth into the twentieth centuries. New instruments were added, others fell into disuse. Ensembles became larger and incorporated different styles of music into one ensemble. The names of some of the modes changed. Perhaps modal configurations changed also. What remained constant is the one essential element for musical survival: the "fit," the congruence, the harmony, the consonance between the values of the society and the implicit values of the music system.

The grammar of gamelan compositions also remained constant.

Gamelan grammar includes musical forms built by a process of subdivision and expansion, the primary subdivisions marked by a convergence or coincidence of a number of musical lines. These musical forms are units marked at the end by a gong, repetitive cyclical musical units that in themselves are neither beginnings, middles, nor ends.

The introduction of notation at the end of the nineteenth century did not at first affect the internal relationships of the Javanese gamelan oral tradition or the external relationships of the music system to the society. By itself, notation would not necessarily have made any difference to the Javanese oral tradition. What notation did was to make possible a reordering of those relationships when pressures arose from the surrounding environment. Now that musical notation is widespread and imperatives for change are felt by many musicians, musical notation is a prominent factor in the realignment of musical values.

Beginning in the twentieth century and reaching a climax with independence in 1949, Javanese society underwent a vast emotional upheaval in trying to restructure a king-centered, stratified society in order to become a modern state. One of the pursuits of the nationalists was rapid, innovative economic development, an activity that rated very low on the traditional scale of values. Public education for all meant an elimination of the monopoly of knowledge by an elite. The use of the Indonesian language in official life lessened the status-reinforcing aspect of the Javanese language, with its carefully controlled and manipulated levels of speech. The new spirit of dynamism and change, and the growing importance of the individual also contributed to undermining the ethos of the traditional arts.

These changes came so suddenly and were so cataclysmic that the traditional arts could not adjust nor evolve slowly in accordance with oral traditions. The result is a complex of traditional arts that continue to remain popular, but in a curious way are out of phase with the thrust of the culture as a whole. All these changes have occurred within the lifetimes of mature Javanese, and among the intellectuals they have created a painful ambivalence.

In an address given on a college campus in the United States in 1968, the former ambassador from Indonesia, the Honorable Soedjatmoko, said:

> Art is an expression of the totality of a culture. It mirrors not only the concept of beauty and artistic form, but it also reflects, though less directly, through the perception and feelings it visibly expresses and through its function in a society, the value system that infuses that culture.... Apart from the enjoyment we find in it, it is one of the roots that feeds our modern sense of national identity and, as such, it is a source of our national pride and

strength, as well as an expression of the continuity of our history as a nation. At the same time, apart from a source of pride and strength, this music and dance also reflects a problem, one of our central problems. . . . Why do I speak about music, dance and traditional culture in connection with these problems of modernization? In order to make clear that it is almost impossible for a modern Indonesian just to lose himself completely, as he would often wish to, in the enjoyment of the traditional arts.[1]

His Excellency Soedjatmoko, a *priyayi* as well as a modern Indonesian with a Western education, is able to state eloquently the problem that besets and depresses the traditional musician. The modern composer is able to do more than state the problem. He can try to alter traditional gamelan music in such a way that it more closely reflects "the value system that infuses the culture." He can try to make the Javanese see their own beliefs, hopes, interests, and even their anxieties. Presented symbolically, wholly, and thereby made meaningful, problems become understandable, perhaps even soluble. It is this role of psychic physician that is one of the crucial functions of the artist in society. In a country such as Java, which is experiencing fundamental alterations of its basic structure, the role of the creative artist is not only very important but also inevitably painful.

Clifford Geertz, building on the categories of Redfield, Toynbee, and Childe, makes the distinction between two types of intellectuals, or those who consciously consider the problems of their society. There are the "literati," whose concern is to preserve old values and traditions, and the "intelligentsia," who try to bridge the gap between old symbolic forms and new thought patterns, or new societal constructs.[2]

As Geertz points out, in Java the literati and intelligentsia aspects are likely to be combined in one man. This is certainly true of Ki Wasitodipuro and Ki Nartosabdho, both of whom are preservers of old gamelan traditions as well as innovators. They are deeply involved in traditional media and for the most part compose within traditional gamelan structures and modes.

But certain aspects of their compositions indicate transition and change of a major order, not a slow, natural evolution, but a deliberate, quick turn toward a particular direction. Writing compositions in three-four meter is a basic change from the age-old structures divisible by two. The use of Western contrapuntal vocal techniques, particularly thematic development, are a substantive change. The emergence of the composer who orchestrates, conducts, and controls the total performance of a composition is a change which veers away dramatically from an oral tradition. Gamelan compositions that cannot be categorized within the traditional modal structures indicate an attempt to expand the expressive possibilities of the gamelan. At the same time, these pieces place greater emphasis on the composer as a unique personality, as an individual with a personal state-ment to make. The use of the kempul to mark Pan-American dance rhythms (3 + 3 + 2) obliterates its old function as a principal subdivider of a musical unit. These are not surface changes or superficial additions. They are deep and meaningful attempts to change gamelan structure. They demonstrate the ways in which modern gamelan composers are trying to make the old traditions relevant today, and to bring the gamelan traditions into phase with the society around them.

It is an interesting irony that these innovations, which in essence are an attempt to prevent gamelan traditions from becoming museum tradi-tions or fossilized, are just the ones attacked most bitterly by the literati. One sometimes hears the contemptuous remark that modern composers are "only writing for the tourists." In the deepest possible sense, the modern composers are writing for the Javanese living today.

The question of aesthetics or the question of what is beautiful has been deliberately avoided in this study for many reasons. The problem of aesthetics is difficult to handle within one's own culture; cross-culturally it becomes well-nigh impossible, as too many factors exist that are largely inaccessible to the outsider. Nonetheless, the aesthetic criterion is the one most frequently used against new-style compositions and one which I find to be at least partially valid. In this respect several points need to be stressed. First, one does not expect a stylistic innovator to be the same person who perfects that style, particularly when the composer is moving from a long-established and sophisticated oral tradition into a fledgling written tradition. Second, modern composers are trying to reach an all-Java if not a Pan-Indonesian audience, who do not share the feeling for and knowledge of the cumulative meanings and ethos of traditional Javanese gamelan music. These cumulative meanings make subtlety possible. Finally, an aesthetic criterion that subsumes all other criteria is itself an innovation and is to some extent Western.

In a traditional society in which music is closely linked to religion and ritual, in which the music system supports the entire edifice of belief, the question of beauty is always subordinate to the question of efficacy. Mean-ingfulness, relevance, and simple usefulness (does the music produce the desired result?) are infinitely more important than the creation of sensually delightful sound patterns. In the best of all possible music systems meaning-fulness and beauty coincide. In a society where musical sound has magical qualities, pure beauty of sound can never be more important than the meaningfulness of sound. The emphasis on the aesthetic criterion that one finds in Java today is only a further indication of the movement away from a music system that is integrated into, and integral to, Javanese society as a whole. Composers write innovative compositions and are attacked on aesthetic grounds. In this curious way, both the innovators and the anti-innovators, the intelligentsia and the literati, are proclaiming the fact that Javanese gamelan music is no longer ritualistic, and no longer part of a total harmony encompassing the world, the king, and the cosmos.

More and more, art in Java is becoming a product. One buys tickets to see a *wayang orang* performance. The person one sits next to is not necessarily one's neighbor. The audience is not necessarily the community whose presence at an artistic event strengthens communality and a shared belief system. With the decline in the use of music as ritual, aesthetic meaning tends to subsume all others.

Where will it lead? Are the innovations of Ki Wasitodipuro and Ki Nartosabdho necessary sorts of innovations? Are they drastic enough or too drastic? Can these men and others like them keep Javanese gamelan traditions from becoming objects of interest only to the tourist, the musicologist, and the antiquarian? Already, some Southeast Asian musical traditions have become museum traditions. Musicologists make bad prophets. As an outsider, I can only view musical developments in Java with compassion and a silent hope.

Appendix 1

Toward a Theory of the Derivation of Central Javanese Gamelan Gongan

Preface

The motivation for constructing the theory that follows is to demonstrate explicitly how the various *gongan* forms are structurally related to each other. My debt to the students in my proseminar on gamelan theory is enormous. They provided a constant source of criticisms, suggestions, and a forum for discussion without which my thoughts would have remained embryonic. In particular, the original ideas and critical suggestions of Alan Templeton and Stanley Hoffman are now indistinguishable from my own contributions. At a later stage, R. Anderson Sutton suggested important corrections. We read and reread Javanese theorists in an effort to incorporate their intuitions and basic understandings about their music system. The writings of Ki Sindoesawarno, R. L. Martopangrawit, R. M. Kodrat Poerbapangrawit, and Sulaiman Gitosaprodjo were especially helpful and insightful.

Introduction and Background

Javanese gamelan compositions consist of a sequence of temporal/melodic units of 2 beats, or multiples of 2 beats whose final beat is marked by a gong. The term *gongan*, notated as "g," refers to this temporal/melodic unit, whatever its length. The *gongan* is, theoretically at least, infinitely repeatable. The basic repeated unit, the *gongan*, is structured by the principle of subdivision. For example, a 4-beat *gongan* would be marked at the end by the stroke of a gong on the fourth beat. This unit would be subdivided at midpoint, at beat 2, by another instrument. A third instrument would subdivide the unit again by playing either on beats 1 and 3 or on all 4 beats. (See diagram 1.)

Diagram 1

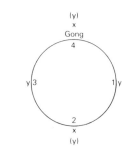

1, 2, 3, 4 = beats
      x = second instrument
      y = third instrument

Redundant instrumental markers of units are enclosed in parentheses in diagram 1. The number of subdivisions of a *gongan* and the particular instruments that mark the different subdivisions are prime determiners of the form of the *gongan*.

Another way to illustrate the same principle is to subdivide a line rather than a circle (diagram 2).

Diagram 2

unit (g)   ———————————————
subdivision   ———————— ————————

Each subdivision may be further subdivided, the process theoretically repeatable infinitely.

unit (g)   ——————————————————————————
first level subdivision   ———————————— ————————————
second level subdivision   —————— —————— —————— ——————
third level subdivision   —— —— —— —— —— —— —— ——

Correlated with the principle of subdivision is the general rule that the instrumental register becomes higher with increasingly small subdivisions. A good term for this principle of subdivision and rising register is *stratification*, applied to gamelan by Mantle Hood (1963:452).

> Unlike the primary tradition of the Western orchestra, founded on a large harmonic complex which moves in vertical structures, the gamelan moves in as many as twenty-five different horizontal strata. For a time in the Middle Ages Western church music was also composed on this principle of stratification: three different voices performed in such a way that the

lowest voice had note values of long duration, the middle voice had a melody that was more active, and the highest voice the most active line. When, as in gamelan, these strata are increased up to twenty-five different lines, the resulting complexity is one which requires a considerable exposure to appreciate.

Javanese gamelan *gongan* are cyclical rather than linear. The gamelan musicians continue to play a given cycle which corresponds to a given form, until the leader (usually the rebab player or the drummer) gives the signal to move to another cycle after the end-marking gong. Therefore, it is at the end-marking gong that two different cycles connect. (The exception to this general rule is that an *irama* change often occurs at a point in the *gongan* other than the end-marking gong). The process of cycle change and cycle connection is illustrated by diagram 3.

Diagram 3

This could represent, for example, the movement from the form Mérong kethuk 2 kerep to the form Minggah Ladrang.

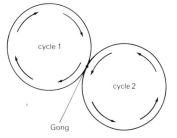

Diagram 4 illustrates the fact that different instruments operate on different cycles within the large cycle (*gongan*). The greatest number of instruments coincide with the large gong. In other words, the greatest number of individual cycles coincide with the gong cycle.

Diagram 4

a = instrument marking first
level subdivision
b = instrument marking second
level subdivision
c = instrument marking third
level subdivision

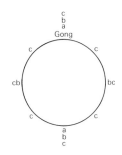

A Theory of Javanese Gamelan **Gongan** *Forms*

This theory posits as the basic structural unit of Javanese gamelan music a repeated *gongan* (g + g), or a concatenated gong unit. There were several reasons for the decision to use a 2-gong structure rather than a 1-gong structure as the largest unit of the analysis.

1. All Javanese gamelan forms (*gongan*) are cyclical. Repetition of *gongan* is such an inherent part of the musical system that it seemed intuitively correct to introduce the concept of recursiveness at the beginning of the theory.

2. The 2-gong structure is the smallest repeated unit that can be isolated, or that *occurs* in the simplest form, Sampak. A 2-gong unit is necessary to conclude (*suwuk*) this form.

3. The criterion of simplicity is served by positing a 2-gong structure (g + g) rather than a 1-gong structure as the largest unit of the analysis. The 4-kenong-per-gong forms are analysed as a repeated *gongan* with the middle gong deleted (ϕG). Were the 4-kenong-per-gong forms treated as single units, the derivation of these forms would be exactly twice as long as presented here. Also, the simplest way to describe the derivation of the 4-kenong-per-gong forms from the 2-kenong-per-gong forms is to posit a deletion of the first gong marker of a concatenated 2-*gongan* unit. *Gongan* forms differ from each other in two basic ways: (1) they differ in the number of beats per *gongan*, and (2) they differ in regard to which subdivision of the *gongan* is marked by the instrument *kethuk*.

Definitions

Dhing-dhong: The Javanese recognize two levels of stress, called *dhing* and *dhong*. Stress in this system refers primarily to relative position rather than to relative length or accent. *Dhing* is a secondary level of stress, *dhong* is a primary level of stress. Thus the second of two elements is termed D (*dhong*), or strong stress, and the first is termed d (*dhing*), or weak stress. The *dhing-dhong* stress unit always occurs in the order, *dhing* followed by *dhong*. The *dhing-dhong* stress unit applies at every level of subdivision of the *gongan*. For example:

	gongan							g
first level of subdivision				d				D
second level of subdivision		d		D		d		D
third level of subdivision	d	D	d	D	d	D	d	D

It should be noted that the *dhing-dhong* unit defines a hierarchical subdivision of the *gongan*. *Dhing-dhong* units are not concatenated, or added together, but rather are subdivisions. As levels of subdivision are added to the *gongan*, every *dhing* becomes a *dhing-dhong* at the next higher level of subdivision. ("Higher" refers to the higher *number* of subdivisions.) Similarly, every *dhong* becomes a *dhing-dhong* at the next higher level of subdivision. The process of subdivision that occurs within a *gongan* contrasts with the process of concatenation that occurs between two *gongan*.

Keteg: Inseparable from the *dhing-dhong* concept, that is, secondary-primary stress unit, is the concept of *keteg*, or basic pulse. *Keteg*, literally "heartbeat," always falls on a *dhong*. Although *keteg* can be thought of as basic pulse, *keteg* may be played in fast (*druta*), medium (*madya*), or slow (*wilambita*) tempos. It is the ratio of *keteg* per gong, *keteg* per kenong, and *keteg* per kethuk that determines form, not the tempo at which *keteg* are played. In all forms except Sampak, *keteg* is manifested by the bonang barung. The *dhong* of the level of subdivision played by bonang barung manifests *keteg*. (In Sampak, *keteg* is manifested by kenong).

    Keteg is notated as a dot. The dot in this theory is not strictly equatable with the saron part *balungan*. *Keteg* often coincides with *balungan*, particularly in Irama I, but Javanese cipher notation rarely indicates *keteg* expansion in Irama II, and often does not indicate *keteg* precisely in Irama III, and Irama IV. It is not necessary to indicate *keteg* precisely in the notation as Javanese performers know intuitively that all levels of the hierarchy above the level of *keteg* double the number of strokes per gong in any Irama expansion. The model below illustrates the relation of *keteg* to the level of expansion of *dhing-dhong* played by the bonang barung.

first level of subdivision	d	D
second level of subdivision	d D d D	
third level of subdivision	d D d D d D d D (bonang barung)	
	. . . . KETEG	

KETEG = *dhong* of the level of subdivision played by bonang barung.

Keteg-kethuk pattern: In every form (except Sampak) there is a pattern of relationship between the *keteg* and the kethuk levels of subdivision. These patterns are given special names by the Javanese, indicating the ratio of *keteg* per kethuk in a given pattern. The patterns are given below. Kethuk is notated as "t".

kethuk ngganter	t . or t .
kethuk kerepan	. t . .
kethuk kerep	. . . t . . . .
kethuk arang/awis	. . . . t . . . .

Kenong unit: The *kenong unit*, called *kenongan*, is defined as the sequence of *keteg-kethuk patterns* that is marked at the end by kenong. (See diagram 5.)

Diagram 5

FORM

Srepegan

kempul			P		P	
kenong		N	N	N	N	
kethuk	t	t	t	t	
saron		3	2	3	2	

bonang barung – – – – – – – –
KETEG   .   .   .   .

keteg-kethuk pattern   kenong unit   gong unit

                                                P

    t .   t Ṇ   t Ṇ t Ṇ

Levels of Subdivision

     g   g   0. kempul marks g
  d D d D   1. kenong marks dD (saron plays on dD)
d D d D d D d D   2. bonang marks dD, kethuk marks d

Ayak-ayakan   (fragment)
  kethuk 1 ngganter/
    2 ngganter

kempul				P			P	
kenong		N		N		N		N
kethuk	t		t		t		t	
saron	2	3	2	1	2	3	2	1

bonang – – – – – – – – – – – – – – – –
KETEG   .   .   .   .

keteg-kethuk pattern   kenong unit   gong unit

                                                      P

    ț .   ṭ Ṇ   ṭ Ṇ ṭ Ṇ
    or   or   or   P
    t .   t . t Ṇ   t . t Ṇ t . t Ṇ

Levels of Subdivision

  N   N   N   N
      g   g   0. kempul marks g
  d   D   d   D   1. kenong marks dD
 d D d D d D d D   2. kethuk marks d, (saron)
d D d D d D d D d D d D d D d D   3. bonang barung marks dD

Diagram 5 (*continued*)

Ladrang
  kethuk 2 kerepan, Irama I

kethuk, kempul, kenong, gong		t		(P)*		t		N
saron	3	2	3	7	3	2	7	6

KETEG/bonang barung — ̣— ̣ — ̣ — ̣ — ̣ — ̣ — ̣ — ̣

		t		P		t		N/(Ǥ)**
	7	6	3	2	5	3	2	7

— ̣ — ̣ — ̣ — ̣ — ̣ — ̣ — ̣ — ̣

		t		P		t		N
	3	5	3	2	6	5	3	2

— ̣ — ̣ — ̣ — ̣ — ̣ — ̣ — ̣ — ̣

		t		P		t		N/G
	5	3	2	7	3	2	7	6

— ̣ — ̣ — ̣ — ̣ — ̣ — ̣ — ̣ — ̣

keteg-kethuk pattern   kenong unit   gong unit

. ṭ . .   . ṭ . . . ṭ . N   . t .(P)* t . N
                                               . t . P . t . N/(Ǥ)**
                                               . t . P . t . N
                                               . t . P . t . N/G

Levels of Subdivision

```
                                    (g)                                      g   0.
                    d                D                    d                   D   1.
          d         D         d      D         d          D          d        D   2.
    d  D  d  D  d   D   d   D   d   D   d   D   d   D   d   D   d   D   d   D   d  D   3.
  d D d D d D d D d D d D d D d D d D d D d D d D d D d D d D d D d D d D d D d D d D  4.
dDdDdDdDdDdDdDdDdDdDdDdDdDdDdDdDdDdDdDdDdDdDdDdDdDdDdDdDdDdDdDdDdDdDdDdDdD  5.
```

0. G marks second g, delete first gong marker (Ǥ)
1. kenong marks dD
2. kempul marks d
3. kethuk marks d
4. (saron plays dD)
5. bonang barung marks dD

---

*In Central Javanese style, first kempul is deleted in this form.
**Deleted G is discussed below, gong deletion function.

Gamelan formal structures are determined by which instruments mark which levels of subdivision in any given form. All markers of formal structure are either hanging gongs or horizontal pot gongs. (The saron is not a determiner of formal structure. While the saron often plays on *keteg*, it does not consistently do so and therefore cannot be a marker of formal structure. It is included in the models that follow only for the orientation of those familiar with the gamelan repertoire. From here on, *keteg*, in the models and diagrams, will be written KETEG to aid the reader in distinguishing the abstraction *keteg* from particular instruments [especially *kethuk*] appearing in the same model.)

Instrumental symbols used in this theory are

Hanging Gongs	Horizontal Pot Gongs
gong ageng = G	kenong = N
siyem (gong suwukan) = S	kethuk = t
kempul = P	bonang barung = _

The horizontal pot gongs are consistent in function. Kenong and bonang barung mark both *dhing* (d) and *dhong* (D) at whatever level of subdivision they occur. The kethuk marks only *dhing* (d) at the level of subdivision at which it occurs.

The primary function of hanging gongs is to mark the end point of the *gongan* unit. In the simplest forms, Sampak, Srepegan, and Ayak-ayakan, the kempul (P) marks the end point of the *gongan*. When other gongs occur in Sampak, Srepegan, and Ayak-ayakan, they mark the end point of a series of concatenated *gongan*. In the forms Lancaran, Bubaran, Ladrang, and Ketawang, where gong ageng (G) is used to mark the *gongan*, kempul is found at the level of subdivision above kenong and marks only *dhing* at that level. In the forms Lancaran and Bubaran, gong siyem (S) may be used to mark the *gongan*, and gong ageng (G) to mark the final *gongan*. This use of gong ageng (G) is similar to that found in Sampak, Srepegan, and Ayak-ayakan in which gong ageng (G) or gong siyem (S) marks a series of concatenated *gongan*.

Diagram 5 illustrates the relationships between *keteg-kethuk pattern*, *kenongan*, *gongan*, and the increasing levels of subdivision as the formal structures become larger. In this example, Javanese cipher notation is used for the orientation of those readers familiar with the gamelan repertoire.

Functions that yield forms

In the derivation of gamelan formal structures there are two basic processes that generate new *gongan* forms. These processes are called in this theory the *Irama function* and the *Kethuk function*.

1. Irama function ($\Rightarrow$)

   a. The Irama function expands a form by subdividing the highest level dD unit (Sampak) or, alternatively, the level of subdivision played by bonang barung. (If bonang panerus, gendèr panerus, or gambang are playing one level subdivision above bonang barung, it is still the dD unit at the level of subdivision of the bonang barung which is subdivided, and all levels above bonang barung.)

"d" becomes "dD", "D" becomes "dD"

or

"dD" becomes "dDdD"

or

"." becomes ". ."

   This subdivision of dD, or doubling of _keteg_, means that _keteg/_ bonang barung moves "up" (higher number) one level of subdivision, but does not affect the position of the kethuk, or all other instruments

Diagram 6 (Irama function)

P   P

t . tN t . tN t . tN t . tN   Ayak-ayakan, Irama I
_____

(_keteg-kethuk pattern_: t .)

becomes ($\rightarrow$)

P   P

t . . t N t . . t N t . . t N t . . t N   Ayak-ayakan,
_____   Irama II

(_keteg-kethuk pattern_: t .)

or


```
                    g              0. kempul marks gongan
          d         D              1. kenong
      d   D   d     D              2. (saron)
  d D d D d D d D  KETEG           3. bonang barung/kethuk
```

becomes ($\rightarrow$)

```
                          g                0. kempul marks gongan
              d           D                1. kenong
      d       D       d   D                2.
  d   D   d   D   d   D   d   D            3. (saron)/kethuk
d D d D d D d D d D d D d D d D  KETEG      4. bonang barung
```

"below" (lower number) the level of *keteg*. This results in a change in the *keteg-kethuk pattern*, or *keteg* and kethuk do not stay in the same relationship to each other. (See diagram 6.)

b. Alternative and equivalent definition: The Irama function starts at the *keteg* level, doubles the number of *keteg*, thus doubling the density (ratio per gong) of all instruments above *keteg*. The Irama function results in the *keteg*/bonang barung and all instruments above (higher number) *keteg* being moved up one level in the subdivision of the *gongan*. All levels below (lower number) the *keteg* level of subdivision are unaffected.

$$\overset{\text{N}}{\underset{\text{t . t N t . t G}}{}} \rightarrow \overset{\text{N}}{\underset{\text{t . t N t . t G}}{}}$$

The terms Irama I, II, III, and IV do not refer to specific levels of subdivision but to the successive application of the Irama function alone on any given structure. Thus the only difference between Ayak-ayakan Irama I and Ayak-ayakan Irama II is that Ayak-ayakan Irama II has one more level of subdivision than Ayakan-ayakan I, and *keteg*/bonang barung is on this additional level.

2. Kethuk function (⇛)

a. The kethuk function subdivides the number of kethuk per *kenongan* to generate another *kenongan* with twice as many kethuk per kenong.

b. Alternative and equivalent definition: The kethuk moves up one level of subdivision of the *gongan* thus resulting in twice as many kethuk per kenong as in the previous form.

$$\text{t N t N/G} \Rrightarrow \text{t . t N t . t N/G}$$

The Irama and Kethuk functions are ordered. While they can operate independently of one another, the Kethuk function cannot be applied until an Irama expansion has occurred at the next higher level. (See diagram 7.)

The Irama function and the Kethuk function operate independently and/or together on *gongan* and are the most powerful of the rules that can generate new *gongan* forms. They are the core of this theory of gamelan *gongan* forms and can generate, by themselves, the majority of gamelan *gongan*.

Alone, however, the Irama function and the Kethuk function cannot generate every form. Less explicit, less powerful, and less often applied functions must be introduced to complete the derivations.

3. Gong deletion function (ϕG)

The Gong deletion function operates upon the middle gong of a re-

Diagram 7

FORM	*keteg-kethuk pattern*	*kenongan*	*gongan* (*first gong deleted*)
Ladrang, kethuk 2 kerepan, Irama I	. t . .	. t . P . t . N	. t . (P) . t . N . t . P . t . N(Ǥ) . t . P . t . N . t . P . t . N/G

Irama function, (⇒), operating upon the form Ladrang, Irama I,
yields the form Ladrang, Irama II.
Or, as notated in this theory
⇒ (Ladrang, Irama I) → Ladrang, Irama II*

| Ladrang, kethuk 2,
Irama II | . . . t . . . . | . . . t . . . P
. . . t . . . N | . . . t . . . (P)
. . . t . . . N
. . . t . . . P
. . . t . . . N(Ǥ)
. . . t . . . P
. . . t . . . N
. . . t . . . P
. . . t . . . N/G |

Kethuk function, (⇒), operating upon the form Ladrang, kethuk 2,
Irama II, yields the form, Minggah, kethuk 4 kerepan, Irama I
Or, as notated in this theory
(Ladrang, kethuk 2, Irama II) → Minggah, kethuk 4 kerepan, Irama I

| Minggah, kethuk 4
kerepan, Irama I | . t . . | . t . . . t . .
. t . . . t . N | . t . . . t . .
. t . . . t . N
. t . . . t . .
. t . . . t . N(Ǥ)
. t . . . t . .
. t . . . t . N
. t . . . t . .
. t . . . t . N/G |

---

* The change to Irama II is not normally notated as such in Java. A composition played in Irama I and/or Irama II is notated as Irama I, although the number of *keteg*, often equated with the dot, has doubled in Irama II.

Diagram 7 (*continued*)

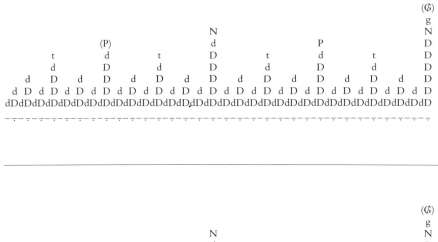

Subdivision
Ladrang, kethuk 2 kerepan, Irama I

```
              (G̸)                                      G
               g                                        g
        N              N              N              N        0.  φ+G
 (P)    d       P      D      P       d      P       D        1.  kenong
  t  d  t  D  t  d  t  D  t  d  t  D  t  d  t  D              2.  kempul
  d  D  d  D  d  D  d  D  d  D  d  D  d  D  d  D              3.  kethuk
 d D d D d D d D d D d D d D d D d D d D d D d D d D d D d D  4.  (saron)
dDdDdDdDdDdDdDdDdDdDdDdDdDdDdDdDdDdDdDdDdDdDdDdDdDdDdDdDdD  KETEG 5. bonang barung
‾ ‾ ‾ ‾ ‾ ‾ ‾ ‾ ‾ ‾ ‾ ‾ ‾ ‾ ‾ ‾ ‾ ‾ ‾ ‾ ‾ ‾ ‾ ‾ ‾ ‾ ‾ ‾
```

Ladrang, kethuk 2, Irama II

```
                                                        G
                                                        g
                N                              N        0.  φ+G
        P               d               P      D        1.  kenong
    t       d       t       D       t       d       t       D        2.  kempul
    d       D       d       D       d       D       d       D        3.  kethuk
  d  D  d  D  d  D  d  D  d  D  d  D  d  D  d  D       4.  (saron)
 d D d D d D d D d D d D d D d D d D d D d D d D d D d D d D d D      5.
dDdDdDdDdDdDdDdDdDdDdDdDdDdDdDdDdDdDdDdDdDdDdDdDdDdDdDdDdD  KETEG 6. bonang barung
‾ ‾ ‾ ‾ ‾ ‾ ‾ ‾ ‾ ‾ ‾ ‾ ‾ ‾ ‾ ‾ ‾ ‾ ‾ ‾ ‾ ‾ ‾ ‾ ‾ ‾ ‾ ‾
```

(Kethuk remains at level 3. KETEG/bonang barung move from level 5 to level 6.)

Minggah, kethuk 4 kerepan, Irama I

```
                                                        G
                                                        g
                N                              N        0.  φ+G
                d                              D        1.  kenong
        d               D               d      D        2.
  t  d  t  D  t  d  t  D  t  d  t  D  t  d  t  D        3.
  d  D  d  D  d  D  d  D  d  D  d  D  d  D  d  D        4.  kethuk
 d D d D d D d D d D d D d D d D d D d D d D d D d D d D d D  5.  (saron)
dDdDdDdDdDdDdDdDdDdDdDdDdDdDdDdDdDdDdDdDdDdDdDdDdDdDdDdDdD  KETEG 6. bonang barung
‾ ‾ ‾ ‾ ‾ ‾ ‾ ‾ ‾ ‾ ‾ ‾ ‾ ‾ ‾ ‾ ‾ ‾ ‾ ‾ ‾ ‾ ‾ ‾ ‾ ‾ ‾ ‾
```

(Kethuk moves from level 3 to level 4. KETEG/bonang barung remain at level 6.)

peated *gongan* unit and results in the elimination of the middle gong. Deletion gong occurs between the forms Ayak-ayakan and Lancaran and results in a *gongan* with four *kenongan* per gong rather than two *kenongan* per gong. (See diagram 8.)

Diagram 8

Schema   *Subdivision*

Ayak-ayakan,   P   P   g   marked by kempul
  Irama I,   ṭ Ṇ ṭ Ṇ ṭ Ṇ ṭ Ṇ   1. kenong
  kethuk 1   2. kethuk/(saron)
  ngganter   KETEG   3. bonang barung

(Ayak-ayakan, Irama I, kethuk 1 ngganter)
→ (Ayak-ayakan, Irama I, kethuk 2 ngganter)

            P   P   g   marked by kempul
t . tṆt . tṆt . tṆt . tṆ   1. kenong
                                   2. (saron)
                      KETEG   3. bonang barung/kethuk

ϕG (Ayak-ayakan, Irama I, kethuk 2 ngganter)
→ Lancaran, Irama I

            ϕ g   marked by G or S
t . tṆt . tṆt . tṆt . tṆ/G   1. kenong
                                   2. (saron)
                   KETEG   3. kethuk/bonang barung

The Lancaran form, which results from the operation of the kethuk function and the gong deletion function upon Ayak-ayakan, is not yet complete. One more function is needed to complete the derivation. This final function is termed the "Plus kempul" function.

4. Plus kempul function (+ P)

There is a strong tendency in the derivation of *gongan* to delete all markers of the hierarchical subdivisions between kethuk and kenong. This general tendency is most striking in the later stages of Derivation B. Each time the kethuk function operates upon a form to yield another form, the kethuk moves up one level of the subdivision while the kenong remains in the same position. The level of subdivision left vacant by the "upward" movement of the kethuk remains vacant, resulting in an increasingly long list of subdivisions, or unmarked levels of subdivision, notated as ϕ. (See diagram 9.)

Diagram 9

Mérong, kethuk 4 awis, Irama I   Mérong, kethuk 8 awis, Irama I

g ϕ+G   g ϕ+G
1. kenong   1. kenong
2. ϕ 2. ϕ
3. ϕ 3. ϕ
4. kethuk   4. ϕ
   etc.   5. kethuk
                                                    etc.

However, there are a comparatively small number of forms, albeit among the most popular in the repertoire, which insert a subdivision between kethuk and kenong. These forms are Lancaran, Bubaran, Minggah Ladrang Kethuk 2 Irama I–IV, and Ketawang Kethuk 2 Irama I–II. The kempul, which in earlier forms is used as an end-marking gong, becomes the divider of the *kenongan*. The kempul always marks only *dhing* and is usually deleted in the first *kenongan*. (The first kempul is not always deleted in archaic pieces, that is, certain Kebogiro, or in gamelan pieces outside the Central Javanese area, or in Yogyakarta style Ketawang.) This special use of the kempul serves to differentiate some forms from others that are otherwise formally identical: Minggah Ladrang, kethuk 2, Irama III from Mérong, kethuk 2 awis; or, Ketawang, kethuk 2, Irama II from Ketawang Gendhing, kethuk 2 kerep. The factor of greater identifiability may have influenced the retention of the special use of the kempul in later derivations but does not account for the initial use of the kempul in forms Lancaran and Kebogiro, which are differentiated from comparable forms—Ayak-ayakan, Irama I—by the number of kenong per gong.

This grammar of gamelan *gongan* is written as a sequence of derivations: *Derivation A*, 1 kethuk per kenong, 2 kethuk per kenong, et cetera; *Derivation B*, 2 kethuk per kenong, 4 kethuk per kenong, et cetera. All derivations begin with Sampak. (See chart at end of this appendix.)

While a certain chronology is implicit and intentional in this theory, I do not mean to say that all *gongan* originate from Sampak. The Irama function (or the kethuk function) can be applied in reverse, resulting in a contracted *gongan* as easily as in a forward movement resulting in an expanded *gongan*. The pieces Ayak-ayakan, Srepegan, and Sampak are often performed in the order given above, each change in piece manifesting the Irama function operating in reverse. I do believe, however, that the forms Kebogiro, Lancaran, Ayak-ayakan, and Monggang represent archaic and in some sense "original" *gongan* forms.

Key to Notational Symbols Used in this Theory

$\Rightarrow$ = Irama function

$\twoheadrightarrow$ = Kethuk function

ϕ = Deletion

$\rightarrow$ = Becomes

$+P$ = Plus kempul function

$\Rightarrow$ (Srepegan) = Irama function operating upon Srepegan

$\twoheadrightarrow$ (Ayak-ayakan) = Kethuk function operating upon Ayak-ayakan

ϕG (Ayak-ayakan) = Deleting gong function operating upon Ayak-ayakan

((dD) dD) = dD subdivided into dDdD, or

d   D

d D d D

(((dD) dD) dD) = dD subdivided into dDdDdDdD, or

d   D

d D d D

dDdDdDdD

Gamelan Gongan Grammar

Derivation A

1 kethuk per kenong
2 kenong per gong

Derivation level

Sampak → ((dD) dD)

Schema:

P   P
N Ṇ N Ṇ

Subdivision: *Horizontal and pot gong markers*

             g   g+g → P P
KETEG 1 kenong/bonang barung   1 dD → N Ṇ

1. ⇒ (Sampak) → Srepegan
   Srepegan → (((dD) dD) dD)

   Schema:

             P   P
        t Ṇ t Ṇ t Ṇ t Ṇ

   Subdivision:

             g   g+g → P P
             1 kenong/saron   1 dD → N N
   KETEG 2 kethuk/   2 dD → – –̣
               bonang barung   d → t

2. ⇒ (Srepegan) → Ayak-ayakan, Irama I
   Ayak-ayakan, Irama I → ((((dD) dD) dD) dD)

   Schema:

                 P   P
          ṭ Ṇ ṭ Ṇ ṭ Ṇ ṭ Ṇ

   Subdivision:

             g   g+g → P P
             1 kenong   1 dD → N N
             2 kethuk/saron   2   d → t
   KETEG 3 bonang barung   3 dD → – –̣

3. ⇒ (Ayak-ayakan, Irama I) → Ayak-ayakan, Irama II
    Ayak-ayakan, Irama II → (((((dD) dD) dD) dD) dD)

Schema:

$$\begin{array}{cccc} & P & & P \\ . \; \underset{.}{t} \; . \; \underset{.}{N} \; . \; \underset{.}{t} \; . \; \underset{.}{N} \; . \; \underset{.}{t} \; . \; \underset{.}{N} \; . \; \underset{.}{t} \; . \; \underset{.}{N} \end{array}$$

Subdivision:

	g		g+g	→ P P
	1 kenong		1 dD	→ N N
	2 kethuk/saron		2 d	→ t
	3 ϕ		3	
KETEG	4 bonang barung		4 dD	→ – –

Derivation A

2 kethuk per kenong
2 kenong per gong
(Begins from Derivation A, 1 kethuk per kenong, 2 kenong per gong)

Derivation level

1. ⇒ (Sampak) → Srepegan
    Srepegan → (((dD) dD) dD)

2. ⇒ (Srepegan) → Ayak-ayakan, Irama I
    Ayak-ayakan Irama I → ((((dD) dD) dD) dD)

To this point all derivations are the same. Now begins the part of Derivation A which differs from all other derivations. Ayak-ayakan appears in both Derivation A, 1 kethuk per kenong and Derivation A, 2 kethuk per kenong. This is because Ayak-ayakan has two different forms with two different *keteg-kethuk patterns.* Derivation A, 1 kethuk per kenong illustrates the use of kethuk 1 ngganter in the form ṭ Ṇ. Derivation A, 2 kethuk per kenong illustrates the use of kethuk 2 ngganter in the form t . t Ṇ.

2′. ⇛ (Ayak-ayakan, kethuk 1 ngganter) →
    Ayak-ayakan, kethuk 2 ngganter, Irama I/Monggang*
    Ayak-ayakan, kethuk 2 ngganter → ((((dD) dD) dD) dD)

---

* Monggang differs from Ayak-ayakan, kethuk 2 ngganter, Irama I in that the two concatenated *gongan* are differentiated in Monggang by a smaller gong marking the first *gongan* and a larger gong marking the second.

Schema:

$$P \qquad\qquad P$$

t . t Ṇ t . t Ṇ t . t Ṇ t . t Ṇ

Subdivision:

KETEG	g 1 kenong 2 saron 3 kethuk/ bonang barung	g+g → P P 1 dD → N N 2 3 dD → – ⸗ d → t

3. ⇒ (Ayak-ayakan, Irama I) → Ayak-ayakan, Irama II/ Ködok-Ngorek*
    Ayak-ayakan, Irama II → (((((dD) dD) dD) dD) dD)

Schema:

$$P$$

ṭ . ṭ Ṇ ṭ . ṭ Ṇ

ṭ . ṭ Ṇ ṭ . ṭ Ṇ/P

Subdivision:

KETEG	g 1 kenong 2 (saron) 3 kethuk 4 bonang barung	g+g → P P 1 dD → N N 2 3 d → t 4 dD → – ⸗

4. ⇒ (Ayak-ayakan, Irama II) → Ayak-ayakan, Irama III
    Ayak-ayakan, Irama III → ((((((dD) dD) dD) dD) dD) dD)

Schema:

. ṭ . . . ṭ . Ṇ

. ṭ . . . ṭ . Ṇ/S

. ṭ . . . ṭ . Ṇ

. ṭ . . . ṭ . Ṇ/S

Subdivision:

KETEG	g 1 kenong 2 φ 3 kethuk/(saron) 4 5 bonang barung	g+g → S S 1 dD → N N 2 3 d → t 4 5 dD → – ⸗

*Kodok-Ngorek, like Monggang, differs from the equivalent Ayak-ayakan form by the differentiation of the gong markers of the two concatenated *gongan*.

4a.* ⇒ (Ayak-ayakan, Irama III) → Ketawang, kethuk 2 kerepan, Irama I
   +P

Schema:

$$
\begin{array}{ccccccc}
. & \d{t} & . & (\d{P}) & . & \d{t} & . & \d{N} \\
. & \d{t} & . & P & . & \d{t} & . & \d{N}/G \\
. & \d{t} & . & (\d{P}) & . & \d{t} & . & \d{N} \\
. & \d{t} & . & P & . & \d{t} & . & \d{N}/G
\end{array}
$$

Subdivision:

g			g+g	→ G G
	1 kenong		1 dD	→ N N
	2 kempul		2 d	→ P
	3 kethuk		3 d	→ t
	4 (saron)		4	
KETEG	5 bonang barung		5 dD	→ − ⫶

(This form is represented by the piece *Puspawarna*.)

5.   ⇒ (Ketawang, kethuk 2 kerepan, Irama I) →
   Ketawang, kethuk 2, Irama II →
   (((((((dD) dD) dD) dD) dD) dD) dD)

Schema:

$$
\begin{array}{ccccccccccc}
. & . & . & \d{t} & . & . & . & (\d{P}) & . & . & . & \d{t} & . & . & . & \d{N} \\
. & . & . & \d{t} & . & . & . & P & . & . & . & \d{t} & . & . & . & \d{N}/G \\
. & . & . & \d{t} & . & . & . & (\d{P}) & . & . & . & \d{t} & . & . & . & \d{N} \\
. & . & . & \d{t} & . & . & . & P & . & . & . & \d{t} & . & . & . & \d{N}/G
\end{array}
$$

Subdivision:

g			g+g	→ G G
	1 kenong		1 dD	→ N N
	2 kempul		2 d	→ P
	3 kethuk		3 d	→ t
	4 (saron)		4	
	5		5	
KETEG	6 bonang barung		6 dD	→ − ⫶

(This form is also represented by *Puspawarna*.)

---

* The subscript *a* is used to differentiate forms within one box that are at the same plane vertically on the chart (have same relationship of kethuk per kenong) and the same plane horizontally (have the same derivation level) but differ in the presence or nonpresence of kempul. This occurs repeatedly in respect to various minggah and mérong structures in Derivation B.

5a. ⇒ (Ayak-ayakan, Irama III) →
Ketawang Gendhing, kethuk 2 kerep, Irama I →
((((((((dD) dD) dD) dD) dD) dD) dD)

Schema:

```
.   .   .   ṭ   .   .   .   .   .   .   ṭ   .   .   .   Ṇ
.   .   .   ṭ   .   .   .   .   .   .   ṭ   .   .   .   Ṇ/G
.   .   .   ṭ   .   .   .   .   .   .   ṭ   .   .   Ṇ
.   .   .   ṭ   .   .   .   .   .   .   ṭ   .   .   .   Ṇ/G
```

Subdivision:

	g	g+g	→ G G
	1 kenong	1 dD	→ N N
	2 φ	2	
	3 kethuk	3 d	→ t
	4	4	
	5 (saron)	5	
KETEG	6 bonang barung	6 dD	→ – ṭ

(This form is represented by *Kabor*)

6. ⇒ (Ketawang Gendhing, kethuk 2 kerep, Irama I) →
Ketawang Gendhing, kethuk 2 kerep, Irama II →
(((((((((dD) dD) dD) dD) dD) dD) dD) dD)

Schema:

```
.   .   .   .   .   .   ṭ   .   .   .   .   .   .   ṭ   .   .   .   .   .   N
.   .   .   .   .   .   ṭ   .   .   .   .   .   .   ṭ   .   .   .   .   .   N/G
.   .   .   .   .   .   ṭ   .   .   .   .   .   .   ṭ   .   .   .   .   .   N
.   .   .   .   .   .   ṭ   .   .   .   .   .   .   ṭ   .   .   .   Ṇ/G
```

Subdivision:

	g	g+g	→ G G
	1 kenong	1 dD	→ N N
	2 φ	2	
	3 kethuk	3 d	→ t
	4	4	
	5 (saron)	5	
	6	6	
KETEG	7 bonang barung	7 dD	→ – ṭ

Derivation A

4 kethuk per kenong
Same as Derivation A, 2 kethuk per kenong through derivation level 5.
6′. ↠ (Ketawang Gendhing, kethuk 2, Irama II) →
Ketawang Gending, kethuk 4, kerep, Irama I →
$(((((((((dD)\,dD)\,dD)\,dD)\,dD)\,dD)\,dD)\,dD)$

Schema:

```
. . . t . . . . . . . . . t . . . . . . . . t . . . . . . . . t . . . N
. . . t . . . . . . . . . t . . . . . . . . t . . . . . . . . t . . . N/G
. . . t . . . . . . . . . t . . . . . . . . t . . . . . . . . t . . . N
. . . t . . . . . . . . . t . . . . . . . . t . . . . . . . . t . . . N/G
```

Subdivision:

g		g+g → G G
1 kenong		1 dD → N N
2 φ		2
3 φ		3
4 kethuk		4 d → t
5 (saron)		5
6		6
KETEG 7 bonang barung		7 dD → – –

(This form is represented by the piece *Krawitan*.)

7. ⇒ (Ketawang Gendhing, kethuk 4 kerep, Irama I) →
Ketawang Gendhing, kethuk 4, Irama II →
$((((((((((dD)\,dD)\,dD)\,dD)\,dD)\,dD)\,dD)\,dD)\,dD)$

Schema:

```
. . . . . . . t . . . . . . . . . . . . . . t . . . . . . . .
. . . . . . . t . . . . . . . . . . . . . . t . . . . . . N
. . . . . . . t . . . . . . . . . . . . . . t . . . . . . . .
. . . . . . . t . . . . . . . . . . . . . . t . . . . . . N/G
. . . . . . . t . . . . . . . . . . . . . . t . . . . . . . .
. . . . . . . t . . . . . . . . . . . . . . t . . . . . . N
. . . . . . . t . . . . . . . . . . . . . . t . . . . . . . .
. . . . . . . t . . . . . . . . . . . . . . t . . . . . N/G
```

Subdivision:

g
 1 kenong
 2 ϕ
 3 ϕ
 4 kethuk
 5
 6 (saron)
 7
KETEG 8 bonang barung

g+g   → G G
1 dD → N N
2
3
4 d → t
5
6
7
8 dD → − ⊤

(This form is represented by *Krawitan*, Irama II.)

Derivation B

2 kethuk per kenong
4 kenong per gong

Derivation level

1. ⇒ (Sampak) → Srepegan
Srepegan → (((dD) dD) dD)

2. ⇒ (Srepegan) →
Ayak-ayakan, Irama I, kethuk 1 ngganter →
((((dD) dD) dD) dD)

Schema: P   P
         t N t N t N t N

Subdivision:

g
 1 kenong
 2 kethuk/(saron)
KETEG 3 bonang barung

g+g → P P
1 dD → N N
2 d → t
3 dD → − ⊤

2.1*⇒ (Ayak-ayakan, kethuk 1 ngganter, Irama I) →
Ayak-ayakan, kethuk 2 ngganter, Irama I →
((((dD) dD) dD) dD)

*2.1, 2.2, and 2.3 are operations necessary to get from Ayak-ayakan, Irama I, 1 kethuk per kenong, 2 kenong per gong to Gangsaran, Kebogiro and Lancaran, that is, (1) change kethuk per kenong relationship, (2) delete gong, and (3) add kempul. This transition is the most complex of this descriptive system.

Schema: P   P

t . t Ṇ t . t Ṇ t . t Ṇ t . t Ṇ

Subdivision:

g		g+g	→ P P
1	kenong	1	dD	→ N N
2	(saron)	2		
KETEG 3	kethuk/bonang barung	3	dD	→ − ‗
		d	→ t

2.2   ⌀G (Ayak-ayakan, kethuk 2 ngganter) →
       Lancaran, incomplete

Schema: (⌀̵G)

t . t Ṇ t . t Ṇ t . t Ṇ t . t Ṇ/G

2.3   +P (Lancaran, incomplete) →
       Gangsaran Lancaran/Kebogiro, Irama I →
       ((((dD) dD) dD) dD)

Schema: (⌀̵G)

ṭ (Ṗ) t Ṇ t Ṗ t Ṇ t Ṗ t Ṇ t Ṗ t Ṇ/G

Subdivision:

g		g+g	→ ⌀+G
1	kenong	1	dD → N N
2	kempul/(saron)	2	d → P
KETEG 3	kethuk/bonang barung	3	dD → − ‗
		d	→ t

3.   ⇒ (Lancaran, Irama I) →
      Lancaran, Irama II/Bubaran, Irama I →
      (((((dD) dD) dD) dD) dD)

Schema:

ṭ (Ṗ) ṭ Ṇ ṭ Ṗ ṭ Ṇ/(⌀̵G)

ṭ Ṗ ṭ Ṇ ṭ Ṗ ṭ Ṇ/G

Subdivision:

g		g+g → ⌀+G	
1	kenong	1	dD → N N
2	kempul	2	d → P
3	kethuk/(saron)	3	d → t
KETEG 4	bonang barung	4	dD → − ‗

4. ⇒ (Bubaran, Irama I) →
   Bubaran, Irama II/Ladrang, kethuk 2 kerepan, Irama I →
   ((((((dD) dD) dD) dD) dD) dD)

   Schema:

   ```
   .  ṭ  .  (P̣)  .  ṭ  .  Ṇ
   .  ṭ  .  P̣   .  ṭ  .  Ṇ/(G̸)
   .  ṭ  .  P̣   .  ṭ  .  Ṇ
   .  ṭ  .  P̣   .  ṭ  .  Ṇ/G
   ```

   Subdivision:

g		g+g	→ ⌀+G
1	kenong	1 dD	→ N N
2	kempul	2 d	→ P
3	kethuk	3 d	→ t
4	(saron)	4	
KETEG 5	bonang barung	5 dD	→ – ¬

   (This form is represented by the piece *Remeng.*)

5. ⇒ (Ladrang, kethuk 2 kerepan, Irama I) →
   Ladrang, kethuk 2, Irama II →
   (((((((dD) dD) dD) dD) dD) dD) dD)

   Schema:

   ```
   .  .  .  ṭ  .  .  .  (P̣)  .  .  .  ṭ  .  .  .  Ṇ
   .  .  .  ṭ  .  .  .  P̣   .  .  .  ṭ  .  .  .  Ṇ/(G̸)
   .  .  .  ṭ  .  .  .  P̣   .  .  .  ṭ  .  .  .  Ṇ
   .  .  .  ṭ  .  .  .  P̣   .  .  .  ṭ  .  .  .  Ṇ/G
   ```

   Subdivision:

g		g+g	→ ⌀+G
1	kenong	1 dD	→ N N
2	kempul	2 d	→ P
3	kethuk	3 d	→ t
4	(saron)	4	
5		5	
KETEG 6	bonang barung	6 dD	→ – ¬

   (This form is represented by *Remeng*, Irama II.)

5a.   φP (Minggah Ladrang, kethuk 2, Irama II) →
Mérong, kethuk 2 kerep, Irama I

Schema:

```
.  .  .  ṭ  .  .  .  .  .  .  .  .  ṭ  .  .  .  N̩
.  .  .  ṭ  .  .  .  .  .  .  .  .  ṭ  .  .  .  N̩/(Ǥ)
.  .  .  ṭ  .  .  .  .  .  .  .  .  ṭ  .  .  .  N̩
.  .  .  ṭ  .  .  .  .  .  .  .  .  ṭ  .  .  .  N̩/G
```

Subdivision:

g		g+g	→ φ+G
1	kenong	1 dD	→ N N
2	φ	2	
3	ketuk	3 d	→ t
4		4	
5	(saron)	5	
KETEG 6	bonang barung	6 dD	→ – ṭ

(This form is represented by the piece *Gambir Sawit*, Mérong section.)

6.   ⇒ (Minggah Ladrang, kethuk 2, Irama II) →
Minggah Ladrang, kethuk 2, Irama III →
(((((((((dD) dD) dD) dD) dD) dD) dD) dD)

Schema:

```
.  .  .  .  .  .  ṭ  .  .  .  .  .  (P). .  .  .  .  .  ṭ  .  .  .  .  .  N̩
.  .  .  .  .  .  ṭ  .  .  .  .  .  P . .  .  .  .  .  ṭ  .  .  .  .  .  N̩/(Ǥ)
.  .  .  .  .  .  ṭ  .  .  .  .  .  P . .  .  .  .  .  ṭ  .  .  .  .  .  N̩
.  .  .  .  .  .  ṭ  .  .  .  .  .  P . .  .  .  .  .  ṭ  .  .  .  .  .  N̩/G
```

Subdivision:

g		g+g	→ φ+G
1	kenong	1 dD	→ N N
2	kempul	2 d	→ P
3	kethuk	3 d	→ t
4		4	
5	(saron)	5	
6		6	
KETEG 7	bonang barung	7 dD	→ – ṭ

6a. ⇒ (Mérong, kethuk 2 kerep, Irama I) →
    Mérong, kethuk 2, Irama II/Mérong, kethuk 2 awis, Irama I →
    (((((((((dD) dD) dD) dD) dD) dD) dD) dD)

Schema:

```
. . . . . . t . . . . . . . . . . . . . . . t . . . . . . Ṇ
. . . . . . ṭ . . . . . . . . . . . . . . . ṭ . . . . . . Ṇ/(Ǥ)
. . . . . . ṭ . . . . . . . . . . . . . . . ṭ . . . . . . Ṇ
. . . . . . ṭ . . . . . . . . . . . . . . . ṭ . . . . . . Ṇ/G
```

Subdivision:

g		g+g → φ+G
1 kenong		1 dD → N N
2 φ		2
3 kethuk		3 d → t
4		4
5		5
6 (saron)		6
KETEG 7 bonang barung		7 dD → – ̤

(This form is represented by the piece *Lara Njala*.)

7. ⇒ (Minggah Ladrang, kethuk 2, Irama III) →
   Minggah Ladrang, kethuk 2, Irama IV →
   ((((((((((dD) dD) dD) dD) dD) dD) dD) dD) dD)

Schema:

```
. . . . . . . . . . . . . ṭ . . . . . . . . . . . . (Ṗ)
. . . . . . . . . . . . . ṭ . . . . . . . . . . . . Ṇ
. . . . . . . . . . . . . ṭ . . . . . . . . . . . . Ṗ
. . . . . . . . . . . . . ṭ . . . . . . . . . . . . Ṇ/(Ǥ)
. . . . . . . . . . . . . ṭ . . . . . . . . . . . . Ṗ
. . . . . . . . . . . . . ṭ . . . . . . . . . . . . Ṇ
. . . . . . . . . . . . . ṭ . . . . . . . . . . . . Ṗ
. . . . . . . . . . . . . ṭ . . . . . . . . . . . . Ṇ/G
```

Subdivision:

g		g+g	→ ϕ+G
1	kenong	1 dD	→ N N
2	kempul	2 d	→ P
3	kethuk	3 d	→ t
4		4	
5		5	
6	(saron)	6	
7		7	
KETEG 8	bonang barung	8 dD	→ _ ⁻

7a. ⇒ (Mérong, kethuk 2 awis, Irama I) →
   Mérong, kethuk 2, Irama II →
   (((((((((dD) dD) dD) dD) dD) dD) dD) dD) dD)

Schema:

```
. . . . . . . . . . . . . . . . t . . . . . . . . . . . . . . . .
. . . . . . . . . . . . . . . . t . . . . . . . . . . . . . . . . N
. . . . . . . . . . . . . . . . t . . . . . . . . . . . . . . . .
. . . . . . . . . . . . . . . . t . . . . . . . . . . . . . . . . N/(Ǥ)
. . . . . . . . . . . . . . . . t . . . . . . . . . . . . . . . .
. . . . . . . . . . . . . . . . t . . . . . . . . . . . . . . . . N
. . . . . . . . . . . . . . . . t . . . . . . . . . . . . . . . .
. . . . . . . . . . . . . . . . t . . . . . . . . . . . . . . . . N/G
```

Subdivision:

g		g+g	→ ϕ+G
1	kenong	1 dD	→ N N
2	ϕ	2	
3	kethuk	3 d	→ t
4		4	
5		5	
6	(saron)	6	
7		7	
KETEG 8	bonang barung	8 dD	→ _ ⁻

Derivation B

4 kethuk per kenong
4 kenong per gong

Same as Derivation B, 2 kethuk per kenong, through derivation level 4.

5.   ⇒ (Minggah Ladrang, kethuk 2, Irama II) →
     ϕP Minggah, kethuk 4 kerepan, Irama I →
     (((((((dD) dD) dD) dD) dD) dD) dD)

Schema:

```
. ṭ . . . ṭ . . . ṭ . . . ṭ . N
. ṭ . . . ṭ . . . ṭ . . . ṭ . N/(Ꞡ)
. ṭ . . . ṭ . . . ṭ . . . ṭ . N
. ṭ . . . ṭ . . . ṭ . . . ṭ . N/G
```

Subdivision:

	g		g+g → ϕ+G
	1 kenong		1 dD → N N
	2 ϕ		2
	3 ϕ		3
	4 kethuk		4 d → t
	5 (saron)		5
KETEG	6 bonang barung		6 dD → _ ⊤

(This form is represented by the piece *Gambir Sawit*, Minggah section.)

6.   ⇒ (Minggah, kethuk 4 kerepan, Irama I) →
     Minggah, kethuk 4, Irama II/Mérong, kethuk 4 kerep, Irama I →
     ((((((((dD) dD) dD) dD) dD) dD) dD) dD)

Schema:

```
. . . ṭ . . . . . . ṭ . . . . . . ṭ . . . . . . ṭ . . . N
. . . ṭ . . . . . . ṭ . . . . . . ṭ . . . . . . ṭ . . . N/(Ꞡ)
. . . ṭ . . . . . . ṭ . . . . . . ṭ . . . . . . ṭ . . . N
. . . ṭ . . . . . . ṭ . . . . . . ṭ . . . . . . ṭ . . . N/G
```

Subdivision:

g		g+g	→	φ+G
1 kenong		1	dD →	N N
2 φ		2		
3 φ		3		
4 kethuk		4	d →	t
5		5		
6 (saron)		6		
KETEG 7 bonang barung		7	dD →	_ $\bar{-}$

(This form is represented by the piece *Tukung*, Mérong section.)

7. ⇒ (Mérong, kethuk 4 kerep, Irama I) → Minggah, kethuk 4, Irama III/
Mérong, kethuk 4, Irama II/Mérong, kethuk 4 awis, Irama I →
$((((((((((\text{dD})\,\text{dD})\,\text{dD})\,\text{dD})\,\text{dD})\,\text{dD})\,\text{dD})\,\text{dD})\,\text{dD})$

Schema:

```
. . . . . . . ṭ                     ṭ . . . . . .
. . . ṭ . . . ṭ                     ṭ . . . . . . . Ṇ
. . . . . . . ṭ                     ṭ . . . . . .
. . . . . . . ṭ                     ṭ . . . . . . . Ṇ/(Ǥ)
. . . . . . . ṭ                     ṭ . . . . . .
. . . . . . . ṭ                     ṭ . . . . . . . Ṇ
. . . . . . . ṭ                     ṭ . . . . . .
. . . . . . . ṭ                     ṭ . . . . . Ṇ/G
```

Subdivision:

g		g+g	→	φ+G
1 kenong		1	dD →	N N
2 φ		2		
3 φ		3		
4 kethuk		4	d →	t
5		5		
6		6		
7 (saron)		7		
KETEG 8 bonang barung		8	dD →	_ $\bar{-}$

(This form is represented by the piece *Slebrak*, Mérong section.)

8. ⇒ (Mérong, kethuk 4 awis, Irama I) →
Mérong, kethuk 4, Irama II →
$(((((((((((\text{dD})\,\text{dD})\,\text{dD})\,\text{dD})\,\text{dD})\,\text{dD})\,\text{dD})\,\text{dD})\,\text{dD})\,\text{dD})$

Schema:

```
. . . . . . . . . . . . . . ṭ . . . . . . . . . . . . . . . _ _
. . . . . . . . . . . . . . ṭ . . . . . . . . . . . . . . . . .
. . . . . . . . . . . . . . ṭ . . . . . . . . . . . . . . . . .
. . . . . . . . . . . . . . ṭ . . . . . . . . . . . . . .Ṇ
. . . . . . . . . . . . . . ṭ . . . . . . . . . . . . . . . .
. . . . . . . . . . . . . . ṭ . . . . . . . . . . . . . . . .
. . . . . . . . . . . . . . ṭ . . . . . . . . . . . . . . . .
. . . . . . . . . . . . . . ṭ . . . . . . . . . . . .Ṇ/(Ǥ)
. . . . . . . . . . . . . . ṭ . . . . . . . . . . . . . . . .
. . . . . . . . . . . . . . ṭ . . . . . . . . . . . . . . . .
. . . . . . . . . . . . . . ṭ . . . . . . . . . . . . . . . .
. . . . . . . . . . . . . . ṭ . . . . . . . . . . . . . .Ṇ
. . . . . . . . . . . . . . ṭ . . . . . . . . . . . . . . . .
. . . . . . . . . . . . . . ṭ . . . . . . . . . . . . . . . .
. . . . . . . . . . . . . . ṭ . . . . . . . . . . . . . . . .
. . . . . . . . . . . . . . ṭ . . . . . . . . . . . . .Ṇ/G
```

Subdivision:

	g		g+g	→	φ+G
	1	kenong	1	dD →	N N
	2	φ	2		
	3	φ	3		
	4	kethuk	4	d →	t
	5		5		
	6		6		
	7	(saron)	7		
	8		8		
KETEG	9	bonang barung	9	dD →	_ ⊤

Derivation B
8 kethuk per kenong
4 kenong per gong

Same as Derivation B, 4 kethuk per kenong, through derivation level 5.

6. ⇶ (Minggah, kethuk 4, Irama II) →
Minggah, kethuk 8 kerepan, Irama I →
(((((((((dD) dD) dD) dD) dD) dD) dD) dD)

Schema:

. ṭ . . . ṭ . . . ṭ . . . ṭ . . . ṭ . . . ṭ . . . ṭ . . . ṭ . N
. ṭ . . . ṭ . . . ṭ . . . ṭ . . . ṭ . . . ṭ . . . ṭ . . . ṭ . N/(Ḡ)
. ṭ . . . ṭ . . . ṭ . . . ṭ . . . ṭ . . . ṭ . . . ṭ . . . ṭ . N
. ṭ . . . ṭ . . . ṭ . . . ṭ . . . ṭ . . . ṭ . . . ṭ . . . ṭ . N/G

Subdivision:

g		g+g	→ ϕ+G
1 kenong		1 dD	→ N N
2 ϕ		2	
3 ϕ		3	
4 ϕ		4	
5 kethuk		5 d	→ t
6 (saron)		6	
KETEG 7 bonang barung		7 dD	→ _ _

(This form is represented by the piece *Lambang Sari*.)

7. ⇒ (Minggah, kethuk 8 kerepan, Irama I) →
Minggah, kethuk 8, Irama II/Mérong, kethuk 8 kerep, Irama I →
((((((((((dD) dD) dD) dD) dD) dD) dD) dD) dD)

Schema:

. . . ṭ . . . . ṭ . . . . . . ṭ . . . . . . ṭ . . . .
. . . ṭ . . . . ṭ . . . . . . ṭ . . . . . . ṭ . . N
. . . ṭ . . . . . . ṭ . . . . . . ṭ . . . . . . ṭ . . . .
. . . ṭ . . . . ṭ . . . . . . ṭ . . . . . . ṭ . . N/(Ḡ)
. . . ṭ . . . . . . ṭ . . . . . . ṭ . . . . . . ṭ . . . .
. . . ṭ . . . . ṭ . . . . . . ṭ . . . . . . ṭ . . N
. . . ṭ . . . . . . ṭ . . . . . . ṭ . . . . . . ṭ . . . .
. . . ṭ . . . . . . ṭ . . . . ṭ . . . . . . ṭ . . N/G

Subdivision:

	g		g+g	→ ∅+G
	1	kenong	1	dD → N N
	2	∅	2	
	3	∅	3	
	4	∅	4	
	5	kethuk	5	d → t
	6		6	
	7	(saron)	7	
KETEG	8	bonang barung	8	dD → _ _

(This form is represented by the piece *Jalaga*.)

8. ⇒ (Mérong, kethuk 8 kerep, Irama I) → Minggah, kethuk 8, Irama III/
Mérong, kethuk 8, Irama II/Mérong, kethuk 8 awis, Irama I →
(((((((((((dD) dD) dD) dD) dD) dD) dD) dD) dD) dD)

Schema:

```
. . . . . . . t . . . . . . . . . . . . . t . . . . . . . .
. . . . . . . t . . . . . . . . . . . . . t . . . . . . . .
. . . . . . . t . . . . . . . . . . . . . t . . . . . . . .
. . . . . . . t . . . . . . . . . . . . . t . . . . . N
. . . . . . . t . . . . . . . . . . . . . t . . . . . . . .
. . . . . . . t . . . . . . . . . . . . . t . . . . . . . .
. . . . . . . t . . . . . . . . . . . . . t . . . . . . . .
. . . . . . . t . . . . . . . . . . . . . t . . . . . . N/(Ḡ)
. . . . . . . t . . . . . . . . . . . . . t . . . . . . . .
. . . . . . . t . . . . . . . . . . . . . t . . . . . . . .
. . . . . . . t . . . . . . . . . . . . . t . . . . . . . .
. . . . . . . t . . . . . . . . . . . . . t . . . . . N
. . . . . . . t . . . . . . . . . . . . . t . . . . . . . .
. . . . . . . t . . . . . . . . . . . . . t . . . . . . . .
. . . . . . . t . . . . . . . . . . . . . t . . . . . . . .
. . . . . . . t . . . . . . . . . . . . . t . . . . . N/G
```

Subdivision:

	g		g+g	→ ϕ+G
	1 kenong		1	dD → N N
	2 ϕ		2	
	3 ϕ		3	
	4 ϕ		4	
	5 kethuk		5	d → t
	6		6	
	7 (saron)/ϕ		7	
	8 ϕ/(saron)		8	
KETEG	9 bonang barung		9	dD → _ ‾

(This form is represented by the piece *Pangrawit*, Pelog Pathet Lima, Yogyakarta style.)

9. ⇒ (Mérong, kethuk 8 awis, Irama I) → Minggah, kethuk 8, Irama IV/ Mérong, kethuk 8, Irama II →

(((((((((((dD) dD) dD) dD) dD) dD) dD) dD) dD) dD) dD)

Schema:

```
. . . . . . . . . . . . . t . . . . . . . . . . . . . .
. . . . . . . . . . . . . t . . . . . . . . . . . . . .
. . . . . . . . . . . . . t . . . . . . . . . . . . . .
. . . . . . . . . . . . . t . . . . . . . . . . . . . .
. . . . . . . . . . . . . t . . . . . . . . . . . . . .
. . . . . . . . . . . . . t . . . . . . . . . . . . . .
. . . . . . . . . . . . . t . . . . . . . . . . . . . .
. . . . . . . . . . . . . t . . . . . . . . . . . . . N
. . . . . . . . . . . . . t . . . . . . . . . . . . . .
. . . . . . . . . . . . . t . . . . . . . . . . . . . .
. . . . . . . . . . . . . t . . . . . . . . . . . . . .
. . . . . . . . . . . . . t . . . . . . . . . . . . . .
. . . . . . . . . . . . . t . . . . . . . . . . . . . .
. . . . . . . . . . . . . t . . . . . . . . . . . . . .
. . . . . . . . . . . . . t . . . . . . . . . . . . . .
. . . . . . . . . . . . . t . . . . . . . . . . N/(Ǥ)
. . . . . . . . . . . . . t . . . . . . . . . . . . . .
. . . . . . . . . . . . . t . . . . . . . . . . . . . .
. . . . . . . . . . . . . t . . . . . . . . . . . . . .
. . . . . . . . . . . . . t . . . . . . . . . . . . . .
```

```
. . . . . . . . . . . . . . ṭ . . . . . . . . . . . . .
. . . . . . . . . . . . . . ṭ . . . . . . . . . . . . .
. . . . . . . . . . . . . . ṭ . . . . . . . . . . . . .
. . . . . . . . . . . . . . ṭ . . . . . . . . . . . . .N
. . . . . . . . . . . . . . ṭ . . . . . . . . . . . . .
. . . . . . . . . . . . . . ṭ . . . . . . . . . . . . .
. . . . . . . . . . . . . . ṭ . . . . . . . . . . . . .
. . . . . . . . . . . . . . ṭ . . . . . . . . . . . . .
. . . . . . . . . . . . . . ṭ . . . . . . . . . . . . .
. . . . . . . . . . . . . . ṭ . . . . . . . . . . . . .
. . . . . . . . . . . . . . ṭ . . . . . . . . . . . . .
. . . . . . . . . . . . . . ṭ . . . . . . . . . . . . .N/G
```

Subdivision:

	g		g+g → ϕ+G
	1 kenong		1 dD → N N
	2 ϕ		2
	3 ϕ		3
	4 ϕ		4
	5 kethuk		5 d → t
	6		6
	7 ϕ/(saron)		7
	8 (saron)/ϕ		8
	9		9
KETEG	10 bonang barung		10 dD → _ ̅

Derivation B

16 kethuk per kenong
4 kenong per gong

Same as Derivation B, 8 kethuk per kenong, through derivation level 6.

7. ⇒ (Minggah, kethuk 8 kerepan, Irama II) →
   Minggah, kethuk 16 kerepan, Irama I →
   (((((((((dD) dD) dD) dD) dD) dD) dD) dD) dD)

Schema:

```
. ṭ . . . ṭ . . . ṭ . . . ṭ . . . ṭ . . . ṭ . . . ṭ . . . ṭ . .
. ṭ . . . ṭ . . . ṭ . . . ṭ . . . ṭ . . . ṭ . . . ṭ . . . ṭ .N
. ṭ . . . ṭ . . . ṭ . . . ṭ . . . ṭ . . . ṭ . . . ṭ . . . ṭ . .
```

```
. t . . . t . . . t . . . t . . . t . . . t . . . t . . . t . N/(G̸)
. t . . . t . . . t . . . t . . . t . . . t . . . t . . . t . .
. t . . . t . . . t . . . t . . . t . . . t . . . t . . . t . N
. t . . . t . . . t . . . t . . . t . . . t . . . t . . . t . .
. t . . . t . . . t . . . t . . . t . . . t . . . t . . . t . N/G
```

Subdivision:

g			g+g	→ ∅+G
1	kenong		1 dD	→ N N
2	∅		2	
3	∅		3	
4	∅		4	
5	∅		5	
6	kethuk		6 d	→ t
7	(saron)		7	
KETEG 8	bonang barung		8 dD	→ _ _

(This form is represented by the piece *Agul-agul*.)

8.   ⇒ (Minggah, kethuk 16 kerepan, Irama I) →
Minggah, kethuk 16, Irama II →
(((((((((((dD) dD) dD) dD) dD) dD) dD) dD) dD) dD)

Schema:

```
. . . t . . . . . . . t . . . . . . . t . . . . . . . t . . . .
. . . t . . . . . . . t . . . . . . . t . . . . . . . t . . . .
. . . t . . . . . . . t . . . . . . . t . . . . . . . t . . . .
. . . t . . . . . . . t . . . . . . . t . . . . . . . t . . . N
. . . t . . . . . . . t . . . . . . . t . . . . . . . t . . . .
. . . t . . . . . . . t . . . . . . . t . . . . . . . t . . . .
. . . t . . . . . . . t . . . . . . . t . . . . . . . t . . . .
. . . t . . . . . . . t . . . . . . . t . . . . . . . t . . . N/(G̸)
. . . t . . . . . . . t . . . . . . . t . . . . . . . t . . . .
. . . t . . . . . . . t . . . . . . . t . . . . . . . t . . . .
. . . t . . . . . . . t . . . . . . . t . . . . . . . t . . . .
. . . t . . . . . . . t . . . . . . . t . . . . . . . t . . . N
. . . t . . . . . . . t . . . . . . . t . . . . . . . t . . . .
. . . t . . . . . . . t . . . . . . . t . . . . . . . t . . . .
. . . t . . . . . . . t . . . . . . . t . . . . . . . t . . . .
. . . t . . . . . . . t . . . . . . . t . . . . . . . t . . . N/G
```

Subdivision:

g		g+g	→ ϕ+G
1 kenong		1 dD	→ N N
2 ϕ		2	
3 ϕ		3	
4 ϕ		4	
5 ϕ		5	
6 kethuk		6 d	→ t
7		7	
8 (saron)		8	
KETEG 9 bonang barung		9 dD	→ _ ⫶

9. ⇒ (Minggah, kethuk 16 kerepan, Irama II) →
   Minggah, kethuk 16, Irama III →
   (((((((((((dD) dD) dD) dD) dD) dD) dD) dD) dD) dD) dD)

Schema:

```
. . . . . . . . . . . . . . . . . . ṭ . . . . . . . . . . . . . . . . . .
. . . . . . . . . . . . . . . . . . ṭ . . . . . . . . . . . . . . . . . .
. . . . . . . . . . . . . . . . . . ṭ . . . . . . . . . . . . . . . . . .
. . . . . . . . . . . . . . . . . . ṭ . . . . . . . . . . . . . . . . . .
. . . . . . . . . . . . . . . . . . ṭ . . . . . . . . . . . . . . . . . .
. . . . . . . . . . . . . . . . . . ṭ . . . . . . . . . . . . . . . . . .
. . . . . . . . . . . . . . . . . . ṭ . . . . . . . . . . . . . . . . . .
. . . . . . . . . . . . . . . . . . ṭ . . . . . . . . . . . . . . . .N
. . . . . . . . . . . . . . . . . . ṭ . . . . . . . . . . . . . . . . . .
. . . . . . . . . . . . . . . . . . ṭ . . . . . . . . . . . . . . . . . .
. . . . . . . . . . . . . . . . . . ṭ . . . . . . . . . . . . . . . . . .
. . . . . . . . . . . . . . . . . . ṭ . . . . . . . . . . . . . . . . . .
. . . . . . . . . . . . . . . . . . ṭ . . . . . . . . . . . . . . . . . .
. . . . . . . . . . . . . . . . . . ṭ . . . . . . . . . . . . . . . . . .
. . . . . . . . . . . . . . . . . . ṭ . . . . . . . . . . . . . . . . . .
. . . . . . . . . . . . . . . . . . ṭ . . . . . . . . . . . . . . .N/(Ǥ)
. . . . . . . . . . . . . . . . . . ṭ . . . . . . . . . . . . . . . . . .
. . . . . . . . . . . . . . . . . . ṭ . . . . . . . . . . . . . . . . . .
. . . . . . . . . . . . . . . . . . ṭ . . . . . . . . . . . . . . . . . .
. . . . . . . . . . . . . . . . . . ṭ . . . . . . . . . . . . . . . . . .
. . . . . . . . . . . . . . . . . . ṭ . . . . . . . . . . . . . . . . . .
```

. . . . ṭ . . . .

. . . . ṭ . . . .

. . . . ṭ   Ṇ

. . . . ṭ . . . .

. . . . ṭ . . . .

. . . . ṭ . . . .

. . . . ṭ . . . .

. . . . ṭ . . . .

. . . . ṭ . . . .

. . . . ṭ . . . .

. . . . ṭ . . . . .Ṇ/G

Subdivision:

g			g+g	→ φ+G
1	kenong		1 dD	→ N N
2	φ		2	
3	φ		3	
4	φ		4	
5	φ		5	
6	kethuk		6 d	→ t
7			7	
8	(saron)		8	
9			9	
KETEG 10	bonang barung		10 dD	→ _ ‗

(This form is represented by the piece *Pangrawit*.)

Conclusion

This theory has attempted to demonstrate the generative processes of gamelan *gongan* structures. The theory illustrates that the same basic operations have been performed on existent formal structures to produce new formal structures over and over again. According to this theory, the necessary instruments for defining formal structures are gong, which defines *gongan*, kenong, which defines *kenongan*, kethuk, which defines *keteg-kethuk pattern*, and bonang barung, which defines *keteg*, or basic pulse. To a lesser extent, the kempul is structurally important for differentiating the form Minggah, kethuk 2 from the form Mérong, kethuk 2. This distinction is lost in later derivations with the result that there is no formal distinction between, for example, Minggah, kethuk 8, Irama II and Mérong, kethuk

8 kerep, Irama I. (The distinction between these forms lies in the performance style of certain instruments playing subdivisions at the level of *keteg* and at levels above *keteg*—bonang barung, gendèr, gendèr panerus, gambang, and kendhang.)

The names for the *keteg-kethuk patterns*, ngganter, kerepan, kerep, and awis/arang, are strictly applicable only to forms played in Irama I. Once the number of *keteg* has expanded to Irama II, in fact, though not in name, the *keteg-kethuk pattern* has changed to the next category: ngganter to kerepan, kerepan to kerep, kerep to awis. Theoretically, at least, the process of generating new forms could continue to produce such forms as Minggah, kethuk 32, Irama I, that is, ⇥ Mérong, kethuk 16 awis, Irama II. The length of formal structures, however, presumably has outer limits.

Perhaps some comment is necessary about the asymmetrical development of the 4-kenong-per-gong forms as contrasted with the 2-kenong-per-gong forms. It has been suggested that the extended development of the 4-kenong-per-gong forms is related to the use of sung poetic forms in the context of the gamelan. It has yet to be demonstrated, however, how a 4-kenong-per-gong form facilitates the setting of poetic lines whose number of lines per stanza varies greatly from verse form to verse form. Also, there is no evidence to suggest that the extended development of the 4-kenong-per-gong forms does not predate the introduction of vocal forms into gamelan performance.

Not discussed here are those occasional forms, called Pamijen, which have 3 or 5 *kenongan* per gong. It would have been possible to include them with an ad hoc rule but it seemed arbitrary to do so.

The fact that it is possible to apply a rigidly formal analysis to a corpus of traditional music that has developed over hundreds of years without benefit of notation or written theory suggests a mystery, or a set of mysteries, not touched upon in this analysis. The processes that have generated these many formal structures are so precise, so "scientific," and so consistent as to seem to have an autonomous existence outside the memories of men, while clearly this is not the case. Gamelan *gongan* structures have been created by men within an oral tradition that is specific and explicit about the correct manner of playing each instrument within each type of *gongan*, but which has not been explicit about the processes of creating new types of *gongan*. The generating processes are implicit within and between existent structures. The structures themselves (or the idea of them in men's minds) carry the seeds of their own further development; this is not a new or surprising idea. But the precision of their development is rather surprising. We have not been accustomed to thinking about a conceptual abstraction such as "a music system" as having the same kind of organic quality as, say, a mollusk, and yet the predictability of the development of gamelan *gongan* seems to suggest something similar to genetic coding.

There have been and continue to be efforts by Javanese musicians to standardize gamelan tunings, to standardize gamelan pedagogy and notation, efforts at least partially motivated by a desire to make gamelan music "scientific" and thus worthy of respect internationally, following the Western pattern of rationalizing Western tonality by its basis in acoustics. And yet, gamelan formal structures lend themselves to a rational analysis, even a mathematical analysis, more easily than do Western formal structures. It would seem that rationalized music systems are in no way dependent upon a written tradition but are inherent in the process of music making, and that what varies is rather the aspect of the music that lends itself to rationalization. Various aspects of gamelan music and Western music, such as tunings, modes, formal structures or styles of improvization, have been described within the theoretical framework of a rationalized structural analysis.[1] The most successful rationalizations of Western music deal with tunings, but rationalizations of gamelan tunings are the least successful. On the other hand, gamelan *gongan* forms are easily rationalized, but Western formal structures are much more resistant. (How much effort has gone into the attempts to define Sonata-allegro form?) Music systems, as products of man's mind/body, exhibit characteristics shared by all other natural systems—aspects that are predictable and those that are not predictable—and thus lend themselves to interpretations both particularistic and generalized.

Derivation of
Central Javanese
Gamelan *Gongan*

Derivation level	Derivation B 4 kenong per gong		
	16 kethuk per kenong	8 kethuk per kenong	4 kethuk per kenong
1. 1 keteg = 1 *kenongan*			
2. 2 keteg = 1 *kenongan*			
3. 4 keteg = 1 *kenongan*			
4. 8 keteg = 1 *kenongan*			
5. 16 keteg = 1 *kenongan*			Minggah kethuk 4 kerepan, Irama I ⇓
6. 32 keteg = 1 *kenongan*		Minggah, kethuk 8 kerepan, Irama I ⇓	(Minggah, kethuk 4, Irama II) ⇐ Mérong, kethuk 4 kerep, Irama I ⇓
7. 64 keteg = 1 *kenongan*	Minggah, kethuk 16 kerepan, Irama I ⇓	(Minggah, kethuk 8, Irama II) ⇐ Mérong, kethuk 8 kerep, Irama I ⇓	(Mérong, kethuk 4, Irama II) (Minggah, kethuk 4, Irama III) Mérong, kethuk 4 awis, Irama I ⇓
8. 128 keteg = 1 *kenongan*	(Minggah, kethuk 16, Irama II) ⇓	(Mérong, kethuk 8, Irama II) (Minggah kethuk 8, Irama III) Mérong, kethuk 8 awis, Irama I ⇓	(Mérong, kethuk 4 awis, Irama II)
9. 256 keteg = 1 *kenongan*	(Minggah, kethuk 16, Irama III)	(Mérong, kethuk 8, Irama II) (Minggah, kethuk 8, Irama IV)	

KEY: ⇒ = expansion of dD by Irama function
⇻ = expansion of kethuk by kethuk function
ϕG = deletion of first gong marker
+P = addition of kempul
ϕP = deletion of kempul

| | Derivation A   2 kenong per gong | | |
2 kethuk per kenong	1 kethuk per kenong	2 kethuk per kenong	4 kethuk per kenong
	Sampak ⇓		
	Srepegan ⇓		
Kebogiro Lancaran, Irama I ⇐ (φG) (+P) ⇓	Ayak-ayakan, Irama I ⇒ ⇓	Ayak-ayakan, Irama I Monggang ⇓	
(Lancaran, Irama II) Bubaran, Irama I ⇓	(Ayak-ayakan, Irama II)	(Ayak-ayakan, Irama II) Kodok-Ngorek ⇓	
(Bubaran, Irama II) Minggah Ladrang, kethuk 2 kerepan, Irama I ⇓		(Ayak-ayakan, Irama III) Ketawang, kethuk 2 kerepan, Irama I(+P) ⇓	
(Minggah Ladrang, ⇐ kethuk 2, Irama II [+P]) Mérong, kethuk 2 kerep, Irama I (φP) ⇓		(Ketawang, kethuk 2, Irama II) Ketawang Gendhing, kethuk 2 kerep, Irama I ⇓	
(Mérong, kethuk 2, Irama II) Mérong, kethuk 2 awis, Irama I (Minggah Ladrang, kethuk 2, Irama III) ⇓		(Ketawang Gendhing, kethuk 2, Irama II)	Ketawang Gendhing, kethuk 4 kerep, Irama I ⇒ ⇓
(Mérong, kethuk 2, Irama II) (Minggah Ladrang, kethuk 2, Irama IV)			(Ketawang Gendhing kethuk 4, Irama II)

Note: The Irama II forms enclosed in parentheses indicate that the form is not normally notated as Irama II, but only as Irama I. All parenthesized forms have undergone a change in *keteg-kethuk pattern* as well as an Irama change. For example, Mérong, kethuk 8 kerep, Irama I becomes, when played in Irama II, Mérong, kethuk 8 awis, but is not designated as such.

Appendix 2

Ki Wasitodipuro and Ki Nartosabdho: Biographical Sketches and List of Compositions Used as the Basis of this Study

Ki Wasitodipuro

Ki Wasitodipuro, formerly known as Ki Tjokrowasito, was born in the Pakualaman Palace in Yogyakarta in 1909. His father held the position of director of the palace musical activities, and Ki Wasitodipuro succeeded his father in that position. Ki is a title bestowed upon men of outstanding distinction and achievement.

In addition to his palace gamelan duties, in 1934 he became the musical director of MAVRO, the radio station in Yogyakarta. He continued in that position during the Japanese occupation when the station was called Jogja Hosokjoku. Since the proclamation of independence in 1945, the station has been known as Radio Republic Indonesia, RRI, Yogyakarta. In 1951 Ki Wasitodipuro was officially appointed the RRI musical director.

In 1961, Ki Wasitodipuro became associated with the newly evolved dance–drama form *sendratari*. He has written the music for various *sendratari Ramayana* held at the temple Prambanan and for the *sendratari* performances choreographed by P.L.T. Bagong Kussudiardjo of Yogyakarta.

He currently holds three positions: director of the Pakualaman gamelan, director of musical activities at RRI Yogyakarta, and musical director for the *sendratari* company of Bagong Kussudiardjo.

Ki Nartosabdho

Ki Nartosabdho, one of eight children, was born in 1925 in Wedi, a small village between Surakarta and Yogyakarta. His earliest education took place in Wedi, where he first attended a Muhammadiyah (Islamic) school and later a school run by a Roman Catholic mission.

In August 1945, when he was twenty years old, he joined the Ngesti Pandowo *wayang orang* company. Ngesti Pandowo is a resident company with its home base in the northern port city of Semarang. Performances are given every night in Semarang except when the company goes on tour to other parts of Java. Ki Nartosabdho remained with Ngesti Pandowo as musical director and drummer for twenty-five years. Simultaneously, he developed a reputation as a *dhalang*, a puppeteer of the shadow-puppet-play.

In 1970 he left his position with Ngesti Pandowo and formed his own recording and performing company, Condong Raos, composed of musicians from Semarang and Surakarta. He remains in great demand as a *dhalang* and continues to make recordings and give concert performances.

A Partial Listing of Compositions by Ki Wasitodipuro

Title	Pathet	Recording	Source of Notation Used in this Study
Jaya Manggala Gita Makakawin		Tape through the	Manuscript through
Pujian	Pélog Barang	courtesy of RRI	the courtesy of the
Lagu Mars : Jepang	Pélog Bem	Yogyakarta	composer
Gendhing Sakura	Sléndro Sanga		
Lagu Dolanan Paman Tani Sagung	Pélog Nem		Published in the magazine *Mekar Sari*, May 1970
Lancaran Keluarga Berencana	Pélog Barang		*Mekar Sari*, June 1970
Lancaran Penghijauan	Sléndro Nem		*Mekar Sari*, June 1970
Sendratari Arjuna Wiwaha		Tape through the courtesy of Bagong Kussudiardjo	
Sendratari Alleluyah		Tape through the courtesy of Bagong Kussudiardjo	
Sendratari Nyai Ratu Kidul		Tape through the courtesy of Bagong Kussudiardjo	

TITLE	PATHET	RECORDING	SOURCE OF NOTATION USED IN THIS STUDY
Sendratari Diponegoro		Tape through the courtesy of Bagong Kussudiardjo	Manuscript through the courtesy of the composer
Gendhing Pangeran Diponegoro	Pélog Nem		
Lagu Gerilya	Pélog Nem		
Lancaran Rudita	Pélog Nem		
Lancaran Mindana	Pélog Nem		
Ketawang Sambang Dalu	Pélog Nem		
Lancaran Umban	Pélog Nem		
Lancaran Aja Ngono	Pélog Nem	Tape of "Konser Gamelan," Yogyakarta, 1968	Manuscript through the courtesy of the composer
Ketawang Wedyasmara	Pélog Nem		
Orde Baru	Pélog Barang		
Kawiwitan Meditasi/ Konsentrasi	Pélog Nem		
Kagok Pangrawit	Pélog Lima		
Bedayan Sundari	Pélog Nem		
Liwung Bayang Kara	Pélog Nem		
Lancaran Catrik	Pélog Nem		
Ginada	Sléndro Manyura		
Sunda Nirmala	Sléndro Manyura		
Ladrang Sri Duhita	Pélog Barang		
Lancaran Gugur Gunung	Pélog Barang		
Gérong Kanon	Pélog Barang		
Lancaran Pawaka	Pélog Barang		
Lancaran Dahana	Pélog Barang		
Nara Karya	Sléndro Manyura		*Lelagon: Dolanan Populèr*, Soeranto, Kediri, 1965
USDEK	Pélog Nem		
Ayo Nyang Ganéfo	Sléndro Manyura		
Holopis Kontul Baris	Sléndro Sanga		
Montor Cilik	Sléndro Sanga		
Campur Sari	Sléndro Sanga		
Kanca Tani	Sléndro Sanga		
Gotong Royong	Sléndro Sanga		
Ganéfo	Sléndro Sanga		
Nekolim	Sléndro Sanga		
Bémo	Sléndro Sanga		
Banting Stir	Pélog Pathet Liwung (Sunda)		
Sendratari Pangeran Mangkubumi			Manuscript through the courtesy of the composer
Gendhing Jahnawi	Pélog Nem		
Lancaran Graksa	Pélog Nem		
Welasan Tandasih	Pélog Lima		
Ladrang Dwi Rocana	Pélog Barang		

A Partial Listing of Compositions by Ki Wasitodipuro (continued)

TITLE	PATHET	RECORDING	SOURCE OF NOTATION USED IN THIS STUDY
Lagu Kelahiran Kristus			From a radio broadcast by RRI Yogyakarta on Christmas eve, manuscript through the courtesy of the composer
Tri Narpati	Pélog Nem		
Ketawang Sasmi Tengrat	Pélog Barang		
Kartika	Pélog Nem		
Wus Miyos	Pélog Nem		
Ing Ratri	Pélog Nem		
Ayak-ayakan Saroja	Pélog Lima	Videotape Sendratari Kelahiran Kristus	Collection of gérong parts compiled by the composer for teaching at RRI Yogyakarta
Ketawang Dana Wara	Pélog Bem		
Dolanan Ok Ok	Pélog Barang		
Ladrang Jati Asih	Pélog Lima		
Lancaran Gembala	Pélog Lima		
Ketawang Kamu Dawuk	Pélog Barang		
Lela Ledung	Pélog Nem		
Ketawang Mas Kumambang	Pélog Lima		
Ladrang Ayun-ayun (Gérong)	Pélog Nem		
Asmarandana Banyumasan	Sléndro Sanga		
Gendhing Janger	Pélog Barang		
Jineman Mijil Wida Waten	Pélog Nem		
Jineman Blibar	Pélog Nem		
Jonjang Banyuwangen	Sléndro Manyura (from Sendratari Gajah Mada)		
Ladrang Gléyong	Pélog Nem		
Grantes	Sléndro Manyura (Sendratari Lutung Kasarung)		
Ketawang Gambuh	Sléndro Manyura (Sendratari Sri Tanjung)		
Dolanan Gembira Loka	Sléndro Sanga		
Lancaran Ilogondang	Sléndro Sanga		
Ketawang Kumudasmara	Pélog Nem (Sendratari Ramayana-Prambanan)		
Kembang Lepang	Sléndro Sanga		
Ketawang Kasatriyan	Sléndro Sanga		

Title	Pathet	Recording	Source of Notation Used in this Study
Ngimpi Nyopir	Sléndro Sanga		
Ladrang Panjang Ilang	Sléndro Sanga (Sendratari Ramayana)		*Buku Gérong* by Ki Wasitodipuro
Ketawang Prihatin	Pélog Lima (Sendratari Hamlet)		
Lagu Bancak Doyok	Pélog Nem (Sendratari Bandung Bandowaso)		
Lagu Pulo Bali	Pélog Barang		
Lagu Repelita	Pélog Nem		
Ketawang Santi	Pélog Nem		
Sesaji	Pélog Nem (Sendratari Gajah Mada)		
Sirepan Ayak Mijil	Sléndro Manyura		
Sensus	Sléndro Sanga		
Ladrang Srenggara	Pélog Lima (Sendratari Sri Tanjung)		
Ketawang Sumekar	Pélog Nem (Sendratari Ramayana)		
Ketawang Sri Lulut	Pélog Barang		
Gérong Suba Kastawa Winangun	Sléndro Sanga (Sendratari Ramayana)		
Gérong Ladrang Sri Widada	Pélog Barang		
Ladrang Suka Bagya	Pélog Barang		
Ketawang Sundari	Pélog Barang		
Lancaran Tahu Tempé	Pélog Nem		
Taman Sari	Pélog Bem (Sendratari Damar Wulan)		
Lancaran Tari Payung	Sléndro and Pélog (Sendratari Gajah Mada)		
Ladrang Clunthang	Sléndro Sanga		
Welasan Rudatin	Pélog Barang (Sendratari Ramayana)		
Welasan Lancar	Pélog Barang		
Welasan Ruwida	Pélog Nem (Sendratari Ramayana)		

A Partial Listing of Compositions by Ki Wasitodipuro (continued)

TITLE	PATHET	RECORDING	SOURCE OF NOTATION USED IN THIS STUDY
Gendhing Mbangun Kuta	Pélog Nem		Manuscript through the courtesy of the composer
Modernisasi Désa	Pélog Nem	Tape of concert "Ciptaan Baru" through the courtesy of Bagong Kussudiardjo	*Buku Gérong* by Ki Wasitodipuro
Dolanan Kuwi Apa Kuwi	Pélog Barang	RRI Yogyakarta	*Tuntunan Nabuh Gamelan*,
Dolanan Tari Bali	Pélog Barang	Lokananta ARD-001A	Sastrodarsono,
Dolanan Sepur Trutuk	Pélog Lima		Surakarta, 1960
Dolanan Kaé Lo Kaé	Sléndro Sanga		
Dolanan Dong Dong Dung	Sléndro Manyura		
Dolanan Ronda Malam	Sléndro Sanga		
Tatanya	Pélog Barang		
Sopir Becak	Pélog Nem		*Lelagon Dolanan Populèr*, Soeranto
Mbangun Désa	Pélog Barang		*Lelagon Djawi Klasik and Modern*, Tarnowidodo, Wonogiri

A Partial Listing of Compositions by Ki Nartosabdho

TITLE	PATHET	RECORDING	SOURCE OF NOTATION USED IN THIS STUDY
Dolanan Sapa Ngira	Sléndro Sanga	Lokananta *Gara-gara* BRD-014	*Dolanan Ngesti Pandawa,* Semarang, 1969
Dolanan Lumbung Désa	Sléndro Sanga		
Dolanan Ayo Praon	Pélog Nem		
Dolanan Mari Kangen	Pélog Nem		
Dolanan Jula-Juli Sunba	Sléndro Sanga		
Dolanan Sapu Tanganmu	Pélog Barang		
Dolanan Caping	Pélog Barang		
Ketawang Ibu Pertiwi	Pélog Lima	Lokananta *Ki Nartosabdho* BRD-017	*Dolanan Ngesti Pandawa,* Semarang, 1969
Ketawang Suba Kastawa	Pélog Nem		
Ketawang Mèh Rahina	Pélog Nem		
Ketawang Suka Asih	Pélog Barang		
Kembang Glepang	Sléndro Sanga	Lokananta *Kembang Glepang* BRD-023	*Dolanan Ngesti Pandawa,* Semarang, 1969
Ladrang Santi Mulya	Pélog Lima		
Ladrang Clunthang Rinengga	Sléndro Sanga		
Ketawang Pangkur Pegatsih	Pélog Lima		
Wandali	Pélog Nem	Lokananta *Ki Nartosabdho* ARD-037	*Dolanan Ngesti Pandawa,* Semarang, 1969
Dolanan Lesung Jumengglung	Sléndro Sanga		
Lagu Suara Suling	Pélog Lima		
Lancaran Mbok Ja Mesem	Sléndro Sanga		
Lagu Aja Lamis	Pélog Nem	Lokananta *Ki Nartosabdho* ARD-039	"Condong Raos," a collection of compositions; manuscript through the courtesy of the composer
Glopa Glapé	Sléndro Sanga		*Dolanan Ngesti Pandawa*
Dolanan Jago Kluruk	Pélog Barang		
Aku Ngimpi	Pélog Nem		"Condong Raos"
Dolanan Kerja Bakti	Pélog Nem	Indah 12011/12 *Wayang Orang Kresno Kembang*	"Condong Raos"
Ketawang Petis Manis	Sléndro Sanga		

A Partial Listing of Compositions by Ki Nartosabdho (continued)

TITLE	PATHET	RECORDING	SOURCE OF NOTATION USED IN THIS STUDY
Pambuka Condong Raos		Tape of concert of new compositions by *Ki Nartosabdho*, Jakarta, June 1971; through the courtesy of the composer.	
Ladrang Balabak	Pélog Lima		
Ladrang Nuswantara	Pélog Nem		
Lancaran Mikat Manuk	Sléndro Manyura		
Gendhing Logondang	Pélog Lima		
Ladrang Logondang	Pélog Lima		
Ketawang Logondang	Pélog Lima		
Eling-eling Banyumas			
Arum Manis			"Condong Raos"
Gendhing Bandi Lori	Pélog Barang		
Ladrang Serang	Pélog Barang		
Lagu Jakarta Endah	Pélog Nem		
Gendhing Glondong Pring	Pélog Nem		
Ladrang Godasih	Pélog Nem		
Lagu Ayo Ngguyu	Pélog Nem		
Ladrang Panjang Ilang	Sléndro Sanga		
Ladrang Panglipur	Pélog Nem		
Ladrang Ronda Ngangsu	Pélog Barang		
Ladrang Sara Yuda	Pélog Nem		"Condong Raos"
Ladrang Sumiyar	Pélog Barang		
Ketawang Sri Ratih	Sléndro Nem		
Lancaran Wira-wiri	Pélog Lima		
Ladrang Wulangan	Pélog Nem		
Ketawang Gambuh Kayungyun	Pélog Lima		*Dolanan Ngesti Pandawa*
Ketawang Mijil Panglilih	Pélog Lima		
Lagu Desaku	Pélog Nem		
Ketawang Dumadi	Sléndro Sanga		
Singa-singa (new arrangement)			
Gudeg Yogya	Pélog Lima		
Cep Menenga	Pélog Nem		
Suwé Ora Jamu	Pélog Nem		*Lelagon Djawi Klasik dan Modern*, Tarnowidodo, Wonogiri

Appendix 3

The Traditional Gendhing Used in the Analysis of Pathet in Chapter 6

Sléndro Pathet
Ladrang and Ketawang with 8 balungan/kenong

GENDHING	PATHET	SOURCE
Ladrang Asmaradana Kenya Tinembe	Sanga	Pak Sumardjo, a drummer from Yogyakarta living and teaching in Malang, East Java
Ladrang Pangkur	Sanga	
Ladrang Cangklèk	Manyura	
Ladrang Clunthang	Sanga	
Ladrang Sumingin	Sanga	
Ketawang Raja Swala	Sanga	
Ladrang Kijing Miring	Manyura	
Ladrang Jangkrik Ginggong	Sanga	
Ladrang Kagok Sumingin	Nem	
Ladrang Dirada Meta	Nem	
Ladrang Kencèng-kencèng	Manyura	
Ladrang Wirang Rong	Sanga	
Ladrang Prabu Mataram	Sanga	
Ladrang Temanten	Manyura	
Ladrang Singra Mangsah	Manyura	
Ladrang Awun-awun	Sanga	
Ladrang Mijil Wedar Ing Tyas	Manyura	
Ladrang Eling-eling Kasmaran	Sanga	
Ladrang Asmaradana	Manyura	
Ladrang Ayun-ayun	Manyura	
Ketawang Madu Murti	Manyura	
Ketawang Langen Gita	Sanga	
Ladrang Sri Karongron	Sanga	
Ladrang Sumirat	Manyura	
Ladrang Tebu Sak Uyon	Manyura	

Sléndro Pathet
Ladrang and Ketawang with 8 balungan/kenong (*continued*)

Gendhing	Pathet	Source
Ladrang Prabu Anom	Manyura	
Ladrang Lengkir	Manyura	
Ladrang Girisa Mengkreng	Sanga	
Ladrang Geger Sakutha	Nem	
Ladrang Girang-girang	Nem	
Ladrang Oyak-oyak	Manyura	
Ladrang Grompol Mataram	Sanga	
Ladrang Sara Yuda	Manyura	
Ladrang Wilujeng	Manyura	
Ladrang Sri Kacarya	Sanga	
Ladrang Lungkeh	Nem	*The Nuclear Theme as a*
Ladrang Royo Hanggolo	Nem	*Determinant of Pathet in*
Ladrang Gondo Yonni	Sanga	*Javanese Music*, Mantle Hood
Ladrang Udan Sejati	Sanga	
Ladrang Celeng Mogok	Manyura	
Ladrang Tlosor	Manyura	
Ladrang Sri Wibawa	Sanga	*Noot Gending lan Tembang*,
Ladrang Sri Sudana	Sanga	Toko Buku Sadubudi; Solo
Ladrang Sri Kasusra	Manyura	
Ladrang Sri Dayinta Minulya	Manyura	
Ladrang Sri Rinengga	Manyura	
Ladrang Sri Biwaddha Mulya	Manyura	
Ladrang Pangkur (also a version in Sanga)	Manyura	Sulaiman Gitosaprodjo, teacher from Surakarta residing in
Ladrang Remeng	Nem	Malang, East Java
Ladrang Sri Yatna	Manyura	*Gending Djawi*, vol. 2,
Ladrang Sri Hutama	Manyura	Probohardjono, Toko Buku
Ladrang Perkumpulan	Sanga	Budhi Ladsana; Solo
Ladrang Moncèr	Manyura	
Ketawang Sukma Ilang	Manyura	*Sekarsari, Gending Djawi*,
Ketawang Pawukir (Ngelik)	Manyura	Darmoredjono Wonogiri,
Ladrang Mugi Rahayu	Manyura	1968
Ladrang Kaki Tunggu Jagung	Nem	*Gendhing-gendhing Nabuhi*
Ladrang Bedat	Nem	*Wajangan Purwa*,
Ladrang Sobrang	Nem	Probohardjono, Yogyakarta, 1957
Ladrang Bindri	Sanga	*Udan Mas, Madjalah Kesenian*,
Ladrang Eling-eling	Manyura	vol. 1, nos. 3 and 6; Solo
Ladrang Bolang-bolang	Nem	
Ladrang Sri Minulya	Sanga	*Gending Djawi*, vol. 1, Probohardjono; Solo
Ladrang Kongas	Nem	*Titiswara* (huruf Djawi),
Ladrang Tentrem	Sanga	Kangdjeng Raden Mas
Ladrang Prasaja	Sanga	Tumenggung Sumonagoro,
Ladrang Suka Wati	Sanga	Surakarta, 1936
Ladrang Kumenyar	Sanga	

GENDHING	PATHET	SOURCE
Ketawang Langen Gita	Sanga	Manuscript of *gendhing-gendhing*
Ladrang Pamikat	Sanga	for *Sendratari Ramayana*,
Ketawang Umbak	Sanga	Martopangrawit
Ladrang Kembang Dhadhap	Manyura	
Ketawang Marta Pura	Manyura	"Gendhing-gendhing
Ladrang Lagu Dhempel	Sanga	Wajangan," manuscript,
Ladrang Uga-uga	Sanga	Sumijanto, Perakit
Ladrang Kagok Maduro	Sanga	Kebudajaan K.D.3.K. Klaten
Ladrang Babar Layar	Sanga	
Ladrang Embat-embat Penjalin	Sanga	
Ketawang Pucung	Manyura	

Ladrang and Ketawang with 4 balungan/kenong

GENDHING	PATHET	SOURCE
Ladrang Gudasih	Nem	Sulaiman Gitosaprodjo, teacher
Ladrang Krawitan	Nem	from Surakarta, residing in
Ketawang Suba Kastawa	Sanga	Malang, East Java
Ladrang Clunthang	Sanga	
Ladrang Utama	Sanga	
Ladrang Utama Minulyo (*céngkok* A)	Sanga	
Ladrang Eling-eling Kasmaran (*céngkok* B)	Sanga	
Ladrang Gonjang-ganjing	Sanga	
Ketawang Mijil Paseban	Sanga	
Ladrang Kembang Tanjung	Sanga	
Ladrang Puspa Warna	Manyura	
Ladrang Sri Katon (in *Sekarsari*, *Gending Djawi*, listed as Pélog Nem)	Manyura	
Ladrang Ginonjing	Manyura	
Ladrang Sri Kaloka	Manyura	
Ladrang Babat Kenceng	Nem	*The Nuclear Theme as a*
Ladrang Uluk-uluk	Sanga	*Determinant of Pathet in*
Ladrang Bronto Asmoro	Sanga	*Javanese Music*, Mantle Hood
Ketawang Barang Ganjur (*céngkok* A)	Sanga	
Ladrang Lèngkèr (*gongan* VII)	Manyura	
Ladrang Liwung	Manyura	
Ladrang Sri Utama	Manyura	*Noot Gending lan Tembang*,
Ladrang Sri Hascarya	Sanga	Toko Buku Sadubudi; Solo
Ladrang Sri Raja Putri	Manyura	
Ladrang Sobah	Nem	*Gending-gending Nabuhi*
Ladrang Peksi Kuwung	Nem	*Wajangan Purwa*,
Ladrang Mangu	Nem	Probohardjono
Ladrang Erang-erang	Nem	

Ladrang and Ketawang with 4 balungan/kenong (continued)

Gendhing	Pathet	Source
Ladrang Sembung Gilang	Sanga	
Ladrang Jangkrik Ginggong	Sanga	
Ladrang Lompong Kèlé	Sanga	
Ladrang Uluk-uluk	Sanga	
Ladrang Gondo Suli	Sanga	
Ladrang Gonjang	Manyura	
Ladrang Randhat	Manyura	
Ladrang Kandha Manyura	Manyura	
Ladrang Manis	Manyura	
Ladrang Kembang Pépé	Manyura	
Ketawang Langen Gita (céngkok A)	Sanga	*Gending Djawi*, vol. 2, Probohardjono
Ketawang Padhang Rembulan	Manyura	*Peladjaran Bawa Gerong*, Kebudajaan Djawa Timur, 1967
Ketawang Suba Kastawa	Sanga	"Gending Sendratari Ramayana," manuscript Martopangrawit
Ladrang Kembang Gadhung	Nem	"Gending Wajangan," manuscript, Sumijanto
Ladrang Plupuh	Nem	
Ladrang Ela-ela	Sanga	
Ladrang Giyak	Sanga	
Ketawang Dolo-dolo	Sanga	

Gendhing Ageng

Gendhing	Pathet	Source
Tali Murda	Nem	*Titilaras Gending Ageng*, vol. 1, Larassumbogo, Murtedjo, and Adisoendjojo, Jakarta, 1953
Babat	Nem	
Sedhet	Nem	
Rendhet	Nem	
Padhang Bulan	Nem	
Nenes	Nem	
Pondhoh	Nem	
Gandes	Nem	
Cluring	Nem	
Klumpuk	Nem	
Gondes	Nem	
Pacul Pethot	Nem	
Kedasih	Nem	
Glondong Pring	Nem	
Prihatin	Nem	
Madu Sari	Sanga	
Candra	Sanga	
Talak Bodin	Sanga	
Mencep	Sanga	
Sumirah	Sanga	
Madu Kocak	Sanga	
Mardi Kengrat	Sanga	
Madu Kengrat	Sanga	

GENDHING	PATHET	SOURCE
Ngeksi Laras	Sanga	
Sumba Gengrat	Sanga	
Madu Kumala	Sanga	
Sardju Ning Tyas	Sanga	
Ngeksi Minulya	Sanga	
Susila	Sanga	
Lungit	Sanga	
Ngeksi Ngestuti	Sanga	
Ngeksi Bronta	Sanga	
Merak Kesimpir	Manyura	
Mendes	Manyura	
Hamong–hamong	Manyura	
Cethi	Manyura	
Lare Hangon	Manyura	
Sekar Gebang	Manyura	
Giwang Kusuma	Manyura	
Kembang Pelem	Manyura	
Pendhul Peté	Manyura	
Kembang Peté	Manyura	
Carang Gantung	Manyura	
Randhu Kentir	Manyura	
Gidro–gidro	Manyura	
Laler Mengeng	Manyura	
Jaka Wuru	Manyura	
Lobong	Manyura	
Glebag	Manyura	
Centhini	Manyura	

Pélog Pathet

GENDHING	PATHET	SOURCE
Ladrang Retna Ningsih	Lima	Sulaiman Gitosaprodjo,
Ketawang Wigar Ing Tyas	Lima	Malang, East Java
Ladrang Bayemtur	Lima	
Ladrang Eling–eling	Lima	
Ketawang Pucung Wuyung	Lima	
Ketawang Pangkur Ngremas	Lima	
Ladrang Sembawa	Lima	
Ketawang Langen Gita	Nem	
Ketawang S'wala Gita	Nem	
Ketawang Gondo Mastuti	Nem	
Ketawang Udan Mas (variously listed as Ketawang, Bibaran, Lancaran)	Nem	
Ketawang Puspa Njala	Nem	
Ladrang Sri Rejeki	Nem	
Ladrang Surung Dayung	Nem	
Ladrang Wirang Rong	Nem	
Ladrang Kopyah Ilang	Nem	
Ladrang Mentok-mentok	Nem	
Ladrang Jambe Thukul	Nem	
Ketawang Manggung Soré	Nem	

Gendhing Ageng (*continued*)

Gendhing	Pathet	Source
Ladrang Sri Sinuba	Nem	
Ladrang Tirto Kencono	Nem	
Ladrang Magelang	Nem	
Ladrang Sri Kretarta	Nem	
Ladrang Kembang Kates	Nem	
Ketawang Kinanthi Sandhung	Barang	
Ketawang Megatruh	Barang	
Ketawang Jali	Barang	
Ketawang Puspa Giwang	Barang	
Ladrang Moncer	Barang	
Ladrang Gleyong	Nem	
Ladrang Sampang	Barang	
Ladrang Sawung Galing	Barang	
Ketawang Sita Mardawa	Barang	*Gending Djawi*, vol. 2,
Ladrang Ayun-ayun	Nem	Probohardjono
Ketawang Boyong	Barang	
Ladrang Penghijauan	Nem	*Sekarsari*, *Gending Djawi*,
Ladrang Among Tani	Nem	Darmoredjono
Ladrang Suwignya	Barang	
Ladrang Slamet	Barang	*Gending Djawi*, vol. 1,
Ladrang Ginonjing	Barang	Probohardjono
Ladrang Sedya Laras	Barang	
Ketawang Pari Joto	Nem	*Peladjaran Bawa Gerong*,
Ketawang Langen Gita Sri Narendra	Barang	Direktorat Djenderal Djatim Kebudajaan
Ketawang Sumedhang	Nem	
Ladrang Langen Asmoro	Nem	*The Nuclear Theme as a*
Ladrang Langen Bronto	Nem	*Determinant of Pathet in*
Ladrang Riyem-riyem	Lima	*Javanese Music*, Mantle Hood
Ladrang Rangu-rangu	Barang	
Ladrang Megarsi	Nem	
Ladrang Horang Haring	Lima	
Ladrang Pacar Cina	Lima	
Ladrang Sri Kuncara	Nem	*Noot Gending lan Tembang*;
Ladrang Megar Semu	Barang	Solo
Ladrang Sri Nassao	Barang	
Ladrang Sri Dayita	Barang	
Ladrang Sri Dayinta Linuhur	Nem	
Ladrang Sri Dirga Yuswa	Barang	
Ladrang Sri Dayunta Wibawa	Barang	
Ladrang Sri Linuhung	Barang	
Ladrang Sri Biwaddha	Barang	
Ladrang Playon	Lima	*Karawitan Wajang Gedog*,
Ladrang Blabak	Lima	Kraton Surakarta
Ladrang Satata	Lima	*Titiswara* (huruf Djawi),
Ladrang Nawung Gita	Lima	Kandjeng Raden Mas
Ladrang Tetep	Lima	Tumenggung Sumonogoro

GENDHING	PATHET	SOURCE
Ladrang Lipur Wuyung	Barang	
Ketawang Melatsih	Barang	"Sendratari Ramayana," manuscript, Martopangrawit
Ketawang Dhenda Ageng	Nem	Naskah *Gending-gending Wajangan*, Sumijanto
Ladrang Crina	Barang	*Tuntunan Nabuh Gamelan*, Sukanto Sastrodarsono, Surakarta, 1960

Ladrang and Ketawang with 4 balungan/kenong

GENDHING	PATHET	SOURCE
Ladrang Wani-wani	Nem	Sulaiman Gitosaprodjo, Malang,
Ladrang Kembang Pépé	Nem	East Java
Ladrang Ginonjing	Barang	
Ladrang Clunthang	Barang	
Ladrang Retna Mulya	Barang	*Noot Gending lan Tembang*;
Ladrang Sri Nindita	Nem	Solo
Ladrang Sri Raharja	Barang	
Lancaran Tropongan	Nem	*Gendhing-gendhing Nabuhi Wajangan Purwa*, Probohardjono
Ketawang Wala Gita	Nem	*Tuntunan Karawitan Gending Djawi*, Kodiron; Solo, 1964
Ketawang Sita Mardawa	Barang	*Gending Djawi*, vol. 2, Probohardjono
Lancaran Udan Mas	Barang	*Udan Mas*, vol. 1, no. 3
Ladrang Sri Kastawa	Barang	*Karawitan Wajang Gedog*, Surakarta
Ladrang Purwoko	Nem	*Naskah Gending-gending Wajangan*, Sumijanto
Kebo Giro	Barang	*Tuntunan Nabuh Gamelan*,
Singa Nebah	Barang	Sastrodarsono
Tejo Sari	Lima	Sulaiman Gitosaprodjo, Malang,
Logondhang	Lima	East Java
Condro Noto	Lima	
Kumbang Mara	Lima	
Lara Njala	Lima	
Randhu Kintir	Nem	
Gambir Sawit Pancerana	Nem	
Manik Maninten	Nem	
Kembang Gayam	Nem	
Sumedhang	Nem	
Rujak Sentul	Nem	
Perkutut Manggung	Barang	
Kuwung-kuwung	Barang	
Bande Lori	Barang	

Ladrang and Ketawang with 4 balungan/kenong (continued)

Gendhing	Pathet	Source
Wido Sari	Barang	
Jangkung Kuning	Barang	
Prawan Pupur	Barang	
Tunggul Kawung	Barang	
Wigati	Lima	*Titiswara*, Sumonagoro
Sewara	Lima	
Karep Mantep	Lima	
Mangu Kadung	Nem	
Surya Sumirat	Nem	
Pami Walkung	Barang	
Mandheg Mangu	Barang	
Ketungkul Lali	Barang	
Lebda Jiwa	Barang	
Bangunsin	Barang	
Untung	Barang	
Dlongeh	Barang	
Mandheg	Barang	
Onang-onang	Nem	*Tuntunan Karawitan*, Kodiroı
Penghijauan	Nem	*Gending Djawi Sekarsari*, Darmoredjono
Gendiyeng	Nem	*Wajang Gedog*, Kraton,
Tejo Noto	Lima	Surakarta
Genjong	Nem	
Andong-andong	Nem	
Gandrung	Nem	
Ranu Manggala	Nem	
Montro	Barang	*Naskah Gending-gending Wajangan* Sumijanto

Appendix 4

Tables Illustrating the Distribution of Melodic Patterns within Each Pathet

TABLE 1.
Frequency of Occurrence and Distribution of Patterns Ending on
Sléndro Pitch Level 1

Contour No.	Pattern	Pathet Nem			Pathet Sanga			Pathet Manyura		
		G	N	P	G	N	P	G	N	P
1	2 3 2 1		9	8	5	21	28	1	12	29
2	5 3 2 1	1	10	12	1	33	11	1	11	21
3	6 3 2 1								3	3
4	3 3 2 1									2
5	2 1 2 1		1	3	3	11	2		2	3
6	6 1 2 1			1	1	2	8			
7	1 1 2 1			4		1	5			6
8	6 5 2 1		2	4		3	1	1		3
9	3 5 2 1		1				2			
10	2 5 2 1					2	1			
11	2 2 2 1						2			1
12	2 6 2 1				1	10	12			2
13	6 6 2 1			4			10			1
14	5 6 2 1		2			4	8		1	1
15	1 6 2 1			1			1			
16	3 5 6 1			18	4	3			6	35
17	6 5 6 1		1	6	1	1			2	
18	1 5 6 1			12			4		3	2
19	5 5 6 1		1	2	1	3	4			
20	2 1 6 1						1			
21	1 1 6 1			2			5			
22	6 1 6 1			1						
23	6 6 6 1			1	1					8
24	1 2 6 1	—	—	—	—	—	—	—	—	—
25	2 2 6 1			5						2
26	6 2 6 1						3			
27	3 2 6 1	—	—	—	—	—	—	—	—	—
28	5 2 6 1	—	—	—	—	—	—	—	—	—
29	5 3 6 1	—	—	—	—	—	—	—	—	—
30	3 2 3 1			1			2		1	3
31	1 2 3 1							1		
32	5 2 3 1	—	—	—	—	—	—	—	—	—
33	5 6 5 1	—	—	—	—	—	—	—	—	—
34	5 2 5 1	—	—	—	—	—	—	—	—	—
35	1 6 1 .			1						3
36	5 6 1 .		2	4			3			
37	1 2 1 .									2
38	1 1 1 1						7			7

TABLE 2.
Frequency of Occurrence and Distribution of Patterns Ending on Sléndro Pitch Level 2

Contour No.	Pattern	Pathet Nem			Pathet Sanga			Pathet Manyura		
		G	N	P	G	N	P	G	N	P
1	3 5 3 2	4	10	16	1	3	34	7	12	23
2	6 5 3 2	12	16	10	4	5	10	13	23	14
3	1 5 3 2									1
4	5 5 3 2			3			1			
5	3 2 3 2	15	13	3		2		1	13	
6	1 2 3 2	2	1	1		1	2		3	
7	2 2 3 2		4	1					2	3
8	1 6 3 2	2	8	2	1	7			2	2
9	5 6 3 2		2			1				
10	3 6 3 2	2	1			1		1	1	2
11	3 3 3 2									1
12	3 1 3 2		3	1					1	4
13	1 1 3 2			3			1			2
14	6 1 3 2		3	5				2	2	4
15	2 1 3 2		1	7				2	1	1
16	5 6 1 2	1	4	6		10	21			
17	1 6 1 2						24		2	3
18	2 6 1 2						1			
19	6 6 1 2						2		3	1
20	3 2 1 2		1	4		3	6	1		5
21	2 2 1 2			3			4			2
22	1 2 1 2	—	—	—	—	—	—	—	—	—
23	1 1 1 2						2			
24	2 3 1 2					1	6			3
25	3 3 1 2	—	—	—	—	—	—	—	—	—
26	1 3 1 2		1						2	4
27	5 3 1 2		1		5	9	4	1		
28	6 3 1 2	—	—	—	—	—	—	—	—	—
29	6 5 1 2	—	—	—	—	—	—	—	—	—
30	5 3 5 2		4	6	1		1	2	8	3
31	2 3 5 2		1	4						
32	6 3 5 2						1			
33	6 1 6 2	—	—	—	—	—	—	—	—	—
34	6 3 6 2	1	5			1	2			
35	2 1 2 .						2			1
36	6 1 2 .			1						
37	2 3 2 .			5			7			
38	2 2 2 2			2			6			11

TABLE 3.

Frequency of Occurrence and Distribution of Patterns Ending on Sléndro Pitch Level 3

Contour No.	Pattern	Pathet Nem			Pathet Sanga			Pathet Manyura		
		G	N	P	G	N	P	G	N	P
1	5 6 5 3	3	5	41		1	6	6	15	17
2	1 6 5 3	1	7	10		1	3	3	7	10
3	2 6 5 3							3		
4	6 6 5 3			3			2			
5	5 3 5 3	—	—	—	—	—	—	—	—	—
6	2 3 5 3		4	8		4	10	1	2	2
7	3 3 5 3		2		1				1	
8	2 1 5 3					1	1	1	1	
9	6 1 5 3	—	—	—	—	—	—	—	—	—
10	5 1 5 3						1			
11	5 5 5 3						1			
12	5 2 5 3								7	
13	2 2 5 3						2			
14	1 2 5 3							1	1	
15	3 2 5 3		1	2					4	2
16	6 1 2 3		4	8			1		2	14
17	2 1 2 3		1	18	1		1		5	13
18	3 1 2 3							1	2	2
19	1 1 2 3									5
20	5 3 2 3	4	6	2	2		9		1	4
21	3 3 2 3			3						
22	2 3 2 3	—	—	—	—	—	—	—	—	—
23	2 2 2 3			13			19			3
24	3 5 2 3		2	7	1		1	1	2	14
25	5 5 2 3			4			2			
26	2 5 2 3			4						1
27	6 5 2 3		14	2				1	12	1
28	1 5 2 3		1					2	7	
29	1 6 2 3						5			
30	6 5 6 3		1	2					4	5
31	3 5 6 3		1	1						
32	1 5 6 3			1						
33	1 2 1 3	—	—	—	—	—	—	—	—	—
34	1 5 1 3	—	—	—	—	—	—	—	—	—
35	3 2 3 .						4			
36	1 2 3 .			2						2
37	3 5 3 .	—	—	—	—	—	—	—	—	—
38	3 3 3 3			1						17

Table 4.
Frequency of Occurrence and Distribution of Patterns Ending on Sléndro Pitch Level 5

Contour No.	Pattern	Pathet Nem			Pathet Sanga			Pathet Manyura		
		G	N	P	G	N	P	G	N	P
1	6 1 6 5	1	3	15	2	8	3		1	3
2	2 1 6 5	1	13	9	35	42	5		2	6
3	3 1 6 5				1					
4	1 1 6 5			1			1			
5	6 5 6 5					2				
6	3 5 6 5	1	5	8	3	1	5			6
7	5 5 6 5			2	2	2				
8	3 2 6 5		4	4	7	9	1			10
9	1 2 6 5	1		1		3	2			
10	6 2 6 5						1			
11	6 6 6 5			5						2
12	6 3 6 5	2	7	14	1	6	3		1	1
13	3 3 6 5			7						3
14	2 3 6 5	1		8	1	2	6			
15	5 3 6 5	1							1	
16	1 2 3 5	—	—	—	—	—	—	—	—	—
17	3 2 3 5		4	7	1	7	5		2	3
18	5 2 3 5				1	4	2			2
19	2 2 3 5	—	—	—	—	—	—	—	—	—
20	6 5 3 5	3	3	19	21	16	7		1	2
21	5 5 3 5			1						
22	3 5 3 5	—	—	—	—	—	—	—	—	—
23	3 3 3 5			7			3			6
24	5 6 3 5	3	1	4	2	12	3			
25	6 6 3 5			2			1			
26	3 6 3 5		5	4	2	3				3
27	1 6 3 5	1	9		22	19	4			
28	2 6 3 5				3	1				
29	2 1 3 5	—	—	—	—	—	—	—	—	—
30	1 6 1 5				6	23	4			
31	5 6 1 5					1	3			
32	2 6 1 5				1	3				
33	2 3 2 5					4				
34	2 6 2 5				1					
35	5 3 5 .	—	—	—	—	—	—	—	—	—
36	2 3 5 .	—	—	—	—	—	—	—	—	—
37	5 6 5 .	—	—	—	—	—	—	—	—	—
38	5 5 5 5			3			8			2

TABLE 5.

Frequency of Occurrence and Distribution of Patterns Ending on Sléndro Pitch Level 6

Contour No.	Pattern	Pathet Nem			Pathet Sanga			Pathet Manyura		
		G	N	P	G	N	P	G	N	P
1	1 2 1 6	2	4	9		5	20	8	4	11
2	3 2 1 6	5	4	10	2	4	11	21	35	4
3	5 2 1 6					3		1		
4	2 2 1 6			2						1
5	1 6 1 6		1			1		1	4	
6	5 6 1 6	7	8	12	2	4	10	4	4	7
7	6 6 1 6					1	2			
8	5 3 1 6	1	3					3	9	1
9	2 3 1 6	2								
10	1 3 1 6	—	—	—	—	—	—	—	—	—
11	1 1 1 6	—	—	—	—	—	—	—	—	—
12	1 5 1 6			1		2	2		6	4
13	5 5 1 6			5			2			7
14	3 5 1 6		3						2	1
15	6 5 1 6	1		1		2	1		1	1
16	2 3 5 6	2	8	4		6	9	1	5	4
17	5 3 5 6	1	4	5		1	1	2	2	7
18	6 3 5 6		7			2	4	2	2	2
19	3 3 5 6			3			1	3	7	8
20	1 6 5 6		1	4		4	28			1
21	6 6 5 6		3			1	1		2	
22	5 6 5 6		4			2				
23	5 5 5 6		7	2		2	14			
24	6 1 5 6		5	1		2		3	1	
25	1 1 5 6						1			
26	5 1 5 6		2	3					2	1
27	2 1 5 6		1		1	1		1	5	
28	3 1 5 6	—	—	—	—	—	—	—	—	—
29	3 2 5 6					2				
30	2 1 2 6	21	20	9		10	9	27	35	14
31	6 1 2 6	—	—	—	—	—	—	—	—	—
32	3 1 2 6			3				5	1	1
33	3 5 3 6	—	—	—	—	—	—	—	—	—
34	3 1 3 6	—	—	—	—	—	—	—	—	—
35	6 5 6 .	—	—	—	—	—	—	—	—	—
36	3 5 6 .			2						4
37	6 1 6 .	—	—	—	—	—	—	—	—	—
38	6 6 6 6			11			7			9

TABLE 6.
Frequency of Occurrence and Distribution of Patterns Ending on Pélog Pitch Level 1

Contour No.	Pattern	Pathet Lima			Pathet Nem			Pathet Barang		
		G	N	P	G	N	P	G	N	P
1a	2 3 2 1		3		4	18	24			
2a	5 3 2 1		3	4		3	7			
c	5 4 2 1	1	4	1		2				
3a	6 3 2 1			1						
4a	3 3 2 1			7			1			
5a	2 1 2 1	12	5	2	4	6	3			
6a	6 1 2 1	1	5							
7a	1 1 2 1		1	8	1		2			
8a	6 5 2 1			1		1				
9a	3 5 2 1	—	—	—	—	—	—	—	—	—
10a	2 5 2 1	—	—	—	—	—	—			
11a	2 2 2 1		1				3			
12a	2 6 2 1	—	—	—	—	—	—	—	—	—
13a	6 6 2 1			2			2			
14a	5 6 2 1			4		1	1			
15a	1 6 2 1	—	—	—	—	—	—	—	—	—
16a	3 5 6 1	1	1			1	9			
17a	6 5 6 1	—	—	—	—	—	—	—	—	—
18a	1 5 6 1					1	2			
19a	5 5 6 1		1	3	1		3			
20a	2 1 6 1	—	—	—	—	—	—	—	—	—
21a	1 1 6 1						1			
22a	6 1 6 1	—	—	—	—	—	—	—	—	—
23a	6 6 6 1						1			
24a	1 2 6 1	—	—	—	—	—	—			
25a	2 2 6 1	—	—	—	—	—	—			
26a	6 2 6 1						3			
27a	3 2 6 1	—	—	—	—	—	—			
28a	5 2 6 1	—	—	—	—	—	—			
29a	5 3 6 1	—	—	—	—	—	—			
30a	3 2 3 1			2			3			
b	4 2 4 1	4	6	3						
31a	1 2 3 1						1			
32a	5 2 3 1	—	—	—	—	—	—	—	—	—
33a	5 6 5 1	—	—	—	—	—	—	—	—	—
34a	5 2 5 1	—	—	—	—	—	—	—	—	—
35a	1 6 1 .	—	—	—	—	—	—	—	—	—
36a	5 6 1 .			1						
37a	1 2 1 .						2			
38	1 1 1 1	1		16			11			

TABLE 7.

Frequency of Occurrence and Distribution of Patterns Ending on Pélog Pitch Level 2

Contour No.	Pattern	Pathet Lima			Pathet Nem			Pathet Barang		
		G	N	P	G	N	P	G	N	P
1a	3 5 3 2	1	3	1	8	18	8	9	15	11
2a	6 5 3 2		2	8	5	16	7	9	28	21
b	6 5 4 2			9						
3a	1 5 3 2	—	—	—	—	—	—	—	—	—
4a	5 5 3 2						2			
b	5 5 4 2			4						
5a	3 2 3 2				1			1		1
6a	1 2 3 2		3		1	2	3	1		
d	7 2 3 2							1	3	
7a	2 2 3 2			1		3				
8a	1 6 3 2						1			
d	7 6 3 2								5	1
9a	5 6 3 2	—	—	—	—	—	—	—	—	—
10a	3 6 3 2								2	3
11a	3 3 3 2			2			3			4
12a	3 1 3 2	1	1			4	2			
13a	1 1 3 2						4			2
14a	6 1 3 2		1		1					
c	6 7 3 2								2	16
15c	2 7 3 2								1	2
16a	5 6 1 2		4	26	1	5				
b	5 6 7 2								1	1
17a	1 6 1 2						7			
b	7 6 7 2								1	7
18a	2 6 1 2	—	—	—	—	—	—	—	—	—
19a	6 6 1 2			1		1	1			
b	6 6 7 2								1	
20a	3 2 1 2	2	7	11		6	12			
b	3 2 7 2							1	1	1
d	4 2 1 2			1						
21a	2 2 1 2		1	1		1				
22a	1 2 1 2	—	—	—	—	—	—	—	—	—
23a	1 1 1 2						2			
b	7 7 7 2									2
24a	2 3 1 2	1		3	2	3	1			
25a	3 3 1 2	—	—	—	—	—	—	—	—	—
26a	1 3 1 2			4	4					
b	7 3 7 2									1
c	1 4 1 2			1						

Contour No.	Pattern	Pathet Lima			Pathet Nem			Pathet Barang		
		G	N	P	G	N	P	G	N	P
27a	5 3 1 2				3		1			
c	5 4 1 2				2	2				
28a	6 3 1 2	—	—	—	—	—	—	—	—	—
29a	6 5 1 2	—	—	—	—	—	—	—	—	—
30a	5 3 5 2					5	1	2	4	1
c	5 4 5 2	1								
31a	2 3 5 2			3			1			3
32a	6 3 5 2	—	—	—	—	—	—	—	—	—
33a	6 1 6 2	—	—	—	—	—	—	—	—	—
34a	6 3 6 2									1
35a	2 1 2 .					1	3			
c	2 7 2 .									3
36c	6 7 2 .									1
37a	2 3 2 .								1	1
38a	2 2 2 2			1			7			5

TABLE 8.
Frequency of Occurrence and Distribution of Patterns Ending on Pélog Pitch Level 3

Contour No.	Pattern	Pathet Lima			Pathet Nem			Pathet Barang		
		G	N	P	G	N	P	G	N	P
1a	5 6 5 3		1	1		3	6	1	6	20
2a	1 6 5 3					3				
d	7 6 5 3		3	1		1		3	9	4
3a	2 6 5 3									3
4a	6 6 5 3			5			1			1
5a	5 3 5 3									1
6a	2 3 5 3	2	3	2		1		1	2	2
7a	3 3 5 3		1			1				
8a	2 1 5 3	—	—	—	—	—	—	—	—	—
9a	6 1 5 3	—	—	—	—	—	—	—	—	—
10a	5 1 5 3	—	—	—	—	—	—	—	—	—
11a	5 5 5 3						3			1
12a	5 2 5 3			1		4				
13a	2 2 5 3	—	—	—	—	—	—	—	—	—
14a	1 2 5 3					1				
15a	3 2 5 3		1	1		1				5
16a	6 1 2 3		1	1	2	3	5			
c	6 7 2 3								4	4
17a	2 1 2 3		2				6			
c	2 7 2 3									11
18a	3 1 2 3	1				4				
19a	1 1 2 3			3		1	7			
20a	5 3 2 3	2	2	6		1	1	1		5
21a	3 3 2 3			3			3			
22a	2 3 2 3								1	
23a	2 2 2 3					2	8			4
24a	3 5 2 3	2				1	2			5
25a	5 5 2 3						1			
26a	2 5 2 3			1		2	3		3	1
27a	6 5 2 3				2	2		5	15	
28d	7 5 2 3				3			1		
29a	1 6 2 3	—	—	—	—	—	—	—	—	—
30a	6 5 6 3					3	1		2	8
31a	3 5 6 3						1			
32a	1 5 6 3	—	—	—	—	—	—	—	—	—
33a	1 2 1 3	—	—	—	—	—	—	—	—	—
34a	1 5 1 3	—	—	—	—	—	—	—	—	—
35a	3 2 3 .	—	—	—	—	—	—	—	—	—
36a	1 2 3 .	—	—	—	—	—	—	—	—	—
37a	3 5 3 .	—	—	—	—	—	—	—	—	—
38a	3 3 3 3			17			14			13

TABLE 9.

Frequency of Occurrence and Distribution of Patterns Ending on
Pélog Pitch Level 4

Contour No.	Pattern	Pathet Lima			Pathet Nem			Pathet Barang		
		G	N	P	G	N	P	G	N	P
1a	5 6 5 4		2	3		3	15			
2a	1 6 5 4		4	8		4	5			
d	7 6 5 4						1			
3a	2 6 5 4	—	—	—	—	—	—	—	—	—
4a	6 6 5 4			3		1	2			
5a	5 4 5 4	—	—	—	—	—	—	—	—	—
6a	2 4 5 4						2			
7a	4 4 5 4	—	—	—	—	—	—	—	—	—
8a	2 1 5 4	—	—	—	—	—	—	—	—	—
9a	6 1 5 4	—	—	—	—	—	—	—	—	—
10a	5 1 5 4	—	—	—	—	—	—	—	—	—
11a	5 5 5 4	—	—	—	—	—	—	—	—	—
12a	5 2 5 4	—	—	—	—	—	—	—	—	—
13a	2 2 5 4						1			
14a	1 2 5 4	—	—	—	—	—	—	—	—	—
15a	3 2 5 4	—	—	—	—	—	—	—	—	—
16a	6 1 2 4	—	—	—	—	—	—	—	—	—
17a	2 1 2 4	—	—	—	—	—	—	—	—	—
18a	3 1 2 4	—	—	—	—	—	—	—	—	—
19a	1 1 2 4	—	—	—	—	—	—	—	—	—
20a	5 4 2 4		2	1		1	3			
21a	4 4 2 4	—	—	—	—	—	—	—	—	—
22a	2 4 2 4	—	—	—	—	—	—	—	—	—
23a	2 2 2 4			3			4			
24a	4 5 2 4	—	—	—	—	—	—	—	—	—
25a	5 5 2 4	—	—	—	—	—	—	—	—	—
26a	2 5 2 4	—	—	—	—	—	—	—	—	—
27a	6 5 2 4	—	—	—	—	—	—	—	—	—
28a	7 5 2 4	—	—	—	—	—	—	—	—	—
29b	7 6 2 4						1			
30a	6 5 6 4	—	—	—	—	—	—	—	—	—
31a	3 5 6 4	—	—	—	—	—	—	—	—	—
32a	1 5 6 4	—	—	—	—	—	—	—	—	—
33a	1 2 1 4	—	—	—	—	—	—	—	—	—
34a	1 5 1 4	—	—	—	—	—	—	—	—	—
35a	4 2 4 .	—	—	—	—	—	—	—	—	—
36a	1 2 4 .	—	·	—	—	—	—	—	—	—
37a	4 5 4 .	—	—	—	—	—	—	—	—	—
38a	4 4 4 4			9						

TABLE 10.

Frequency of Occurrence and Distribution of Patterns Ending on Pélog Pitch Level 5

Contour No.	Pattern	Pathet Lima			Pathet Nem			Pathet Barang		
		G	N	P	G	N	P	G	N	P
1a	6 1 6 5		1			8				
c	6 7 6 5							2	1	4
2a	2 1 6 5	14	23	8	26	22	16			
c	2 7 6 5							1	1	6
3a	3 1 6 5	—	—	—	—	—	—	—	—	—
4a	7 7 6 5		2						2	2
5a	6 5 6 5					1				1
6a	3 5 6 5		2		2		9		4	3
d	4 5 6 5	2	5	2						
7a	5 5 6 5		1		1	2	2			1
8a	3 2 6 5		2		2		2			3
9a	1 2 6 5		1	1						
10a	6 2 6 5	—	—	—	—	—	—	—	—	—
11a	6 6 6 5						2			1
12a	6 3 6 5		2	1	1	2				1
c	6 4 6 5		2		1					
13a	3 3 6 5			5						
c	4 4 6 5		1							
14a	2 3 6 5	1				2	2	1		1
c	2 4 6 5	3	3							
15a	5 3 6 5					2				
16a	1 2 3 5		3	2	2					
b	1 2 4 5		2	2						
17a	3 2 3 5	2							1	3
b	4 2 4 5			4						
18a	5 2 3 5	—	—	—	—	—	—	—	—	—
19b	2 2 4 5			6						
20a	6 5 3 5	1	3	4	4	7	2	5	5	6
b	6 5 4 5		1			1	2			
21a	5 5 3 5		1				7			
b	5 5 4 5			1						
22a	3 5 3 5	—	—	—	—	—	—	—	—	—
23a	3 3 3 5								1	7
24a	5 6 3 5				1	3	1		3	
b	5 6 4 5		1		2					
25a	6 6 4 5					1				
26a	3 6 3 5		3	2				5	4	
b	4 6 4 5			1	1					
27a	1 6 3 5	2	5		3	4		2		
b	1 6 4 5		6				1			
d	7 6 3 5									1
28a	2 6 3 5					1				
b	2 6 4 5						1			
29a	2 1 3 5	—	—	—	—	—	—	—	—	—

Contour No.	Pattern	Pathet Lima			Pathet Nem			Pathet Barang		
		G	N	P	G	N	P	G	N	P
30a	1 6 1 5				2					
b	7 6 7 5							1	6	2
31b	5 6 7 5			2			1			
32a	2 6 1 5	—	—	—	—	—	—	—	—	—
33a	2 3 2 5	—	—	—	—	—	—	—	—	—
34a	2 6 2 5	—	—	—	—	—	—	—	—	—
35a	5 3 5 .	—	—	—	—	—	—	—	—	—
36a	2 3 5 .						3			2
37a	5 6 5 .						2			
38a	5 5 5 5			19			16			7

TABLE 11.

Frequency of Occurrence and Distribution of Patterns Ending on Pélog Pitch Level 6

Contour No.	Pattern	Pathet Lima			Pathet Nem			Pathet Barang		
		G	N	P	G	N	P	G	N	P
1a	7 2 7 6						1			1
b	1 2 1 6		1	1	6	4	9			
2a	3 2 1 6	1	1	8	7	9	17			1
b	3 2 7 6							11	12	12
3a	5 2 1 6		1							
4a	2 2 1 6			1			1			
5a	1 6 1 6		1							
b	7 6 7 6								2	1
6a	5 6 1 6		3			1				
b	5 6 7 6			1	1	2	1	2	2	
7a	6 6 1 6			2						
8a	5 3 1 6		1				1			
b	5 3 7 6							1	2	1
9a	2 3 1 6			2						
b	2 3 7 6								2	
c	2 4 1 6	1								
10a	1 3 1 6	—	—	—	—	—	—	—	—	—
11a	1 1 1 6	—	—	—	—	—	—	—	—	—
12a	1 5 1 6			5						
b	7 5 7 6					2	3		3	
13a	5 5 1 6						2			
b	5 5 7 6									1
14a	3 5 1 6			1						
b	3 5 7 6									1
15b	6 5 7 6							1		2
16a	2 3 5 6	1	2	2		5	17	2	2	5
c	2 4 5 6		1	1			1			
17a	5 3 5 6		1	1		2	10	1	2	1
c	5 4 5 6			3						
18a	6 3 5 6					4	2			2
19a	3 3 5 6			5		3	7	2	1	1
c	4 4 5 6			3						
20a	1 6 5 6		1	1		3				
d	7 6 5 6		1	3						8
21a	6 6 5 6			1		1				3
22a	5 6 5 6					1				
23a	5 5 5 6		2	5			7			1
24a	6 7 5 6								10	3
25a	1 1 5 6			2						
c	7 7 5 6									4
26c	5 7 5 6								7	1
27a	2 1 5 6			3		1				
c	2 7 5 6							18	20	7
28c	3 7 5 6								1	
29a	3 2 5 6	—	—	—	—	—	—	—	—	—

Contour No.	Pattern	Pathet Lima			Pathet Nem			Pathet Barang		
		G	N	P	G	N	P	G	N	P
30a	2 1 2 6	2	2		13	10	11			
c	2 7 2 6							1	3	3
31a	6 1 2 6	—	—	—	—	—	—	—	—	—
32a	3 1 2 6				6					
33a	3 5 3 6						1			
34a	3 1 3 6				6					
c	3 7 3 6								1	
35a	6 5 6 .						1			
36a	3 5 6 .						1			
37a	6 1 6 .	—	—	—	—	—	—	—	—	—
38a	6 6 6 6			5			10			13

TABLE 12.
Frequency of Occurrence and Distribution of Patterns on
Pélog Pitch Level 7

Contour No.	Pattern	Pathet Lima			Pathet Nem			Pathet Barang		
		G	N	P	G	N	P	G	N	P
1a	2 3 2 7						1	2	20	21
2a	5 3 2 7								7	2
d	4 3 2 7							2		
3a	6 3 2 7								2	1
4a	3 3 2 7								1	1
5a	2 7 2 7									2
6a	6 7 2 7							1		1
7a	7 7 2 7									3
8a	6 5 2 7	—	—	—	—	—	—	—	—	—
9a	3 5 2 7	—	—	—	—	—	—	—	—	—
10a	2 5 2 7	—	—	—	—	—	—	—	—	—
11a	2 2 2 7									1
12a	2 6 2 7	—	—	—	—	—	—		—	—
13a	6 6 2 7								1	
14a	5 6 2 7	—	—	—	—	—	—	—	—	—
15a	7 6 2 7	—	—	—	—	—	—	—	—	—
16a	3 5 6 7							3	11	15
17a	6 5 6 7							2	6	5
18a	7 5 6 7						1		4	1
19a	5 5 6 7	—			—	—	—	—	—	—
20a	2 7 6 7								2	2
21a	7 7 6 7								1	2
22a	6 7 6 7						1	1	1	
23a	6 6 6 7	—	—	—	—	—	—	—	—	—
24a	7 2 6 7	—	—	—	—	—	—	—	—	—
25a	2 2 6 7	—	—	—	—	—	—	—	—	—
26a	6 2 6 7	—	—	—	—	—	—	—	—	—
27a	3 2 6 7	—	—	—	—	—	—	—	—	—
28a	5 2 6 7	—	—	—	—	—	—	—	—	—
29a	5 3 6 7	—	—	—	—	—	—	—	—	—
30a	3 2 3 7							1	1	
31a	7 2 3 7	—	—	—	—	—	—	—	—	—
32a	5 2 3 7	—	—	—	—	—	—	—	—	—
33a	5 6 5 7									3
34a	5 2 5 7	—	—	—	—	—	—	—	—	—
35a	7 6 7 .	—	—	—	—	—	—	—	—	—
36a	5 6 7 .									1
37a	7 2 7 .	—	—	—	—	—	—	—	—	—
38a	7 7 7 7									16

TABLE 13.

Profile of Pattern Use in Sléndro Pathet Manyura

	Table No.	Contour No.	Pattern	Nem			Sanga			Manyura		
				G	N	P	G	N	P	G	N	P
Important Patterns	1	1	2 3 2 1		×	×	×	*	*		*	*
Gong		2	5 3 2 1		*	*	*	*			*	*
3 2 1 6		7	1 1 2 1					×				×
2 1 2 6		16	3 5 6 1		*						×	*
Kenong		23	6 6 6 1									×
2 3 2 1		38	1 1 1 1		×			×				×
5 3 2 1	2	1	3 5 3 2		*	*			*	×	*	*
3 5 3 2		2	6 5 3 2	*	*	*		×	*	×	*	*
6 5 3 2		5	3 2 3 2	*	*						*	
3 2 3 2		20	3 2 1 2						×			×
5 6 5 3		30	5 3 5 2			×					×	
6 5 2 3		38	2 2 2 2									*
3 2 1 6	3	1	5 6 5 3		×	*			×	×	*	*
2 1 2 6		2	1 6 5 3		×	*					×	*
Kempul		12	5 2 5 3								×	
2 3 2 1		16	6 1 2 3			×						*
5 3 2 1		17	2 1 2 3			*					×	*
3 5 6 1		19	1 1 2 3									×
3 5 3 2		24	3 5 2 3			×						*
6 5 3 2		25	6 5 2 3	*							*	
2 2 2 2		28	1 5 2 3								×	
5 6 5 3		30	6 5 6 3									×
1 6 5 3		38	3 3 3 3									*
6 1 2 3	4	2	2 1 6 5		*	×	*	*	×			×
2 1 2 3		6	3 5 6 5		×	×			×			×
3 5 2 3		8	3 2 6 5				×	×				*
3 3 3 3		23	3 3 3 5			×						×
3 2 6 5	5	1	1 2 1 6			×	×	*		×		*
1 2 1 6		2	3 2 1 6	×		*			*	*	*	
2 1 2 6		6	5 6 1 6	×	×	*			*			×
Exclusive Patterns		8	5 3 1 6								×	
Gong		12	1 5 1 6								×	
3 1 2 6		13	5 5 1 6			×						×
Kenong		16	2 3 5 6		×			×	×		×	
5 2 5 3		17	5 3 5 6			×						×
1 5 1 6		19	3 3 5 6								×	×
3 3 5 6		28	2 1 5 6								×	
Kempul		30	2 1 2 6	*	*	×		*	×	*	*	*
1 1 2 3		32	3 1 2 6							×		
		38	6 6 6 6			*			×			×

TABLE 14.
Profile of Pattern Use in Sléndro Pathet Nem

Important Patterns	Table No.	Contour No.	Pattern	Nem			Sanga			Manyura		
				G	N	P	G	N	P	G	N	P
Important Patterns	1	1	2 3 2 1	*	×	×	×	*	*		*	*
Gong		2	5 3 2 1		*	*		*	*		*	*
6 5 3 2		16	3 5 6 1			*					×	*
3 2 3 2		17	6 5 6 1		×							
2 1 2 6		18	1 5 6 1			*						
		25	2 2 6 1		×							
Kenong		38	1 1 1 1		×							
5 3 2 1	2	2	6 5 3 2	*	*	*		×	*	×	*	*
6 5 3 2		5	3 2 3 2	*	*						*	
3 2 3 2		1	3 5 3 2		*	*			*	×	*	*
3 5 3 2		8	1 6 3 2	×			×					
6 5 2 3		14	6 1 3 2		×							
2 1 6 5		15	2 1 3 2		×							
2 1 2 6		16	5 6 1 2		×			*	*			
Kempul		30	5 3 5 2		×						×	
5 3 2 1		34	6 3 6 2	×								
3 5 6 1		37	2 3 2 .		×			×				
1 5 6 1	3	1	5 6 5 3	×	*				×	×	*	*
6 5 3 2		2	1 6 5 3	×	*						×	*
3 5 3 2		6	2 3 5 3		×			*				
5 6 5 3		16	6 1 2 3		×							*
1 6 5 3		17	2 1 2 3		*						×	*
2 1 2 3		20	5 3 2 3	×				×				
2 2 2 3		23	2 2 2 3		*			*				
6 1 6 5		24	3 5 2 3		×							*
6 3 6 5		27	6 5 2 3	*						*		
6 5 3 5	4	1	6 1 6 5		*		×					
3 2 1 6		2	2 1 6 5	*	×		*	*	×			×
5 6 1 6		6	3 5 6 5	×	×				×			×
6 6 6 6		11	6 6 6 5		×							
		12	6 3 6 5	×	*			×				
		13	3 3 6 5		×							
		14	2 3 6 5		×				×			
		17	3 2 3 5		×			×	×			
		20	6 5 3 5		*		*	*	×			
		23	3 3 3 5		×							×
		26	3 6 3 5	×								
		27	1 6 3 5	×			*	*				

Table No.	Contour No.	Pattern	Nem			Sanga			Manyura		
			G	N	P	G	N	P	G	N	P
5	1	1 2 1 6			×	×		*	×		*
	2	3 2 1 6	×		*			*	*	*	
	3	5 6 1 6	×	×	*			*			×
	13	5 5 1 6			×						
	16	2 3 5 6		×		×	×			×	
	17	5 3 5 6			×						×
	18	6 3 5 6		×							
	23	5 5 5 6		×				*			
	24	6 1 5 6		×							
	31	2 1 2 6	*	*	×	*	×		*	*	*
	38	6 6 6 6			*		×				×

Key: × = frequent; * = important

TABLE 15.

Profile of Pattern Use in Sléndro Pathet Sanga

	Table No.	Contour No.	Pattern	Nem G	Nem N	Nem P	Sanga G	Sanga N	Sanga P	Manyura G	Manyura N	Manyura P
Important Patterns	1	1	2 3 2 1		×	×	×	*	*		*	*
Gong		2	5 3 2 1		*	*		*	*		*	*
2 1 6 5		5	2 1 2 1				*					
6 5 3 5		6	6 1 2 1						×			
1 6 3 5		7	1 1 2 1						×			×
Kenong		12	2 6 2 1					*	×			
2 3 2 1		13	6 6 2 1						*			
5 3 2 1		14	5 6 2 1						×			
2 1 2 1		21	1 1 6 1						×			
2 6 2 1		38	1 1 1 1						×			×
5 6 1 2	2	1	3 5 3 2		*	*			*	×	*	*
2 1 6 5		2	6 5 3 2	*	*	*		×	*	×	*	*
6 5 3 5		8	1 6 3 2	×			×					
5 6 3 5		16	5 6 1 2					*	*			
1 6 3 5		17	1 6 1 2						*			
1 6 1 5		20	3 2 1 2						×			
2 1 2 6		24	2 3 1 2						×			
Kempul		27	5 3 1 2				×	×				
2 3 2 1		37	2 3 2 .		×				×			
5 3 2 1		38	2 2 2 2						×			×
6 6 2 1	3	1	5 6 5 3	×	*				×	×	*	*
3 5 3 2		6	2 3 5 3		×				*			
6 5 3 2		20	5 3 2 3	×					×			
5 6 1 2		23	2 2 2 3		*				*			
2 3 5 3		24	1 6 2 3						×			
2 2 2 3	4	1	6 1 6 5		*		×					
1 2 1 6		2	2 1 6 5		*	×	*	*	×			×
3 2 1 6		6	3 5 6 5		×	×			×			×
5 6 1 6		8	3 2 6 5				×	×				*
1 6 5 6		12	6 3 6 5		×	*	×					
5 5 5 6		14	2 3 6 5			×			×			
1 6 1 2		17	3 2 3 5			×		×	×			
Exclusive Patterns		20	6 5 3 5			*	*	*	×			
Gong		24	5 6 3 5						*			
5 3 1 2		27	1 6 3 5	×			*	*				
3 2 6 5		30	1 6 1 5				×	*				
Gong/Kenong		38	5 5 5 5						×			
2 6 1 5	5	1	1 2 1 6			×		×	*	×		*
Gong/Kenong/Kempul		2	3 2 1 6	×		*			*	*	*	
1 6 1 5		6	5 6 1 6	×	×	*			*			×
Kenong		16	2 3 5 6	×				×	×		×	
2 6 2 1		20	1 6 5 6						*			
Kenong/Kempul		23	5 5 5 6	×					*			
5 6 1 5		30	2 1 2 6	*	*	×	*	×		*	*	*
		38	6 6 6 6			*			×			×

Key: × = frequent; * = important

TABLE 16.
Profile of Pattern Use in Pélog Pathet Lima

	Table No.	Contour No.	Pattern	Nem			Sanga			Manyura		
				G	N	P	G	N	P	G	N	P
Important Patterns	6	4	3 3 2 1		×							
Gong		5	2 1 2 1	*	×			×				
2 1 2 1		6	6 1 2 1		×							
2 1 6 5		7	1 1 2 1		×							
		30	4 2 4 1		×							
Kenong		38	1 1 1 1			*			*			
2 1 6 5		38	(7 7 7 7)									*
Kempul	7	2	6 5 4 2		×							
1 1 1 1		2	6 5 3 2		×		×	*	×	×	*	*
5 6 1 2		16	5 6 1 2			*						
3 3 3 3		20	3 2 1 2	×	×			×	*			
5 5 5 5	8	4	6 6 5 3		×							
Exclusive Patterns		20	5 3 2 3		×						×	
Kenong		38	3 3 3 3			*			*			*
6 1 2 1		2	1 6 5 4		×			×				
4 2 4 1		38	4 4 4 4		×							
4 5 6 5	9	2	2 1 6 5	*	*	×	*	*	*			
Kempul		2	(2 7 6 5)									×
6 5 4 2		6	(3 5 6 5)					×				
4 4 4 4		6	4 5 6 5	×								
3 3 6 5		13	3 3 6 5		×							
2 2 4 5		19	2 2 4 5		×							
		27	1 6 4 5	×								
		27	1 6 3 5	×								
		38	5 5 5 5			*			*			×
	10	2	3 2 1 6		×		×	×	*			
		2	(3 2 7 6)							*	*	*
		19	3 3 5 6		×			×				
		23	5 5 5 6		×			×				
		38	6 6 6 6		×							

TABLE 17.
Profile of Pattern Use in Pélog Pathet Nem

	Table No.	Contour No.	Pattern	Lima			Nem			Barang		
				G	N	P	G	N	P	G	N	P
Important Patterns	6	1	2 3 2 1					*	*			
Gong		1	(2 3 2 7)								*	*
2 1 6 5		2	5 3 2 1					×				
1 2 1 6		5	2 1 2 1	*	×		×					
2 1 2 6		16	3 5 6 1				×					
		16	(3 5 6 7)								*	*
Kenong		38	1 1 1 1			*			*			
2 3 2 1	7	1	3 5 3 2				×	*	×	×	*	*
3 5 3 2	2	2	6 5 3 2		×		×	*	×	×	*	*
6 5 3 2		16	5 6 1 2		*			×				
2 1 6 5		17	1 6 1 2					×				
2 1 2 6		17	(7 6 7 2)									×
		20	3 2 1 2	×	*		×	*				
Kempul		30	5 3 5 2				×					
2 3 2 1		38	2 2 2 2				×					
1 1 1 1	8	1	5 6 5 4					*				
3 2 1 2		1	5 6 5 3					×				
3 3 3 3		2	1 6 5 4		×			×				
5 6 5 4		16	6 1 2 3					×				
2 1 6 5		17	2 1 2 3					×				
5 5 5 5		17	(2 7 2 3)									*
6 6 6 6		19	1 1 2 3					×				
1 2 1 6		23	2 2 2 3					×				
3 2 1 6		38	3 3 3 3		*			*				*
2 3 5 6	9	2	2 1 6 5	*	*	×	*	*	*			
5 3 5 6		2	(2 7 6 5)									×
2 1 2 6		6	3 5 6 5					×				
Exclusive Patterns		6	(4 5 6 5)	×								
Gong		20	6 5 3 5					×		×	×	×
1 2 1 6		21	5 5 3 5					×				
3 1 2 6		23	3 3 3 5									×
3 1 3 6		38	5 5 5 5			*			*			×
	10	1	1 2 1 6				*		*			
		2	3 2 1 6		×		×	×	*			
		2	(3 2 7 6)							*	*	*
		16	2 3 5 6					×	*			
		17	5 3 5 6						*			
		19	3 3 5 6		×				×			
		23	5 5 5 6		×				×			
		30	2 1 2 6				*	*	*			
		32	3 1 2 6				×					
		34	3 1 3 6				×					
		38	6 6 6 6		×				*			*

TABLE 18.
Profile of Pattern Use in Pélog Pathet Barang

	Table No.	Contour No.	Pattern	Lima G	Lima N	Lima P	Nem G	Nem N	Nem P	Barang G	Barang N	Barang P
Important Patterns	6	1	2 3 2 7								*	*
Gong		1	(2 3 2 1)					*	*			
3 2 7 6		2	5 3 2 7								×	
		2	(5 3 2 1)						×			
Kenong		16	3 5 6 7								*	*
2 3 2 7		16	(3 5 6 1)						×			
3 5 6 7		17	6 5 6 7								×	×
3 5 3 2		38	7 7 7 7									*
6 5 3 2		38	(1 1 1 1)			*			*			
6 5 2 3												
3 2 7 6	7	1	3 5 3 2				×	*	×	×	*	*
6 7 5 6		2	6 5 3 2			×	×	*	×	×	*	*
		8	7 6 3 2								×	
Kempul		14	6 7 3 2									*
2 3 2 7		17	7 6 7 2									×
3 5 6 7		17	(1 6 1 2)						×			
7 7 7 7		38	2 2 2 2						×			×
3 5 3 2												
6 5 3 2	8	1	5 6 5 3						×		×	*
6 7 3 2		2	7 6 5 3								×	
5 6 5 3		15	3 2 5 3									×
2 7 2 3		17	2 7 2 3									*
3 3 3 3		17	(2 1 2 3)						×			
3 2 7 6		20	5 3 2 3			×						×
6 6 6 6		24	3 5 2 3									×
		27	6 5 2 3							×	*	
Exclusive Patterns		30	6 5 6 3									×
Gong		38	3 3 3 3			*			*			*
6 5 6 7												
2 7 5 6	9	2	2 7 6 5									×
		2	(2 1 6 5)	*	*	×	*	*	*			
Kenong		20	6 5 3 5					×		×	×	×
6 5 6 7		23	3 3 3 5									×
7 6 3 2		26	3 6 3 5							×		
3 3 3 5		30	7 6 7 5								×	
6 7 5 6		38	5 5 5 5			*			*			×
5 7 5 6												
	10	2	3 2 7 6							*	*	*
Kempul		2	(3 2 1 6)			×	×	×	*			
6 5 6 7		16	2 3 5 6					×	*			×
6 7 3 2		20	7 6 5 6									×
3 3 3 5		24	6 7 5 6								*	
6 7 5 6		26	5 7 5 6								×	
		38	6 6 6 6			×			*			*

Appendix 5

An Informational Analysis of Pathet

Alan R. Templeton

Introduction

Pathet, usually translated as "mode," is a Javanese criterion for classifying gamelan pieces. Gamelan pieces are played either in a five-tone tuning system called *sléndro* or a seven-tone system called *pélog*. Within each tuning system, pieces are further categorized into one of several *pathet*. In Central Java, the *sléndro pathet* are Nem, Sanga, and Manyura, and the *pélog pathet* are Lima, Nem, and Barang. There are associations of time, mood, and range with *pathet*, but only the determinants of *pathet* in instrumental music will be studied in this appendix. Previous work has been done on the musical determinants of *pathet*—most notably by Kunst and Hood[1]—but, as pointed out in chapter 6, many unsolved problems remain. Becker speculates in chapter 6 that *pathet* is determined by three interlocking factors: (1) melodic pattern, formula, or contour, (2) the pitch level of that pattern, and (3) the position of the pattern within the formal structure of the piece. This appendix will provide support for this definition of *pathet* and elaborate in a quantitative fashion the roles and interactions of contour, pitch, and position in determining *pathet*.

The analysis will be performed on the same set of data described in chapter 6 and given in Appendix 4. These data were obtained from the saron lines of a large number of *sléndro* and *pélog* gamelan pieces, listed in Appendix 3. The *sléndro* and *pélog pathet* will be analyzed separately, but comparisons will be made between them. The saron line was divided into four-note units called *gatra*, the smallest part of a composition that still has meaning.[2] Each *gatra* is characterized by three components: (1) the contour or melodic pattern that describes the relative pitch relationships of the four notes of the *gatra* with one another, (2) the pitch level on which the contour is realized, and (3) the position of the *gatra* within the musical structure as indicated by the end-marking instruments—gong, kenong, and kempul (actually, the kempul class is a catch-all for *gatra* not marked by a gong or kenong). The raw data consist of the number of times a *gatra* characterized by the above three components occurred in each *pathet* in the large repertoire of gamelan music of known *pathet* gathered by Becker. The essential problem is to identify the determinants of *pathet* present in these data and to use the knowledge thus gained to analyze *pathet* further and to test various theories and hypotheses concerning *pathet*.

Methodology

Kunst and Hood based their *pathet* theories upon how frequently certain gong notes (Kunst) or gong *gatra* (Hood) occur in pieces of a specified *pathet*. They identify the important determinants of *pathet* as those musical elements most commonly used in pieces of a given *pathet*. This approach is easily extended to kenong and kempul *gatra* as well as to any musical elements contained within these *gatra* types (for example, kenong end pitch, etc.). To apply this methodology one need only inspect the data given in Appendix 4 and identify the *gatra* that are most commonly used. To do this, the number of occurrences of each *gatra* type given in Appendix 4 must first be converted into frequencies. The frequency of a specific *gatra* is calculated by dividing the number of occurrences of that *gatra* in a given *pathet* by the total number of *gatra* at the same position and in the same *pathet* for the entire sample. This procedure yields a frequency of occurrence that may range between zero and one. A frequency of zero means that the *gatra* never occurs in the position and *pathet* under consideration, while a frequency of one implies that the *gatra* always occurs in the specified position and *pathet*. Such frequencies measure how common a particular *gatra* is with respect to all possible *gatra* that could occur in the same position and *pathet*. Converting to frequencies is necessary because the number of pieces sampled is different for each *pathet*, and different total numbers of gong, kenong, and kempul *gatra* occur within the sample of pieces of the same *pathet*. These differences in sample size influence the number of occurrences given in Appendix 4. For example, the *gatra* marked by a gong that has the sequence of notes 6 5 3 2 G (with G denoting a gong *gatra*) occurs twelve times in Sléndro Pathet Nem and thirteen times in Sléndro Pathet Manyura. This does not mean, however, that the *gatra* 6 5 3 2 G is more frequent in Manyura than Nem. There are a total of 136 gong *gatra* in Pathet Manyura in the sample, but only 105 in Nem. Thus, the frequency of 6 5 3 2 G in Nem is $12/105 = .114$ and in Manyura is $13/136 = .096$; that is, somewhat over 11% of all gong *gatra* are 6 5 3 2 G in Nem and somewhat less than 10% are 6 5 3 2 G in Manyura. The position of the *gatra* can also affect the number of occurrences. As just noted, the *gatra* 6 5 3 2 occurs thirteen times in Manyura when marked by a gong, but it occurs fourteen times in Manyura when marked by a kempul. However, there are 473 kempul *gatra* in Pathet Manyura in the sample, so the frequency of 6 5 3 2 P (P denotes a kempul *gatra*) is $14/473 = .030$, less than a third the frequency of the *gatra* when marked by a gong. These examples illustrate the importance of using frequencies in analyzing *pathet*. In essence, this approach characterizes *pathet* by the frequency distribution over all possible *gatra* (or any other musical element of interest) for a given *pathet*.

The frequency distribution method of analysis is rather simple to execute, but unfortunately it is marred by two serious flaws. First, just because a particular musical element occurs frequently does not imply that it is an important determinant of *pathet*. For example, one of the most commonly occurring *sléndro* kempul *gatra* is 3 5 3 2 P, which accounts for 3% of the kempul *gatra* in Pathet Nem, 7% in Sanga, and 5% in Manyura. Most other kempul *gatra* occur with a frequency of less than .01 (1%). However, because this *gatra* occurs frequently in all the *sléndro pathet*, it has no strong associations with any particular *pathet* and in this sense cannot be an important determinant of *pathet*. Hence, frequencies alone cannot identify the determinants of *pathet*.

Second, any description of *pathet* based upon the few most commonly occurring elements often fails when applied to specific pieces. For example, Kunst's theory of *pathet* is based upon the gong pitch and predicts that Sléndro Pathet Nem pieces should end on the notes 2, 5, or 6. In Becker's sample, over 90% of the Nem pieces do indeed end on one of these notes, but what of the remaining pieces in Pathet Nem that do not? They are in Pathet Nem just as much as any of the other Pathet Nem pieces, but it is difficult to see how these particular pieces fit into Kunst's theory of *pathet*. This is a difficulty of any theory based on the most frequently occurring elements; inevitably there are pieces that use the rarer elements. Any complete theory or description of pathet must be able to predict or describe the *pathet* of these pieces also.

For the above reasons, I do not use the approach of finding the frequency distribution over a class of musical elements in a given *pathet*. Instead, I calculate the frequency distribution over *pathet* given a particular musical element. This approach completely changes the emphasis of the study. When looking at the distribution over musical elements in a given *pathet*, one can answer the question, Which elements occur commonly in this *pathet*? When looking at the distribution over *pathet* given a musical element, one can answer the question, Which *pathet*, if any, is a given musical element most strongly associated with? By answering the second question, the determinants of *pathet* may be identified.

To understand the motivation behind this approach, consider the following hypothetical situation. Suppose a Javanese musician listens to a piece of gamelan music and determines its *pathet*. He obviously hears something in that particular piece that informs him of the piece's *pathet*. No attempt will be made to ferret out the complexities of how a human mind could reach such a decision, but a few speculations can be advanced. First, the musician must have some preconceived ideas about *pathet* before he hears the piece. This does not necessarily mean that he has an explicit theory or definition of *pathet*, but simply that, by having listened to a large number of gamelan pieces, he has developed over the years certain musical associations[3] with the various *pathet*. It is important to note that any element that occurs commonly in all *pathet* would have no strong associations with any particular *pathet*. Hence, from the listener's point of view, such elements are not determinants of *pathet*. It is only by knowing that certain musical elements are associated more often with one *pathet* than with the others that allows the musician to know what each *pathet* should "sound like." As the musician listens to the piece, he interprets what he hears with respect to his prior associations. His opinion about the *pathet* of the piece is conditioned both by all the gamelan music he has heard up to that point and by the specific musical elements he hears in that particular piece. The usefulness of the frequency of a musical element in a large number of pieces breaks down at this point. There are only two frequencies that are meaningful when listening to a particular piece: a frequency of zero (the element does not occur in the piece) and a frequency of one (the element occurs in the piece)—any intermediate frequency is meaningless to the listener. Furthermore, the listener bases his decision about *pathet* specifically on those elements that occur in the particular piece (that is, those with a frequency of one) and the associations that these specific elements have with the various *pathet*.

The approach taken in this appendix will essentially be a "listener's" approach. The question that will be asked is, given that a musical element has occurred in a piece, how much information with respect to the *pathet* of that piece is gained from recognizing that element? The search for the determinants of *pathet* is now changed from the distribution of elements over a large number of pieces to realized individual elements that could occur in particular pieces. This change seems to be a natural one, since *pathet* itself is realized only in individual pieces; that is, *pathet* is a property of a piece.

The method of analysis measures the associations of a musical element with *pathet* by the frequency that element has in pieces of each *pathet*, conditioned by the fact that it has occurred in a piece of unknown *pathet*. More formally, let x be any musical element of interest. Conditioning on the fact that x occurred is equivalent to making the frequency of x equal to one. However, even when x does occur in a piece—for example, a *sléndro* piece—the question still remains as to whether the piece is in Pathet

Nem, Sanga, or Manyura. Hence, let

$P_n(x)$ = the probability of the piece being in Pathet Nem given that x occurred in the piece (or equivalently, the frequency with which x occurs in pieces of Pathet Nem given that it has occurred in a piece of unknown *pathet*)

$P_s(x)$ = the probability of the piece being in Pathet Sanga given that x occurred in the piece

$P_m(x)$ = the probability of the piece being in Pathet Manyura given that x occurred in the piece

These conditional probabilities measure the associations that x has with the three *sléndro pathet*. As a particular piece can be in only one *pathet*, the possible *pathet* of a piece represent mutually exclusive and exhaustive categories. A basic property of probabilities is that the probability of an event that can be subdivided into mutually exclusive subevents is the sum of the probabilities of the subevents. Hence, the probability of musical element x occurring in a piece regardless of *pathet* is the sum of the three conditional *pathet* probabilities; that is,

$$\text{Probability } (x \text{ occurs}) = P_n(x) + P_s(x) + P_m(x).$$

Since the probabilities are already conditioned on the event that x occurred, these probabilities must sum to one:

$$P_n(x) + P_s(x) + P_m(x) = 1.$$

These probabilities do not measure the overall frequency with which x occurs in a large number of pieces, but do measure how x is distributed over *pathet*. The probabilities, however, are easily obtained from the overall frequencies. Suppose that x occurs in *sléndro* pieces with frequency $F_n(x)$ in Nem pieces, $F_s(x)$ in Sanga pieces, and $F_m(x)$ in Manyura pieces. These frequencies measure how common x is in a large number of *sléndro* pieces. These frequencies may be converted to conditional probabilities by the transformation

$$P_n(x) = \frac{F_n(x)}{F_n(x) + F_s(x) + F_m(x)}$$

$$P_s(x) = \frac{F_s(x)}{F_n(x) + F_s(x) + F_m(x)}$$

$$P_m(x) = \frac{F_m(x)}{F_n(x) + F_s(x) + F_m(x)}$$

$$P_n(x) + P_s(x) + P_m(x) = \frac{F_n(x) + F_s(x) + F_m(x)}{F_n(x) + F_s(x) + F_m(x)} = 1.$$

In this manner the conditional probabilities given that x has occurred are obtained from the overall frequencies of x.

The three numbers $P_n(x)$, $P_s(x)$, and $P_m(x)$ measure directly the associations the musical element x has with the three *sléndro pathet*. There are two extremes in the degree of association. At one extreme, x may have equal conditional probability in all *pathet*; that is, $P_n(x) = P_s(x) = P_m(x) = 1/3$. When such an element occurs in a piece, no clue is given as to the *pathet* of the piece as it is equally associated with all *pathet*. At the other extreme, x may be associated exclusively with only one *pathet*. For example, suppose $P_n(x) = 1$ and $P_s(x) = P_m(x) = 0$. Upon hearing x in a piece, a listener would know with certainty that the *pathet* is Nem. Between these two extremes, intermediate probabilities indicate intermediate levels of association between x and *pathet*. However, dealing with three separate numbers is cumbersome, so a single number is needed that measures the degree to which x is informative about *pathet*.

As a first step in developing such an information measure, the concept of the entropy of a frequency distribution is borrowed from probability theory. The entropy of a distribution is the negative of the sum of each of the probabilities multiplied by its respective logarithm.[4] The entropy associated with the conditional probability distribution of x over the three *sléndro pathet* is

$$En(x) = -P_n(x) \cdot \log P_n(x) - P_s(x) \cdot \log P_s(x) - P_m(x) \cdot \log P_m(x).$$

The entropy measures the degree of randomness or uncertainty contained in the distribution. If there is no randomness or uncertainty, one of the probabilities equals one and the others equal zero—as in the previous example in which $P_n(x) = 1$ and $P_s(x) = 0$. Under such circumstances $En(x) = 0$, and this is its minimum value. Therefore, entropy achieves its minimum value of zero when a realized musical element unambiguously defines the *pathet* of the piece. However, suppose $P_n(x) = P_s(x) = P_m(x) = 1/3$. Then $En(x) = -\log(1/3) = \log 3$, and this is the maximum value of the entropy. Therefore entropy is maximum when element x contains no information about *pathet* whatsoever. As the conditional probability distribution deviates further and further from the 1/3, 1/3, 1/3 pattern, the entropy decreases and finally reaches zero when x is associated with only one *pathet*. Therefore, entropy is a convenient measure of uncertainty.

Instead of measuring uncertainty, it is more convenient to measure information in a positive fashion so that low values indicate weak associations with *pathet* and large values indicate strong associations with *pathet*. This is easily accomplished with the measure

$$\log(3) - En(x).$$

This measure inverts the entropy scale so that large values of entropy yield small values of information and small entropy values yield large values of information. When there is no information contained in x (the 1/3, 1/3, 1/3 pattern) this measure is zero; when there is maximum information in x (x occurs in only one *pathet*) the information measure attains its maximum value of log 3. Thus, information ranges on a scale from zero to log 3. A more convenient range would be zero to one, and therefore the measure is rescaled to yield the final information measure:

$$I(x) = \frac{\log 3 - En(x)}{\log 3}.$$

As an example of how these measures can be applied, consider the kempul *gatra* 3 5 3 2 P. This *gatra* occurs with frequency .031 in Nem, .066 in Sanga, and .049 in Manyura. The sum of these frequencies is .146. Dividing each frequency by the sum yields the conditional probabilities $P_n(3\ 5\ 3\ 2\ P) = .031/.146 = .212$, $P_s(3\ 5\ 3\ 2\ P) = .452$, and $P_m(3\ 5\ 3\ 2\ P) = .336$. Finally, applying the information measure to these conditional probabilities yields $I(3\ 5\ 3\ 2\ P) = .040$; that is, this kempul *gatra* contains relatively little information as it occurs commonly in all *pathet*. Now consider the gong *gatra* 3 2 3 2 G, which occurs with frequency .1429 in Nem, 0 in Sanga, and .0074 in Manyura. The conditional probabilities are $P_n(3\ 2\ 3\ 2\ G) = .951$, $P_s(3\ 2\ 3\ 2\ G) = 0$, and $P_m(3\ 2\ 3\ 2\ G) = .049$. This is relatively close to a 1, 0, 0 pattern, and the information measure is correspondingly high: $I(3\ 2\ 3\ 2\ G) = .8221$.

In the development of the information measure, the musical element being studied was purposely kept arbitrary. In the above examples, this element was an entire *gatra* characterized by its position in the piece, its melodic contour, and its pitch level. However, x could also be any subgrouping of these components. For example, let $x = 2G$, where 2G designates a note at pitch 2 in a gong position regardless of the rest of the notes in the gong *gatra*. The frequencies of this subelement are calculated by adding the frequencies of all gong *gatra* ending on pitch level 2. The resulting frequencies are .3714 for Nem, .0753 for Sanga, and .2206 for Manyura. The conditional probabilities are thus $P_n(2G) = .5566$, $P_s(2G) = .1129$, and $P_m(2G) = .3305$, which yield $I(2G) = .1459$. Other elements could be substituted for x, and the element conditioned on is limited only by the nature of the data and the imagination of the investigator.

An Informational Description of Pathet

The techniques described in the previous section were used to obtain an informational description of the determinants of *pathet*. The data were first divided into *sléndro* and *pélog*, and each tuning system was analyzed separately. For both tuning systems, the basic unit of analysis was the *gatra*, as characterized by position, pitch, and contour. The frequency of occurrence of each *gatra* type within a tuning system was calculated for each *pathet*. Next, these frequencies were converted into conditional probabilities to measure the associations that each *gatra* has with all the *pathet*. Finally, the information function was applied to the conditional probability distribution of a *gatra* to calculate the information with respect to *pathet* contained in each individual *gatra*. Furthermore, the frequencies, conditional probabilities, and informations of various subelements were also calculated.

Because of the large number of distinct *gatra* occurring in the data, to do the aforementioned calculations by hand would be an extremely tedious and timeconsuming chore. Hence, a computer program was written in Fortran IV to calculate all the aforementioned quantities on the IBM 360 computer of the University of Michigan. Because of the large amount of output, various averages were taken to summarize the informational patterns observed in a great many individual *gatra* or other musical elements. Only these averages will be presented here, but the output data on each individual *gatra* are available to those who are interested.

The informational analysis of the *sléndro pathet*—Nem, Sanga, and Manyura—will be described first. Table 1 gives the information in individual *gatra* averaged over both pitch and contour for each of the three positions, the average information in pitch level alone for each position, and the average information in contour alone for each position. The average information in individual *gatra* is calculated by summing all the informations associated with all *gatra* types occurring at a given position, and then dividing by the total number of *gatra* types occurring in that position. The information in end pitch at a specific position is calculated by first summing the frequencies over all *gatra* ending on a specific pitch to calculate the frequency with which that pitch occurs in a given *pathet* and in a given position. Then, the conditional probabilities over *pathet* and the information are calculated from these frequencies for that pitch. Finally, the information in end pitch is summed over the five *sléndro* pitches and divided by five to yield the average information in end pitch. For the contours, the frequencies of all *gatra* having the same contour are summed over all five pitch levels to obtain the contour frequency for each *pathet* and position. Then the conditional probabilities and the information in all individual contours are calculated. These informations are then summed over all contours and divided by the total number of contour types that occur for a given position.

The averages shown in table 1 give only a gross picture of the determinants of *pathet*, but several interesting features appear even at this level. The most obvious feature is that a great deal of information about *pathet* is indeed imbedded in individual *gatra*. Hence, *gatra* are or contain very

TABLE 1.
Average Information with Respect to **Sléndro Pathet** *in*
Individual **Gatra,** *End-Pitch Level, and Contour in*
Each of the Three **Gatra Positions**

Position	Average Information		
	Individual *Gatra*	End-Pitch Level	Contour
Gong	.7945	.3638	.4272
Kenong	.5446	.1393	.2825
Kempul	.5338	.0273	.2364

strong determinants of *pathet*. Generally, the most information is found in gong *gatra*, but kenong and kempul *gatra* also contain substantial and approximately equal amounts of information. Therefore, the determinants of *pathet* are spread throughout the entire gamelan piece and occur at all positions. This reinforces the idea that *pathet* is a property of an entire piece and is not just the property of the gong pitch level or the musical contour preceding the gong pitch level.

Although *gatra* at all three positions are strong determinants of *pathet*, the pattern of information in the subelements of end-pitch level (which determines the pitch level of the entire contour) and contour differs greatly with position. These differences indicate that the separation of *gatra* into gong, kenong, and kempul *gatra* is meaningful with respect to *pathet*, and any theory of *pathet* will have to explain this distinction. The differences between positions are most dramatically illustrated by the role of end pitch in determining *pathet*. For gong *gatra*, the information in end pitch alone is roughly half of the total information contained in the entire *gatra*— indicating that some gong pitch levels are strongly associated with *pathet* regardless of contour. For kenong *gatra*, end-pitch information is only about a quarter of the total information, suggesting a reduction, but not a complete elimination, of the association of pitch level with *pathet*. For kempul *gatra*, however, there is essentially no information in pitch level. Thus, the role of end-pitch level in determining *pathet* strongly interacts with position in the piece.

Contour by itself is a fairly strong determinant of *pathet* in all positions, but the effect of contour is most pronounced for gong *gatra*. Thus, in the gong position, both pitch level and melodic contour are used in highly distinctive fashions in certain *pathet*. Note in table 1 that in all positions the information contained in contour alone is always greater than the information contained in pitch alone. Therefore, with regard to sub-elements of *gatra*, melodic contour plays a more important role than pitch level in determining *pathet*.

The amount of information contained in both pitch and contour steadily declines as the position changes from gong to kenong to kempul. It is particularly noteworthy that the information contained in pitch alone and in contour alone is smaller in kempul positions than in kenong positions, yet the total information contained in individual kenong and kempul *gatra* (which consists of a specific pitch level and a specific contour) is roughly the same. This implies that the interaction of pitch and contour is much more important in kempul positions than in kenong positions, and this interaction is least important in gong positions.

A somewhat finer analysis of the determinants of *pathet* may be achieved by categorizing the *gatra* according to their two-note ending pattern. The vast majority of *gatra* used in gamelan music end either in a descending cadence separated by a single pitch level, such as 2 1, or in an ascending cadence separated by a single pitch level, such as 2 3. Consequently, the *gatra* are grouped into descending *gatra*, ascending *gatra*, and remaining *gatra* (*gatra* whose last two notes do not end in a descending or ascending cadence). The average information about *pathet* contained in individual *gatra*, pitch, and contour is calculated for each of these three types. However, since the *gatra* have already been categorized according to the relationship of the last two notes, pitch and contour are somewhat confounded in this case. Finally, by summing the *gatra* frequencies within each of the three categories over both pitch level and contour, the information may be calculated by knowing only that the end cadence is of the descending, ascending, or remaining type. For example, how much information about *pathet* is gained by knowing only that a piece has a gong *gatra* that ends with a descending cadence? The results of this analysis are given in table 2. The patterns previously discussed are still generally valid so only the new features exposed by this finer partitioning will be discussed. One consistent pattern that emerges for *gatra* at all three positions is that descending *gatra* have less information on the average than ascending *gatra*, which in turn have less information than the remaining *gatra*. It is interesting to note that the descending *gatra* are more commonly used than the ascending *gatra*, which in turn are more commonly used than the remaining *gatra*. Hence, the rarer *gatra* on the average have more information than the common *gatra*. The difference in information between descending *gatra*, at one extreme, and remaining *gatra*, at the other, becomes progressively smaller as the position changes from kenong to gong to kempul. Finally, relatively little information is contained in the end cadence alone for all positions; but when the end cadence is coupled with pitch level there is substantial

Table 2.

Average Information in Descending, Ascending, and Remaining
Sléndro Gatra *and Various Subelements for a Given Position*

End-Cadence Category	Position	Average Information			
		Individual *Gatra*	Last Two Pitch Levels*	Contour	End Cadence
Descending *Gatra*	Gong	.7219	.3581	.3784	.0052
	Kenong	.4951	.1572	.0991	.0011
	Kempul	.4783	.0446	.1751	.0011
Ascending *Gatra*	Gong	.8644	.4858	.4429	.1470
	Kenong	.5195	.1712	.3049	.0102
	Kempul	.5716	.0998	.2912	.0025
Remaining *Gatra*	Gong	.9211	.6905	.5344	.1338
	Kenong	.8084	.4269	.5971	.0082
	Kempul	.5865	.1380	.2551	.0164

*As the *gatra* are already categorized according to the relationship of the last two notes, there is some information about contour contained in pitch level. Also, the information in the last two pitch levels is not really calculated for the "remaining" category, but rather the information is calculated by knowing the last pitch level and knowing that the relationship of the last two pitch levels is other than a descending or ascending one.

information in gong positions for all three cadence types and in remaining cadences at kenong positions.

The analysis can be carried into even finer detail by analyzing each end-pitch level separately, as shown in tables 3, 4, and 5. The trend and patterns previously discussed still hold true at each pitch level for the most part, although there are occasional exceptions. Some additional patterns emerge that show considerable heterogeneity among pitch levels in determining *pathet* in all positions. In gong positions, pitch level 5 is a strong determinant of *pathet*—mainly because of its strong association with Patet Sanga. Gong pitches 3 and 1 are somewhat less informative, but are still fairly strong determinants of *pathet*. Gong pitch level 6 is mildly informative of *pathet*, and 2 is least informative. In the kenong position all the end notes still have the same relative positions in terms of amount of information in end-pitch level as do the gong pitch levels, although the absolute amount of information is much smaller. In the kempul position, the relative positions of the pitch levels in degree of information are not very important because all pitch levels are rather uninformative.

Even more detailed analyses are possible, but the results become increasingly cumbersome to record. Only one more characterization of the

TABLE 3.
Information Contained in **Sléndro Gatra** in Gong Positions for Each Pitch Level

					Average Information			
End-Pitch Level	Individual Gatra	Pitch Level	Descending Gatra	Last 2 Pitch Levels in Desc. Gatra	Ascending Gatra	Last 2 Pitch Levels in Asc. Gatra	Remaining Gatra	Last 2 Pitch Levels in Rem. Gatra*
1	.8714	.3768	.7642	.2830	1.0000	1.0000	1.0000	1.0000
2	.7417	.1459	.6334	.2196	.8585	.1298	1.0000	.3900
3	.8939	.4157	.8055	.4815	1.0000	.3692	— no occurrence —	
5	.8168	.6044	.7523	.5762	.8304	.6033	1.0000	1.0000
6	.6883	.2760	.6778	.2303	.7035	.3268	.6845	.3721

*The information in the last two pitch levels is not really calculated for the "remaining" category, but rather the information is calculated by knowing the last pitch level and knowing that the relationship of the last two pitch levels is other than a descending or ascending one.

TABLE 4.
Information Contained in Sléndro Gatra in Kenong Positions for Each Pitch Level

Average Information

End-Pitch Level	Individual Gatra	Pitch Level	Descending Gatra	Last 2 Pitch Levels in Desc. Gatra	Ascending Gatra	Last 2 Pitch Levels in Asc. Gatra	Remaining Gatra	Last 2 Pitch Levels in Rem. Gatra*
1	.6415	.0770	.6323	.1095	.4876	.1535	1.0000	.4329
2	.4627	.0447	.2649	.1125	.7056	.1133	.6212	.1691
3	.4720	.1822	.4463	.1648	.4179	.2149	.7639	.4095
5	.7039	.3284	.6775	.2649	.5724	.3141	1.0000	1.0000
6	.4631	.0640	.4540	.1344	.4552	.0604	.5592	.1233

*The information in the last two pitch levels is not really calculated for the "remaining" category, but rather the information is calculated by knowing the last pitch level and knowing that the relationship of the last two pitch levels is other than a descending or ascending one.

TABLE 5.
Information Contained in Sléndro *Gatra* in *Kempul Positions for Each Pitch Level*

End-Pitch Level	Individual *Gatra*	Pitch Level	Descending *Gatra*	Average Information Last 2 Pitch Levels in Desc. *Gatra*	Ascending *Gatra*	Last 2 Pitch Levels in Asc. *Gatra*	Remaining *Gatra*	Last 2 Pitch Levels in Rem. *Gatra**
1	.5393	.0163	.4782	.0529	.6660	.0823	.4690	.0662
2	.5839	.0202	.5353	.0054	.6040	.2356	.6437	.0017
3	.6205	.0325	.5781	.0692	.5782	.0188	.7759	.2701
5	.4617	.0578	.4193	.0922	.4336	.0671	.7154	.3218
6	.4314	.0099	.3794	.0032	.5607	.0952	.2380	.0300

*The information in the last two pitch levels is not really calculated for the "remaining" category, but rather the information is calculated by knowing the last pitch level and knowing that the relationship of the last two pitch levels is other than a descending or ascending one.

TABLE 6.

Sléndro Gatra *with an Information of* .5 *or More and the* Pathet *with Which They Are Strongly Associated*

Position	Nem			Sanga			Manyura		
					Pathet				
Gong	3232	6362	5365	2321	6661	5235	6521	2653	1523
	1232	5323	2316	2121	5312	6535	1231	2353	5216
	5612	1265	6516	6121	2165	3635	6132	2153	1616
				2621	3165	1635	2132	2123	6356
				3561	5565	2635	3212	3523	3356
				6561	3265	1615	5352	6523	6156
				5561	3235	2615		1253	3126
						2625			
Number of *Gatra*		9			22			20	
Kenong	3521	2352	3565	6121	6565	1615	6321	5253	6563
	561.	6362	3656	1121	5565	5615	1561	1253	5365
	3132	3563	5556	2521	1265	2615	3231	3253	1516
				2621	2365	2325	1612	3123	3356
				2312	5235	5216	6612	1523	3126
				5312	5635	6616			
					2635	3256			
Number of *Gatra*		9			20			15	
Kempul	6561	2352	3563	6121	1112	323.	6321	1532	1312
	6161	612.	1563	3521	5312	6265	3321	2232	3123
	3232	3323	5565	2521	6352	1635	6661	3632	1123
	2132	2523	5535	2621	6362	1615	161.	3332	3333
			6156	5621	2153	5615	121.	3132	5316
				2161	5153	6616			3516
				6261	5553	1656			
				5612	2253	6656			
				1612	1323	5556			
				2612	1623	1156			
Number of *Gatra*		13			30			16	
Total		31			77			51	

sléndro pathet will be given: their distinctiveness from one another, or, alternatively, their ease of identification. One measure of distinctiveness is to count the number of *gatra* strongly associated with only one *pathet*. *Strongly associated* is defined here as an information of .5 or more. The strongly associated *gatra* for each *pathet* and position are listed in table 6.

Note that there are many more *gatra* strongly associated with Pathet Sanga than with either Nem or Manyura. By this criterion, Pathet Sanga should be the most easily distinguished *sléndro pathet*. Another criterion of distinctiveness is to compare by pairs all the *sléndro pathet* to determine how much overlap in *gatra* usage they have and how many *gatra* in the overlap are ambiguous for the *pathet* being compared. *Ambiguous* means that the *gatra* has a conditional frequency greater than 1/3 in both of the *pathet* being compared. By multiplying the frequency of overlap with the frequency of ambiguity, an overall index of distinctiveness may be calculated. The results of the comparisons of pairs of the three *sléndro pathet* are given in table 7. The greatest ambiguity and overlap are between Nem and Manyura, and the least between Manyura and Sanga. When the two measures of ambiguity and overlap are combined in the last column of table 7, they enhance one another revealing that Nem and Manyura are the least distinctive pair of *sléndro pathet* while Sanga is distinct from both Nem and Manyura.

Perhaps the most sensitive indicator of the ease with which the various *sléndro pathet* are distinguished is the expected information in a *gatra* occurring in each of the *pathet*. The expected information contained in a *gatra* differs considerably from the average information in a *gatra*. The average information is calculated by taking the information in a particular *gatra*, for example, $I(g)$, and multiplying this information by the reciprocal of the total number of different *gatra* types that occur in a particular position, n, to yield the number $(1/n) \cdot I(g)$. These numbers are then summed over all *gatra* types occurring in the position under consideration to yield the average information in a *gatra* at a given position and given that the *gatra* has occurred. (This procedure is equivalent to first summing all the $I(g)$'s and then dividing this sum by n). All informations are "weighted" by the same number $(1/n)$ in calculating the average information in a *gatra*, because all *gatra* have the same conditional probability of occurrence of 1. However, the expected information in a particular *pathet* is conditioned only on the position of the *gatra*, and not on the fact that a particular *gatra* has occurred. The frequency data show that some *gatra* are used more often than others. The expected information therefore weights the information in a particular *gatra* by the frequency of that *gatra* in the *pathet* under consideration. Hence, the expected information in *pathet* y is the sum over all possible *gatra* for a particular position of the quantities $F_y(g) \cdot I(g)$. The expected information is a function of both the information contained in a *gatra* and the frequency of the *gatra*. It represents the amount of information one can expect to gain from a randomly chosen *gatra* occurring at a specific position in a piece of a certain *pathet*. Such expected informations are given in table 8 for the three *sléndro pathet* and the three *gatra* positions. Pathet Sanga is once again

TABLE 7.

Pairwise Comparison of the Distinctiveness of the Three Sléndro Pathet

Pathet Compared	Position	Number of *Gatra* Occurring in Either *Pathet*	Number of *Gatra* Occurring in Both *Pathet*	Number of Ambiguous[1] *Gatra*	Percent Overlap[2]	Percent Ambiguous in Overlap[3]	Percent Ambiguous in Total[4]
Nem and Manyura	Gong	53	13	5	24.5	38.4	9.4
	Kenong	83	48	12	57.8	25.0	14.4
	Kempul	115	66	17	57.4	25.8	14.8
	Total	251	127	34	50.6	26.8	13.6
Nem and Sanga	Gong	51	14	2	27.4	14.3	3.9
	Kenong	90	50	9	55.6	18.0	10.0
	Kempul	127	61	14	48.0	22.9	11.0
	Total	268	125	25	46.6	20.0	9.3
Manyura and Sanga	Gong	63	8	1	12.7	12.5	1.6
	Kenong	96	39	2	40.6	5.1	2.1
	Kempul	127	54	10	42.5	18.5	7.9
	Total	286	101	13	35.3	12.9	4.5

1. *Ambiguity* means that the conditional frequency of the *gatra* in both of the *pathet* being compared is greater than 1/3.
2. Percent overlap = 100 × (no. of *gatra* in both *pathet*) ÷ (no. of *gatra* in either *pathet*).
3. Percent ambiguous in overlap = 100 × (no. of ambiguous *gatra*) ÷ (no. of *gatra* in both *pathet*).
4. Percent ambiguous in total = 100 × (no. of ambiguous *gatra*) ÷ (no. of *gatra* in either *pathet*).

TABLE 8.

Expected Information in Individual **Sléndro** *Gatra* **Given Position** *and* **Pathet** *and Given Position Alone*

Position	Pathet			Average (Pathet Unknown)
	Nem	Sanga	Manyura	
Gong	.4865	.7441	.5024	.5777
Kenong	.2757	.4087	.3289	.3378
Kempul	.2662	.3303	.2730	.2898

the most easily identified of the *sléndro pathet*, with Nem and Manyura being roughly equivalent. Pathet Sanga is most distinct because highly informative *gatra* are used more commonly in this *pathet* than in Nem or Manyura. Table 8 also gives the average expected information in a piece of unknown *pathet*. This is calculated by taking the sum over all possible *gatra* of the quantities

$$(1/3) \cdot [F_n(g) + F_s(g) + F_m(g)] \cdot I(g).$$

This sum yields the average over *pathet* of the expected informations associated with each *pathet*. Note that in all three positions the average expected informations are less than the corresponding average informations given in table 1. This implies that the more informative *gatra* are generally used less frequently than the less informative *gatra*, thus illustrating the difference between frequency and informativeness.

A similar analysis was performed on the three *pélog pathet*—Lima, Nem, and Barang. The results are given in tables 9 through 16. These tables illustrate the basic patterns of the musical determinants of the *pélog pathet* contained in saron *gatra*. These patterns show both similarities to and differences from the *sléndro pathet* patterns. Starting with table 9, the amount of information contained in individual *gatra* is larger in *pélog* than in *sléndro*, indicating that *gatra* or elements contained in them are stronger determinants of *pathet* in the *pélog* tuning system than in the *sléndro* tuning system. Moreover, both the subelements of pitch level and contour have larger informations for the most part than the corresponding *sléndro* informations. Another difference is that position no longer affects in any major fashion the information contained in a *gatra* or in the subelements of pitch level and contour—a drastic change from the *sléndro* pattern in which all of these factors strongly interact with position. One common feature is that contour alone is always more important than pitch level alone, although pitch level is a much more important determinant of *pathet* in *pélog* than it is in *sléndro*.

TABLE 9.
Average Information with Respect to Pélog Pathet Contained in Individual Gatra, End–Pitch Level, and Contour in Each of the Three Gatra Positions

Position	Average Information		
	Individual *Gatra*	End-Pitch Level	Contour
Gong	.8493	.3096	.6683
Kenong	.7789	.2747	.5978
Kempul	.7833	.2486	.5678

TABLE 10.
Average Information in Descending, Ascending, and Remaining Pélog Gatra and Various Subelements for a Given Position

End-Cadence Category	Position	Average Information			
		Individual *Gatra*	Last Two Pitch Levels*	Contour	End Cadence
Descending *Gatra*	Gong	.8345	.3987	.6978	.0065
	Kenong	.7487	.3046	.6186	.0026
	Kempul	.7750	.2711	.5916	.0032
Ascending *Gatra*	Gong	.8378	.4100	.5690	.0489
	Kenong	.7966	.3032	.5520	.0088
	Kempul	.8023	.3152	.5337	.0027
Remaining *Gatra*	Gong	.9443	.8983	.8020	.1242
	Kenong	.8558	.6217	.6736	.0125
	Kempul	.7612	.3816	.5841	.0012

*As the *gatra* are already categorized according to the relationship of the last two notes, there is some information on contour contained in pitch level. Also, the information in the last two pitch levels is not really calculated for the remaining category, but rather the information is calculated by knowing the last pitch level and knowing that the relationship of the last two pitch levels is other than a descending or ascending one.

In general, the determinants of the *pélog pathet* are much more evenly distributed across position, pitch level, and contour than are the determinants of the *sléndro pathet*.

Table 10 shows that the information increases as one goes from descending to ascending to remaining *gatra*[5] in a gong or kenong position, just as it does for *sléndro*. However, the difference between the descending *gatra* information and remaining *gatra* information is rather small, indicating that this pattern is less important in *pélog*. Furthermore, the pattern does not hold in the kempul position where all three categories of *gatra* have nearly equal information. The remaining *gatra* have a very large amount of information in pitch level, much larger than for either descending or ascending *gatra*. Such an interaction between pitch and contour of the last two notes is true also for *sléndro*. However, the magnitude of this interaction is considerably less in *pélog*; as in *sléndro*, there is very little information in the end cadence alone. Overall, there is a more even distribution of *pathet* information across end-cadence categories in *pélog* than in *sléndro*.

Various interactions with pitch are illustrated in tables 11, 12, and 13. Pitch levels 2, 3, 5, and 6 contain little information by themselves, while 1, 4, and 7 (in that order, with the exception that 4 does not occur on gong notes) are the most informative.

Finally, the distinctiveness of the *pélog pathet* is greater than that for the *sléndro pathet*, as shown in tables 14, 15, and 16. This is not surprising because more information about *pathet* is in general contained in *pélog gatra* than in *sléndro gatra*. The number of *gatra* strongly associated with a particular *pélog pathet* is large for all three *pathet*, although Barang is the most distinctive by this criterion, mainly because of its strong association with pitch 7. Table 15 also shows that all the *pélog pathet* have little overlap in *gatra* usage, with Barang once again being the most distinct. Finally, the expected informations are high for all positions and for all *pélog pathet*. The *pélog pathet* are thus readily identified by information contained in *gatra* alone. Once again, Pathet Barang is the most easily identified. Also, the expected information of a *gatra* in a *pélog* piece of unknown *pathet* is less than the corresponding average information. Thus, both *pélog* and *sléndro* share the use of the more rarely occurring *gatra* as the stronger determinants of *pathet*.

Before concluding this section, it must be pointed out that this analysis has some limitations that are imposed by the nature of the data set. First, the data consisted of the saron lines only. However, many other musical lines occur in a piece, and hence many potential determinants of *pathet* are totally ignored by this analysis. Furthermore, by treating *gatra* as the unit of analysis, additional potential information is lost. A piece consists of an ordered sequence of *gatra*, and perhaps additional information about *pathet* is contained in the order of the *gatra*, beyond that contained in the individual *gatra* that make up the sequence. Also, the pieces from which the data were gathered consist of many different hierarchical forms. It is known that certain *gatra* contours are used preferentially in certain structures. Consequently, it is conceivable that the determinants of *pathet*

TABLE 11.
Information Contained in Pélog Gatra in Gong Positions for Each Pitch Level

End-Pitch Level	Average Information							
	Individual Gatra	Pitch Level	Descending Gatra	Last 2 Pitch Levels in Desc. Gatra	Ascending Gatra	Last 2 Pitch Levels in Asc. Gatra	Remaining Gatra	Last 2 Pitch Levels in Rem. Gatra*
1	.9591	.5493	.9263	.4996	1.0000	.4240	1.0000	1.0000
2	.7644	.0759	.5553	.1769	.9099	.2399	1.0000	1.0000
3	.7737	.0434	.8365	.3868	.7422	.0108	— no occurrence —	—
4†	—	—	—	—	—	—	—	—
5	.8352	.0564	.8881	.2017	.7286	.0115	1.0000	1.0000
6	.8557	.1326	.8521	.1271	.8431	.7739	.8747	.4913
7	1.0000	1.0000	1.0000	1.0000	1.0000	1.0000	1.0000	1.0000

* The information in the last two pitch levels is not really calculated for the "remaining" category, but rather the information is calculated by knowing the last pitch level and knowing that the relationship of the last two pitch levels is other than a descending or ascending one.
† No occurrence.

TABLE 12.
Information Contained in Pélog Gatra in Kenong Positions for Each Pitch Level

Average Information

End-Pitch Level	Individual Gatra	Pitch Level	Descending Gatra	Last 2 Pitch Levels in Desc. Gatra	Ascending Gatra	Last 2 Pitch Levels in Asc. Gatra	Remaining Gatra	Last 2 Pitch Levels in Rem. Gatra*
1	.7838	.3823	.7555	.3701	.7968	.3904	1.0000	1.0000
2	.8023	.0410	.7167	.1406	.8798	.1378	.8442	.1093
3	.6818	.0279	.5359	.0019	.8143	.0719	.3911	.3911
4	.5635	.3806	.5865	.3716	.4943	.4943	— no occurrence —	
5	.7738	.1241	.7957	.2237	.7149	.0911	1.0000	.4808
6	.7965	.0534	.7841	.0242	.7988	.1096	.8340	.1275
7	.9427	.9134	1.0000	1.0000	.8738	.8269	1.0000	1.0000

*The information in the last two pitch levels is not really calculated for the "remaining" category, but rather the information is calculated by knowing the last pitch level and knowing that the relationship of the last two pitch levels is other than a descending or ascending one.

TABLE 13.

Information Contained in Pélog Gatra in Kempul Positions for Each Pitch Level

Average Information

End-Pitch Level	Individual Gatra	Pitch Level	Descending Gatra	Last 2 Pitch Levels in Desc. Gatra	Ascending Gatra	Last 2 Pitch Levels in Asc. Gatra	Remaining Gatra	Last 2 Pitch Levels in Rem. Gatra*
1	.7914	.3699	.7307	.3698	.8963	.5812	.7977	.4007
2	.8132	.0116	.7975	.0653	.8717	.1610	.7368	.1108
3	.6019	.0287	.6258	.1671	.5897	.0337	.5747	.0118
4	.7190	.3693	.7302	.3820	.6029	.3882	1.0000	1.0000
5	.7964	.0087	.7036	.0121	.9431	.0415	.5870	.0470
6	.7743	.0096	.8359	.0158	.6857	.0011	.8406	.1011
7	.9902	.9424	.9804	.8854	1.0000	1.0000	1.0000	1.0000

*The information in the last two pitch levels is not really calculated for the ''remaining'' category, but rather the information is calculated by knowing the last pitch level and knowing that the relationship of the last two pitch levels is other than a descending or ascending one.

TABLE 14.

Pélog Gatra *with an Information of* .5 *or More and the* **Pathet** *with Which They Are Strongly Associated*

Position	Pathet										
	Lima			Nem				Barang			
Gong	5421	1111	5323	2321	5312	3265	4645	7232	6765	6576	4327
	2121	3132	3523	1121	5412	6365	1216	3272	2765	5356	6727
	6121	3212	4565	5561	6123	6465	3216	5352	3635	3356	3567
	3561	2353	2465	5612	3565	5635	3126	5653	7675	2756	6567
	4241	3123	3235	1312	5565	5645	3136	7653	3276	2726	6767
			2376						5376	2327	3237
Number of *Gatra*	16			20				23			
Kenong	6121	4565	5645	2321	5412	2223	2635	7232	232·	3276	2327
	1121	3265	1645	6521	212·	3523	1615	7632	6723	7676	5327
	2221	1265	5216	5621	1653	6654	1216	3632	2323	5376	6327
	5561	6465	1616	1561	5253	6165	6356	6732	6523	2376	3327
	4241	4465	5616	2232	1253	6565	6656	2732	6765	6756	6627
	5612	2465	5316	6612	3123	2365	5656	5672	2765	5756	3567
	5452	1245	2456	2312	1123	5365	2156	7672	3235	2756	6567
	2123	5535	7656			6645	2126	6672	3335	3756	2767
			5556					3272	7675	2726	7767
										3736	3237
Number of *Gatra*	25			30				38			
Kempul	5421	4212	2245	2321	1232	3563	2645	3232	7653	7675	6327
	6321	2212	5545	2221	1632	5654	565·	7632	2653	3276	3327
	3321	2312	3635	3561	3132	7654	1216	3632	5353	7676	2727
	1121	1312	4645	1561	1612	2454	5316	6732	3253	5376	6727
	6521	1412	6616	1161	1112	2254	7576	2732	6723	5576	7727
	5621	5253	2316	6661	5312	7624	5516	5672	2723	3576	2227
	4241	4444	1516	6261	212·	6545	2126	7672	6563	6576	3567
	561·	4565	3516	1231	6123	5535	3536	3272	6765	6756	6567
	6542	1265	5456	121·	2123	5635	656·	7772	2765	7756	7567
	5542	3365	4456	5532	5523	1645	356·	7372	7765	5756	7567
	2232	1235	1656					6362	6565	2756	2767
	5612	1245	1156					272·	3235	2726	7767
		4245	2156					672·	3335	2327	5657
								232·	7635	5327	567·
											7777
Number of *Gatra*	38			40				56			
Total	79			90				117			

TABLE 15.
Comparison of the Distinctiveness of the Three Pélog Pathet by Pairs

Pathet Compared	Position	Number of Gatra Occurring in Either Pathet	Number of Gatra Occurring in Both Pathet	Number of Ambiguous[a] Gatra	Percent Overlap[b]	Percent Ambiguous in Overlap[c]	Percent Ambiguous in Total[d]
Lima	Gong	53	6	2	11.3	33.3	3.8
and	Kenong	111	11	3	9.9	27.3	2.7
Barang	Kempul	151	23	5	15.2	21.7	3.3
	Total	315	40	10	12.7	25.0	3.2
Lima	Gong	53	11	2	20.7	18.2	3.8
and	Kenong	99	36	17	36.4	47.2	17.2
Nem	Kempul	135	44	19	32.6	43.2	14.1
	Total	287	91	38	31.7	41.8	13.2
Nem	Gong	61	10	3	16.4	30.0	4.9
and	Kenong	112	17	10	15.2	58.8	8.9
Barang	Kempul	153	30	12	19.6	40.0	7.8
	Total	326	57	25	17.5	43.9	7.7

a. *Ambiguity* means that the conditional frequency of the *gatra* in both *pathet* being compared is greater than 1/3.

b. Percent overlap = 100 × (no. of *gatra* in both *pathet*) ÷ (no. of *gatra* in either *pathet*).

c. Percent ambiguous in overlap = 100 × (no. of ambiguous *gatra*) ÷ (no. of *gatra* in both *pathet*).

d. Percent ambiguous in total = 100 × (no. of ambiguous *gatra*) ÷ (no. of *gatra* in either *pathet*).

TABLE 16.

Expected Information in Individual **Pélog** *Gatra Given Position and* **Pathet** *and Given Position Alone*

Position	Pathet			Average (Pathet Unknown)
	Lima	Nem	Barang	
Gong	.6406	.6081	.7344	.6610
Kenong	.5821	.5050	.7019	.5963
Kempul	.5241	.5119	.6477	.5613

interact with formal structure, but this cannot be studied with the present data set. Therefore, the analysis may not have identified all the determinants of *pathet* simply because many potential determinants are excluded from the data.

In summary, the informational analysis supports the idea presented in chapter 6 that *pathet* is determined by three interlocking factors: (1) melodic pattern or contour, (2) pitch level of the pattern, and (3) position of the pattern in the hierarchical structure of the piece. The *sléndro pathet* and *pélog pathet* differ greatly in the strength with which these factors determine *pathet*, in the relative roles of the factors and other musical elements contained within them, and in the type of interactions that exist between the factors.

Determination of the Pathet of an Individual Gamelan Piece

The previous section described *pathet* as manifested in a large number of pieces. By using the conditional probability approach the determinants of *pathet* are measured in terms of the information gained when a particular *gatra* occurs in a piece. Consequently, it should be possible to use the results of the informational description to analyze the *pathet* of individual gamelan pieces. In this section a technique is developed for doing this based on the output from the informational description. There are two major reasons for doing so. First, by analyzing pieces of known *pathet*, I may ascertain the accuracy with which the determinants of *pathet* have been identified. Second, such a technique would provide a useful tool to the musicologist who is interested in *pathet* as it is realized in gamelan pieces and could eventually lead to even greater insight into the meaning of *pathet*.

As previously mentioned, a listener's decision about *pathet* is conditioned both by the particular *gatra* he hears in the piece and by the prior associations that he has about those particular *gatra* with respect to *pathet*. The informational analysis previously described measures through conditional probabilities the associations of each *gatra* with *pathet* on the basis of a large repertoire of gamelan music. Consequently, the informational description corresponds to the prior associations a listener would have after listening to a large number of gamelan pieces. A technique will now be proposed that involves a second stage of conditioning—the conditioning of the *pathet* probabilities for a particular *gatra* upon all the *gatra* that preceded it in a piece. Thus, *pathet* is analyzed in a two-stage conditioning process such that the impact of a *gatra* on the *pathet* of the piece is determined both by the conditional probabilities calculated from a large repertoire of music and by all the previously occurring *gatra* in that specific piece and their respective associations with *pathet*.

Consider a piece of *sléndro* gamelan music that consists of several *gatra*. Before hearing the piece a listener would not know the *pathet*, but he would start hearing clues about the *pathet* with the very first *gatra*. For example, suppose the first *gatra* is 3 2 3 5 P (P denoting a kempul end marker). Looking up the conditional probability for this *gatra* from the results of the informational analysis, the probability of the piece being in Sléndro Pathet Nem is .4593, for Sanga .3268, and for Manyura .2139. These conditional probabilities yield an information of .0418. Suppose that the next *gatra* in the piece is 6 5 3 2 N (N denoting a kenong end marker). The conditional probabilities for this *gatra* are .3889 for Nem, .0968 for Sanga, and .5142 for Manyura yielding an information of .1486. However, the probabilities of the piece being in the various *pathet* should not only be a function of the conditional probabilities associated with 6 5 3 2 N but also a function of those of the previously heard *gatra* 3 2 3 5 P. In other words, the impact of 6 5 3 2 N on *pathet* should be determined not only by its own associations, but also by the particular context it has in the piece under consideration. From probability theory, the probability of an event consisting of a sequence of independent subevents is the product of the probabilities of the subevents. *Independence* here means that there is no information contained in the order of the sequence of events. As the *gatra* were the unit of analysis, any information in the order of the *gatra* was thrown out when the data were gathered. Hence, independence of the *gatra* arises at least as an artifact from the nature of the data set. Therefore, the probability that both the *gatra* 3 2 3 5 P and 6 5 3 2 N are in a piece of Pathet Nem is $(.4593) \cdot (.3889) = .1786$, $(.3268) \cdot (.0968) = .0316$ for Sanga, and $(.2139) \cdot (.5142) = .1100$ for Manyura. Notice that the sum of the above three probabilities is .3202 which is less than one. This means that the event that the piece is in either Nem, Sanga, or Manyura is less than certainty—a statement that is musically false. This occurs because, from a strict probabilistic view, one *gatra* may be in a piece of one *pathet* and another *gatra* may be in a piece of another *pathet*. This is meaningless musically when analyzing a single piece, which can have only one *pathet*. Therefore, the probabilities must be rescaled so that the probability of the event that a piece is in Nem, Sanga, or Manyura is one. This is easily accomplished by dividing the probabilities by their sum. Hence, the corrected probabilities for the piece being in a certain *pathet* after hearing the sequence 3 2 3 5 P 6 5 3 2 N is .1786 ÷ .3202 = .5578 for Nem, .0988 for Sanga, and .3434 for Manyura. Furthermore, the information measure can be applied to these probabilities to find that the total information in the sequence 3 2 3 5 P 6 5 3 2 N is .1614. Now suppose that the next *gatra* is 3 5 6 5 P. The conditional probabilities for this *gatra* are .4102 for Nem, .2554 for Sanga, and .3344 for Manyura, with an information of .0165. Multiplying these conditional probabilities by the respective *pathet* probabilities obtained from the sequence 3 2 3 5 P 6 5 3 2 N and dividing the resulting numbers by their sum yields the probabilities after hearing 3 2 3 5 P 6 5 3 2 N 3 5 6 5 P, .6203 for Nem. .0684 for Sanga, and .3113 for Manyura. The total information is .2327. This algorithm is continued until all the *gatra* have been included and the probabilities for the entire piece being in each of the possible *pathet* are calculated.

To go through this algorithm for a long gamelan piece, or for several pieces, is a rather tedious chore; and thus, a Fortran IV program was written to do these routine calculations on the IBM 360 computer of the University of Michigan. This program analyzed the *pathet* of individual pieces of gamelan music in the way previously described, but with an additional built-in level of "forgetfulness" (that is, a level of acceptance of novelty). For example, if the level of forgetfulness is set at 6%, each of the conditional probabilities for the three *pathet* is multiplied by (1.00 − .06) = .94 so that the sum is now .94 instead of one. Then the quantity .06 ÷ 3 = .02 is added to each modified conditional frequency so that they once again sum to one. This procedure is equivalent to throwing away 6% of the information obtained from the analysis of the repertoire given in Appendix 4 and redistributing it evenly across *pathet*. There are two major reasons for doing so. First, a perfect memory can be a liability because it makes the concept of *pathet* a very conservative and rigid one. Thus, any deviation from the pre-established norms could lead to non-sensical answers about *pathet* because no novelty is allowed. Second, the conditional probabilities are based only on a sample of gamelan music and not on all gamelan pieces. Therefore, the conditional probabilities from the sample are not likely to be completely quantitatively accurate for gamelan music in general. By putting a level of forgetfulness into the program, one expresses both the degree of confidence in the sample as a reflection of gamelan music in general (which at this point is purely sub-jective) and also allows novel expressions of *pathet* to be analyzed.

TABLE 17.
Sléndro *Pieces Analyzed for* Pathet

True *Pathet*

Nem	Sanga	Manyura
Ladrang Remeng	Jangkrik Ginggong	Gendhing Perkutut Manggung
Ladrang Dirada Meta	Ladrang Embat-embat Penjalin	Ladrang Asmaradana
Ladrang Bedat	Ketawang Raja Swala	Ladrang Pangkur
Ladrang Sobrang	Ladrang Kagok Madura	Ladrang Moncer
Gendhing Lara Nangis	Gendhing Onang-onang	Ladrang Geger Sakuta
	Gendhing Genjong	Ladrang Slamet
	Ladrang Lagu Kadhempel	Ladrang Ginonjing
		Ladrang Sumirat
		Ketawang Pawuku
		Ketawang Puspa Giwang
		Ketawang Pucung
		Gendhing Lobang

This program was used to analyze the *pathet* of twenty-four *sléndro* gamelan pieces, listed in table 17. *Sléndro* pieces were chosen because there is less information about *pathet* contained in *sléndro gatra* on the average than in *pélog gatra*. Identifying the *pathet* of *sléndro* pieces is a far greater challenge, although the algorithm previously discussed can be readily applied to *pélog* pieces also. The pieces were analyzed at three levels of forgetfulness: 0%, 6%, and 15%. After a piece was analyzed, a set of decisions was made. A "definite identification" of *pathet* was made if one of the *pathet* had a probability of .95 or higher. It should be pointed out that the .95 probability decision level is arbitrary, and that it also implies that .05 (5%) of the pieces definitely identified may have their *pathet* incorrectly identified by chance alone. This type of error is purely statistical in nature and is not a reflection upon the accuracy of the analysis. It can be reduced by raising the decision level, but in that case fewer definite identifications can be made. In any event, for those pieces in which none of the *pathet* had a probability of .95 or greater, a "most likely" decision was made by identifying the *pathet* with the greatest probability of the three. The results of this analysis are given in table 18, and a specific example of the *pathet* analysis of a piece is given in table 19. As can be seen, the 0% and 6% levels yield the same identification results with 18 out of 22 definite identifications being correct and 2 out of 2 most likely identifications being correct. The 15% level gives the lowest percentage of correct definite identifications—only 16 out of 20—but the total number of correct identi-

TABLE 18.
Pathet Identification of Twenty-four Sléndro Pieces

Level of "Forgetfulness"		True Pathet				Types of Incorrect Definite Identifications
		Nem	Sanga	Manyura	Total	
0%	Number of Pieces	5	7	12	24	1 Nem piece identified as Manyura
	Number of Definite Identifications	5	7	10	22	
	Number of above Correct	4	7	7	18	3 Manyura pieces identified as Nem
	Number of "Most Likely" Identifications	0	0	2	2	
	Number of above Correct	—	—	2	2	
6%	Number of Pieces	5	7	12	24	1 Nem piece identified as Manyura
	Number of Definite Identifications	5	7	10	22	
	Number of above Correct	4	7	7	18	3 Manyura pieces identified as Nem
	Number of "Most Likely" Identifications	0	0	2	2	
	Number of above Correct	—	—	2	2	
15%	Number of Pieces	5	7	12	24	1 Nem piece identified as Manyura
	Number of Definite Identifications	5	6	9	20	
	Number of above Correct	4	6	6	16	3 Manyura pieces identified as Nem
	Number of "Most Likely" Identifications	0	1	3	4	
	Number of above Correct	—	1	3	4	

TABLE 19.
Analysis of **Pathet** *of the* **Sléndro** *Piece* **Ladrang Slamet**
(*True* **Pathet** *is Manyura*) *at the* 0% *Level of "Forgetfulness"*

Gatra	Probability Nem	Probability Sanga	Probability Manyura	Accumulated Information
2 1 2 3 P	.5428	.0310	.4262	.2692
2 1 2 6 N	.4376	.0100	.5524	.3305
3 3 . . P	.0419	.0000	.9581	.8415
6 5 3 2 N	.0320	.0000	.9680	.8710
5 6 5 3 P	.0683	.0000	.9680	.7732
2 1 2 6 N	.0436	.0000	.9517	.8369
2 1 2 3 P	.0549	.0000	.9451	.8065
2 1 2 6 G	.0552	.0000	.9448	.8055
. . 6 . P	.0458	.0000	.9542	.8306
1 5 1 6 N	.0001	.0000	.9999	.9994
3 5 6 1 P	.0000	.0000	1.0000	.9997
6 5 3 2 N	.0000	.0000	1.0000	.9998
6 6 . . P	.0000	.0000	1.0000	.9997
1 5 1 6 N	.0000	.0000	1.0000	1.0000
1 1 3 2 P	.0000	.0000	1.0000	1.0000
2 1 2 6 G	.0000	.0000	1.0000	1.0000

fications (both definite and most likely) is the same in all cases—20 out of 24. As previously mentioned, one would expect about 1 misidentification out of 20 in the definite decision class due to chance alone, but in fact there are 4 out of 22 for the 0% and 6% levels. Thus, there are more errors present than one would expect by chance alone. There are several reasons for this higher than expected error rate. First, many sources of potential information about *pathet* are totally ignored because of the nature of the data, and the decision on *pathet* is based solely on information contained in the saron line grouped into *gatra*. Taking this into consideration, it is rather remarkable that such an accurate identification of *pathet* is possible as so many of the potential determinants available to a human listener were omitted. Second, the four errors that were made are revealing in themselves. All the Pathet Sanga pieces were correctly identified. This is not surprising because the informational analysis predicted that Pathet Sanga is the most distinct of the three *sléndro pathet* and has the highest expected information per *gatra*. All four errors are confusions between Nem and Manyura. Once again, this is not surprising because the analysis indicated that these two *pathet* are the least distinct pair and are less strongly determined by information contained in *gatra*. However, the most remarkable fact is that a confusion of Pathet Nem and Manyura is not an uncommon error made by the Javanese themselves. This algorithm for determining

TABLE 20.
Pathet *Analysis of Sixty-five* Sléndro *Gong Units*

Level of "Forgetfulness"	Two *Ladrang Remeng* Gong Units Scored as Incorrectly Identified*			Two *Ladrang Remeng* Gong Units Scored as Correctly Identified		
	0%	6%	15%	0%	6%	15%
Percentage of Definite Identifications	63.1	53.8	49.2	63.1	53.8	49.2
Percentage of above Correct	80.5	82.9	84.4	82.9	85.7	87.5
Percentage of "Mostly Likely" Identifications	36.9	46.2	50.8	36.9	46.2	50.8
Percentage of above Correct	50.0	60.0	57.6	54.2	63.3	60.6
Percentage of Total Correct Identifications (both definite and "most likely")	69.2	72.3	70.8	72.3	75.4	73.8
Number of Incorrect Definite Identifications:						
Nem for Manyura	3	2	2	3	2	2
Manyura for Nem	4	3	2	4	3	2
Nem for Sanga	1	1	1	0	0	0
Total	8	6	5	7	5	4
Number of Incorrect "Most Likely" Identifications:						
Nem for Manyura	5	6	5	5	6	5
Manyura for Nem	3	4	5	3	4	5
Nem for Sanga	1	1	2	0	0	1
Sanga for Manyura	1	1	1	1	1	1
Sanga for Nem	1	0	1	1	0	1
Manyura for Sanga	1	0	0	1	0	0
Total	12	12	14	11	11	13

* See text for explanation.

pathet, therefore, not only successfully identifies *pathet* in the majority of cases, but makes the same type of errors that Javanese make. It thus provides an excellent simulation of the human process of deciding *pathet*. This also indicates that the determinants of *pathet* contained in *gatra* have been accurately characterized by the informational analysis.

The level of forgetfulness had little effect when the *pathet* of an entire piece was analyzed. A better indication of the importance of this factor is brought forth when the pieces are broken down into gong units and the *pathet* of each unit is analyzed separately. The 24 pieces break down into 65 gong units with 19 in Nem, 19 in Sanga, and 27 in Manyura. The results of this analysis are summarized in table 20. There are double entries because of the ambiguity of the piece *Ladrang Remeng*. This is a piece said to be in Pathet Nem (and indeed the analysis on the entire piece yields a definite decision of Pathet Nem), but some Javanese think that part of the piece is in Pathet Sanga. The analysis here resulted in two of the gong units being definitely in Nem, one gong unit being definitely in Sanga, and the fourth gong unit being most likely in Sanga but very possibly in Nem. This analysis therefore supports the view that _Ladrang Remeng_ is indeed partially in Pathet Sanga. On the left side of table 20, these two gong units identified as Sanga (one definitely, one most likely) are counted as errors; on the right side, they are scored as correct. In either event, the basic pattern remains the same. First, fewer definite decisions are made when analyzing gong units as opposed to analyzing entire pieces, and there are also fewer correct decisions. This is expected simply because there are usually fewer _gatra_—and hence fewer sources of information—in gong units than in pieces. Second, as the level of forgetfulness goes up, the number of definite decisions goes down, but the percentage of correct definite decisions goes up. Thus, fewer decisions are made, but more of them are right, when there is some "forgetting" or "acceptance" of novelty and hence less rigidity in judging _pathet_. Finally, the total percentage correctly identified either as definitely or most likely is maximum at the 6% level. Hence having very rigid and conservative standards in judging _pathet_ is undesirable; and, similarly, throwing out too much of the information gained from the base repertoire is undesirable. Some compromise between prior association and acceptance of novelty must be reached for an optimal identification of _pathet_.

Testing Hypotheses

Up to now the analysis has only produced a quantitative description of _pathet_—albeit a very detailed and accurate one—but it is in no way an explanation or theory of _pathet_. It is much easier to identify those _gatra_ or musical elements that are strong determinants of _pathet_ than to explain why they are strong determinants.

The first step in producing a theory of _pathet_ is to obtain a set of hypotheses that explain certain observed aspects of _pathet_. Once the validity of these hypotheses is established by some criterion, they can, it is hoped, eventually be ordered into a complete theory. The informational analysis can prove to be a useful tool in producing and validating hypotheses. First, the quantitative accuracy of the description of the determinants of _pathet_ offers much insight into _pathet_ that could conceivably guide one into making certain hypotheses. At the very least, the accuracy of the description gives the musicologist an idea of just how much he will have to explain; for example, any theory of _pathet_ based on just gong notes or gong _gatra_ is _a priori_ inadequate. In essence, an accurate description is a prerequisite for an accurate explanation. Second, any hypothesis or theory of *pathet* must be consistent with the informational description of *pathet*. This provides a means of testing a hypothesis once it is given. Examples will now be given which illustrate the two uses of the informational analysis in suggesting hypotheses and testing hypotheses.

In the informational description of the *sléndro* and *pélog pathet*, it was noted that there is more information in *pélog gatra* than in *sléndro gatra*. This suggests that there might be a determinant of *pathet* manifested in the *gatra* that is present in *pélog* but absent in *sléndro*. Furthermore, it was noted that there is proportionally more information in pitch level at all positions in *pélog* than in *sléndro*. The hypothesis can therefore be made more specific; that is, this added element in *pélog* is somehow manifested in the end-pitch levels of the *gatra*. Next, by breaking down the information pitch by pitch, it was seen that most of this information is concentrated in pitch levels 1, 4, and 7. Finally, looking at the associations these particular end-pitch levels have with the *pélog pathet* reveals that end pitches 1 and 4 never occur in Pathet Barang *gatra*, while end pitch 7 never occurs in Lima and only very rarely in Nem. None of the *sléndro* end pitches had such an exclusive distribution over *pathet*. The hypothesis can therefore be made that although *pélog* is a seven-tone tuning system, the operation of *pathet* restricts the use of *gatra* end pitches to a subset of five for Barang and six for Lima and Nem, and that this determinant of *pathet* (a restriction of end pitch to a subset of the possible notes) does not operate in the five-tone *sléndro* tuning system. Furthermore, this hypothesis is consistent with the informational description of *pathet*.

One hypothesis that has been suggested for the *sléndro pathet* is that Pathet Sanga is simply Pathet Manyura transposed down one pitch level. To test this hypothesis, a computer program was written to find those *gatra* most strongly associated with Manyura and then to transpose them down one pitch level. The *pathet* (if any) that these transposed *gatra* were most strongly associated with was then recorded. If the hypothesis is true, these *gatra* should be primarily associated with Pathet Sanga. Also, this procedure was performed on the other two *pathet*, and the pitches were transposed up one level as well. This was done to get an idea of the general effect on *pathet* of transposition compared with the effect seen when transposing down one pitch level from Pathet Manyura. The results of this analysis are given in tables 21 and 22. In not a single case did even a simple majority of transposed *gatra* shift to another single *pathet*. Furthermore, the strongest tendency observed is a change from Sanga to Manyura while transposing Sanga *gatra* down one pitch level, and not the other way around as the hypothesis suggests. Consequently, this hypothesis can be rejected as being inconsistent with the informational analysis. This

TABLE 21.

Effect of Transposing Down One Pitch on the
Associations of Gatra *with the* Sléndro Pathet

Base *Pathet*	Position of *Gatra*	Number of Untransposed *Gatra* Associated with Base *Pathet**	Percentage of Transposed *Gatra* with Maximum Conditional Frequency in *Pathet*			
			Nem	Sanga	Manyura	None
Manyura	Gong	36	16.7	38.9	13.9	30.6
	Kenong	37	32.4	37.8	18.9	10.8
	Kempul	48	20.8	43.8	20.8	14.6
	Total	121	23.1	40.5	18.2	18.2
Sanga	Gong	32	12.5	3.1	53.1	31.3
	Kenong	43	23.3	7.0	46.5	23.3
	Kempul	59	28.8	20.3	32.2	18.6
	Total	134	23.1	11.9	41.8	23.1
Nem	Gong	22	13.6	36.4	22.7	27.3
	Kenong	41	17.1	46.3	9.8	26.8
	Kempul	51	31.4	31.4	23.5	13.7
	Total	114	22.8	37.7	18.4	21.1

* All of these *gatra* have maximum conditional frequency in the base *pathet*.

TABLE 22.

Effect of Transposing Up One Pitch on the
Associations of Gatra *with the* Sléndro Pathet

Base *Pathet*	Position of *Gatra*	Number of Untransposed *Gatra* Associated with Base *Pathet**	Percentage of Transposed *Gatra* with Maximum Conditional Frequency in *Pathet*			
			Nem	Sanga	Manyura	None
Manyura	Gong	36	13.9	47.2	19.4	19.4
	Kenong	37	10.8	43.2	29.7	16.2
	Kempul	48	18.8	35.4	29.2	16.7
	Total	121	14.9	41.3	26.4	17.4
Sanga	Gong	32	25.0	3.1	43.8	28.1
	Kenong	43	46.5	7.0	34.9	11.6
	Kempul	59	25.4	15.3	37.3	22.0
	Total	134	32.1	9.7	38.1	20.1
Nem	Gong	22	18.2	13.6	36.4	31.8
	Kenong	41	24.4	26.8	29.3	19.5
	Kempul	51	33.3	29.4	19.6	17.6
	Total	114	27.2	25.4	26.3	21.1

* All of these *gatra* have maximum conditional frequency in the base *pathet*.

is not surprising because it was previously demonstrated that contour alone is more important than pitch alone, and of course contour is unaffected by transposing. However, it must be borne in mind that the rejection of this hypothesis is based only on the determinants of *pathet* contained in saron *gatra*; it may well be that some other determinants of *pathet* not studied here—for example, gendèr patterns—may have such a relationship.

In this appendix, techniques have been developed to identify the determinants of *pathet* contained in *gatra*, to analyze the manifestation of *pathet* in individual gamelan pieces, and to test hypotheses about *pathet*. The techniques depend upon the principles of conditional probability and information that are in no way specific to the problem of *pathet* or even to the field of music. These techniques can be applied to discover the determinants of any system of categorization.

Funds for computer time provided by the University of Michigan School of Music and Society of Fellows are gratefully acknowledged.

Alan R. Templeton is associate professor of biology and genetics at Washington University in Missouri. While studying for a master's degree in statistics and a doctoral degree in human genetics he played in the University of Michigan gamelan ensemble. After completing his graduate degrees, he spent two years as a Junior Fellow of the Society of Fellows of the University of Michigan researching the theory of gamelan music.

Notes

Notes to Chapter 1

1. Jaap Kunst, *Music in Java*, 2 vols. (The Hague: Martinus Nijhoff, 1949), 1:152.

2. E. R. Leach, *Political Systems of Highland Burma* (London: G. Bell and Sons, 1954), pp. 251, 263.

3. W. H. Rassers, *Panji, The Culture Hero: A Structural Study of Religion in Java* (The Hague: Martinus Nijhoff, 1959), p. 224.

4. For a full description of the process of gongmaking see Edward Jacobson and J. H. Van Hasselt, *De Gong-Fabricatie Te Semarang* (Leiden: D. J. Brill, 1907). An English translation by Andrew Toth has been published in the journal *Indonesia*, no. 19 (April, 1975) Modern Indonesia Project, Cornell University.

5. Kunst, *Music in Java*, p. 162.

6. *Old Javanese* is a term which refers to the Javanese literary language used from approximately the ninth to the fifteenth century. Old Javanese is still used in Bali as a literary language. *Kawi* is a synonymous term.

7. Javanese *wayang kulit*, *wayang orang*, and *sendratari* stories are usually based upon the Javanese versions of the Hindu epics, *Mahabharata* and *Ramayana*.

8. James L. Peacock, *Rites of Modernization: Symbolic and Social Aspects of Indonesian Proletarian Drama* (Chicago: University of Chicago Press, 1968), pp. 61, 62.

9. Excerpts from a newspaper article by Muhadjir published in *Kompas*, 28 July 1970. The author points out the changes that occur when *lenong* is taken from its village context and staged inside a commercial theater.

Notes to Chapter 2

1. The term *foreign* as applied to instruments used in the gamelan is more closely linked to duration of residence in Java than to place of origin. The present-day gamelan drums, kendhang gendhing, ketipung, and ciblon are based on ancient Indian models, but no one today would call them Indian drums. The Western bass drum, however, now found in nearly every *wayang orang* and *ketoprak* gamelan for use in scenes of marching armies, is still new enough to be incompletely incorporated. Other imports such as Turkish bell trees and European trumpets were at certain times and places played with gamelan but are rarely heard today. The rebab, while probably not indigenous, has been played in Java long enough and has assumed a role important enough to be considered a Javanese instrument.

2. R. M. Ng. Poerbatjaraka and Tardjan Hadidjaja, *Kepustakaan Djawa* (Djakarta and Amsterdam: Penerbit Djambatan, 1952), p. 1.

3. Ki Sindoesawarno, *Ilmu Karawitan* (Published in stencil form, Akademi Seni Karawitan Indonesia, Surakarta, 1955), vol. 1, p. 9. The passage in Indonesian is as follows: "Menurut istilah dulu, maka adalah sesuatu jang disebut nada, jaitu jang didengar oleh

telinga manusia. Nada itu ada jang ditimbulkan, ada jang timbul dari sendirinja. Nada jang ditimbulkan itu ada dua, jang satu disebut swara, jang lainnja swabawa. Swara itu jang njaring, rata dan indah, swabawa jang tidak njaring, tidak rata dan tidak indah. Nada jang timbul dari sendirinja disebut nadha anahata, jaitu nada didalam hati, atau nada didalam sunji.''

4. The idea that Javanese notation might be a European innovation was first suggested to me by A. L. Becker. Subsequent research confirmed this hypothesis. See Sindoesawarno, *Ilmu Karawitan*, p. 22, and Purbodiningrat, note 5 below.

5. Professor Ir. Purbodiningrat, ''Gamelan,'' in the magazine *Sana-Budaja* 1, no. 4 (December 1956): 203. Published by the museum Sana-Budaya, Yogyakarta. The passage in Indonesian is as follows: ''Untuk gending² Eropa telah terdapat titiraras-titiraras jang menjebabkan bahwa gending² jang kuno pada saat sekarang masih terdapat dan dapat dipeladjari oleh siapa-pun jang dapat membatja titiraras² itu. Lain dari pada itu dalam gending² itu dapat dirasakan bagaimana perasaan sipentjipta waktu menjusun gending² itu. Seperti telah diketahui oleh umum dalam gending² Eropa terdapat gending² jang namanja sama akan tetapi dari matjam² pentjipta.

Timbulnja pikiran di Jogjakarta untuk mengadakan titiraras untuk gending² Djawa terdorong oleh perasaan sajang apabila kelak gending² kuno tidak dikenal lagi oleh bangsa kita berhubung dengan pertumbuhan masjarakat. Dari sebab itu mulai pada abad ke XIX telah dimulai mentjari suatu titiraras untuk gending² Djawa.''

6. Jaap Kunst, *Music in Java*, 2d rev. ed., 2 vols. (The Hague: Martinus Nijhoff, 1949) 1:349

7. As listed by Professor Ir. Purbodiningrat in his article ''Gamelan'' (see note 5 above), pp. 203–204, these experiments are:

(1) Titilaras kraton Jogjakarta jang lama, ca. 1886
(2) Titilaras Pakualaman, ca. 1878
(3) Titilaras tangga. (No date given by Professor Ir. Purbodiningrat. Ki Sindoesawarno suggests the date as about 1890 in his book *Ilmu Karawitan*. This notation system is more commonly referred to by the Javanese term Titilaras andha, or ladder notation.
(4) Titilaras ranté. No date given by Professor Ir. Purbodiningrat. Ki Sindoesawarno suggests the date as about 1870 in his article ''Radyapustaka dan Nut-angka'' in the magazine *Radyapustaka* (1960):61.
(5) Titilaras kraton Jogjakarta jang baru, ca. 1897.
(6) Titilaras Kepatihan. No date given by Professor Ir. Purbodiningrat. Ki Sindoesawarno gives the date as about 1890, in *Radyapustaka*, p. 61.
(7) Ponotitilaras, 1942.

Other experiments discussed by Ki Sindoesawarno in *Ilmu Karawitan* are Titilaras sariswara, by Ki Hadjar Dewantara, p. 21; and Titilaras damina, by Machjar Angga Kusumadinata, p. 23.

8. This is the notation system called by Kunst (*Music in Java*, p. 349) ''checkered script'' notation. Kunst favored this notation above the others and hoped that it would be adopted throughout Java. This system notates the saron part in primary focus, and the gong, kenong, kempul, and kethuk in secondary focus. No instrument of higher density than the saron barung is notated at all. This notation system presents a visual model of Kunst's tripart analysis of gamelan into (1) nuclear melody, (2) colotomic, and (3) panerusan parts. It may be an example of a visual model affecting aural perception.

9. The Galin-Paris-Chevé notation system is presented in Emile Chevé, *Methode Galin-Paris-Chevé: Methode Elémentaire de Musique Vocale* (Paris: Chez Les Auteurs, 1884).

10. While based upon a European model, *Kepatihan* notation has been adapted to certain structural principles of Javanese music. The temporal sequence of the gong unit is subdivided into kenong phrases, marked at the end by a kenong. The kenong phrase is subdivided into four-note saron phrases, or *gatra*, defined by the Javanese as the smallest meaningful unit of music. While these structural units are clearly marked in *Kepatihan* notation, and not so clearly marked in the other notations, there seems to be no intrinsic reason why the same adaptations could not have taken place with the other forms of notation had their use become widespread.

11. The analysis of oral traditions owes much to the seminal work of Albert Lord, *The Singer of Tales* (New York: Atheneum, 1965).

12. Lord, *The Singer of Tales*, pp. 4–5.

13. Technologies reinforce one another, and in Java the homogenizing effect of printed books is strengthened by the wide dissemination of phonograph records, radio broadcasts, and cassette tapes all teaching Central Javanese, especially Surakarta style, gamelan.

14. The only notable exception to this general trend is the gamelan style which accompanies the East Java dramatic form *ludruk*. *Ludruk* gamelan always play the Surabaya variant of East Javanese gamelan style.

15. This analysis is heavily indebted to the works of Marshall McLuhan, especially *The Gutenberg Galaxy* (Toronto: University of Toronto Press, 1962).

16. This same priority given to the overall flow and form of a composition, rather than to any particular part, is reflected again in the great reluctance of Javanese musicians to break off a piece in mid-*gongan*. If a particular section or transition proves difficult for some of the members of the ensemble, it is much preferred to continue through the whole gong section and then repeat it entirely rather than repeating many times a small, troublesome section. The common Western practice of going over and over a small phrase of a piece is unheard of in Javanese gamelan practice. Only in extreme situations in which the outline of the piece is hopelessly obscured will the drummer or rebab player order the ensemble to stop and begin again.

17. Soetandija, "Gending Emeng minggah Ladrang Nalongsa dan Ladrang Wreda-Muspra" (Thesis for the Sarjana Muda degree, Akademi Seni Karawitan Indonesia, Surakarta, n.d.), p. 11.

Notes to Chapter 3

1. Robert Van Niel, "The Course of Indonesian History," in *Indonesia*, ed. Ruth McVey (New Haven: Human Relations Area File Press, 1963), p. 299.

2. Soemarsaid Moertono, *State and Statecraft in Old Java: A Study of the Later Mataram Period, 16th to 19th Century* (Ithaca: Modern Indonesia Project Monograph Series, Cornell University, 1968), pp. 3, 4.

3. The idea of the relationship between gamelan structure and Javanese calendrical cycles was first suggested to me by A. L. Becker.

4. Clifford Geertz, *The Religion of Java* (Glencoe, Illinois: Free Press, 1960), pp. 38, 39.

5. Soebardi, "Calendrical Traditions in Indonesia," *Madjalah Ilmu Sastra Indonesia* [Journal of Indonesian cultural studies], 3, no. 1 (March 1965):53.

6. Moertono, *State and Statecraft*, p. 3.

7. Albert Lord, *The Singer of Tales* (New York: Atheneum, 1965), p. 28.

8. Selosoemardjan, *Social Change in Jogjakarta* (Ithaca: Cornell University Press, 1962), pp. 17, 18.

9. Selosoemardjan, *Social Change*, p. 28.

10. Theoretically, a man could be a nationalist and a *priyayi*. The most notable example is the Sultan of Yogyakarta, Hamengkubuwono IX, a former leader of guerilla activity during the Indonesian revolution and now vice president of the Republic of Indonesia.

11. For a fuller discussion of the *wayang kulit* as a form of ancestor worship the reader is referred to W. H. Rassers, *Panji, The Culture Hero: A Structural Study of Religion in Java* (The Hague: Martinus Nijhoff, 1959), and Harsja W. Bachtiar, "The Religion of Java: A Commentary", *Bhratara* [Indonesian journal of cultural studies] 5, no. 1 (January 1973): 85–118.

12. Soewojo Wojowasito, *Kamus Kawi (Djawa Kuna) Indonesia*, Malang, East Java: Team Publikasi Ilmiah Fakultas Keguruan Sastra dan Seni, IKIP, 1970), p. 213.

13. Bernard Vlekke, *Nusantara: A History of Indonesia* (The Hague: W. van Hoeve, 1965), p. 53.

14. A. Teeuw, *Modern Indonesian Literature* (The Hague: Martinus Nijhoff, 1967), p. 29.

15. A. Teeuw, *Modern Indonesian Literature*, p. 22.

16. A. Teeuw, *Modern Indonesian Literature*, p. 35.

17. A. Teeuw, *Modern Indonesian Literature*, p. 36.

18. Dr. M. Amir, "Pertukaran dan Pertikaian Pikiran" [Exchange of ideas and controversy], in *Polemik Kebudajaan*, ed. Achdiat Ki Mihardja (Djakarta, 1950), pp. 96–114. Translation by Claire Holt, in *Art in Indonesia: Continuities and Change* (Ithaca: Cornell University Press, 1967), p. 213.

19. W. T. Wertheim, *Indonesian Society in Transition: A Study of Social Change*, 2d rev. ed. (The Hague and Bandung: W. van Hoeve, 1959), pp. 303–305.

20. Holt, *Art in Indonesia: Continuities and Change*, p. 213.

21. A. Teeuw, *Modern Indonesian Literature*, p. 39.

22. Soekanto, "Konservatori Karawitan dan Kebudajaan Nasional," *Sana-Budaja* no. 2 (February 1953), p. 24. Djawatan Kebudajaan Kem. P. P. dan K., Jogjakarta, Madjalah Bulana Kebudajaan.

"Disitulah nanti akan terdjadi hasil² bagi para ahli seni-suara Indonesia angkatan baru, karena disitulah para ahli tersebut berkesempatan mengadakan seribu satu matjam, eksperimin², sehingga achirnja mereka dengan puas dapat menemukan apa jang mereka selalu tjari, ialah seni-suara Indonesia jang sungguh² berdasar atas sendi kebudajaan nasional."

Just opposite this statement is a full-page photograph of Ki Wasitodipuro playing the rebab with a grand piano in the background.

23. *Kroncong* is the product of a synthesis between old Portuguese popular music played on guitar or ukelele and the music of the region in which it finds itself. The instrumentation of *kroncong* always includes a guitar plus other stringed instruments such as ukelele, bass guitar, or cello. Often a flute and/or violin is added. Each region of Indonesia superimposes its own identifying characteristics on the *kroncong* of its area. In central Java, *kroncong* shows clear gamelan influence, while in Ambon, one of the eastern islands, *kroncong* resembles missionary church music.

24. K. M. Soerjatmadja, "Konservatori Karawitan Indonesia," *Sana-Budaja* 1, no. 5 (May 1957), p. 207. Published by the museum Sana-Budaya, Yogyakarta.

25. An eloquent and intelligent statement of this awkward position can be found in the lecture, "Perkembangan Seni Karawitan" [The development of the art of gamelan music], given at the Akademi Seni Karawitan Indonesia in Surakarta, on 18 February 1971,

by one of the faculty members, Sumarsam. Copies of this lecture are available at the school.

26. J. A. Dungga and L. Manik, *Musik di Indonesia dan Beberapa Persoalannja* [Music in Indonesia and some of its problems] (Djakarta: Balai Pustaka, 1952), p. 83.

"Tapi ini adalah tjara mendjalankan maksud-maksud diatas, tapi alangkah sulitnja melakukannja, soal-soal psychologis segera muntjul didepan kita. Pengaruh bentuk musik dan susunan-nada modern bukan sadja sudah masuk sedalam-dalamnja dalam djiwa kita, tapi suluruh berpikir kita sudah setjara *modern*, setjara sekarang. Dan tjara merasa kitapun sudah lain, bukan karena kita sudah berhadapan langsung dengan dunia internasional, negeri luaran, tapi djuga pengaruh revolusi kita. Kita sudah beladjar berpikir dan merasa tjepat dan berani, seperti dikehendaki keadaan sekitar dan dunia sekarang, jang penuh dinamik, pergolakan, konflik dsb. Kita sudah biasa dengan kesulitan hidup dan pemetjahannja sekali, biasa dengan kemadjuan teknik, ilmu pengetahuan dsb. Dalam musik djiwa ini tak tertampung lagi oleh musik asli jang manapun, dari gamelan Djawa dsb, termasuk apa jang disebut musik rakjat jang mempunjai kedudukan dan keindahannja tersendiri. Djiwa ini menghendaki bentuk musik jang bisa menggambarkan pula, extase-extase rasa dll., bukan semata-mata *verpozing*, hiburan sedang omong-omong dan makan katjang goreng, seperti umumnja pada musik asli kita. Kalau Jaap Kunst (dalam bukunja *De Inheemse muziek en de Zending* tsb., hal 5, alinea penghabisan) menga-takan, bahwa kebanjakan musik kita bersifat magis-religieus jang disukai dan di pudjinja itu, maka kita katakan, kita tak dojan musik magis-magis-primitif lagi, dan rasa religieus kita sudah lain.

"Suata tjontoh baik, bahwa djiwa kita sudah lain ialah waktu diputarkan buat pertama kali dikota Djakarta film Usmar Ismail 'Enam djam di Djokja', jang memulai suatu scene pertempuran dengan iringan bunji gamelan. Spontan keluar dari mulut orang-orang: 'Kok gamelan, mengapa bukan mars bersemangat'."

Notes to Chapter 4

1. Herbert Luethy, *Indonesia in Travail* (New Delhi: Congress for Cultural Freedom, 1966), pp. 78, 79.

2. A. L. Becker, "The Indonesian Elections as *Wayang*." Address to the Southeast Asian Association of Ontario, Guelph, Ontario, October 1971.

3. Bernard Vlekke, *Nusantara: A History of Indonesia* (The Hague: W. van Hoeve, 1965), p. 59.

4. This analysis is based upon a tape recording of the performance by RRI, Radio Republic Indonesia, in Yogyakarta, and a text of the composition given to Judith Becker by the composer.

5. In addition to a complete *sléndro/pélog* gamelan the work calls for the following ensembles and instruments:

a. Gamelan Corobalèn (4 or 6 tones)

1. bonang gambyong: 4 or 6 "female" (large, flat) bonang kettles in one row
2. bonang klenang: 4 or 6 "male" (small, high) bonang kettles in one row
3. bonang penontong: bonang with exceptionally broad rim
4. kenong
5. kempul/gong
6. kendhang

(Instrumentation for the Gamelan Corobalèn is from the program notes of a performance given by the Akademi Seni Karawitan: "The presentation of the art of gamelan playing," presented by Proyek Pelita Departemen Pendidikan dan Keguruan, Surakarta.)

b. Gamelan Kodok-Ngorek *(3 tones, usually uses only 2)*

1. bonang klenang: four racks of 8 gongs each, each rack played by two musicians
2. 2 large gongs hanging from one rack
3. 1 kenong used as a kethuk
4. 2 kenong
5. 2 drums: kendhang gendhing and ketipung
6. 1 rojèh: pair of cymbals hung from a small rack and hit with a mallet
7. 3 sléndro saron: 1 demung, and 2 barung

(These instruments are later additions, the result of the desire of Sultan Hamengku-buwono I to expand the repertoire of the Kodok-Ngorek Gamelan.)

8. 1 bell tree (byong)

c. Gamelan Monggang *(3 tones)*

1. four racks of bonang kettles: each containing 3 gongs, called klenang
2. 2 large gongs on one rack
3. 1 kenong used as a kethuk
4. 2 kenong
5. 2 drums: kendhang gendhing and ketipung
6. 1 rojèh: pair of cymbals

(Instrumentation for Gamelan Kodok-Ngorek and Gamelan Monggang is from Professor Ir. Purbodiningrat, "Gamelan," *Sana-Budaja* 1, no. 4 (December 1956): 194. Published by the museum Sana-Budaya, Yogyakarta.

d. kemanak

A pair of small bronze instruments in the shape of a dried banana peel, held in the left hand and struck by a tool in the right hand. Today, they are very rarely heard outside the courts. They have been discovered at the site of medieval ruins in East Java and are also pictured on Candi Panataran (A.D. 1347) in East Java. They are still used in the accompaniment of the highly sacred *Bedhaya* dances at the palace of the Susuhunan in Surakarta and at the Pakualaman palace in Yogyakarta.

e. kecèr

Small plates of bronze, mounted on a wooden frame and struck with unmounted plates of bronze. Although still common in Bali, their use is very limited in Java.

f. bedhug

A large, pegged drum associated with Islam. A bedhug hangs on the porch of every mosque and signals the noon prayer. In some of the princely gamelan of Central Java, the bedhug can be found as a signalling instrument and replaces the kendhang, the usual gamelan drum, in the Sekatèn Gamelan. (The Sekatèn Gamelan, or Gamelan Sekati, is a large, old-fashioned type of gamelan owned by the Sultan of Yogyakarta and the Susuhunan of Surakarta and used for the largest Moslem festival, the Garebeg Mulud in Central Java.)

The texts that are used in the composition are as follows:

a. Negara-kertagama

Written in the fourteenth century to honor an East Javanese king, Hayam Wuruk. The author, whose pen name was Prapanca, was a member of the Buddhist court clergy. The book contains a chronicle of events at the Majapahit court from A.D. 1353 to

1364. (See Dr. Th. G. Pigeaud, *Java in the Fourteenth Century*, 5 vols. (The Hague: Martinus Nijhoff, 1960, 1963).

b. Pararaton

The oldest extant specimen of Javanese historiography. Written in the fourteenth century, also during the Majapahit era, it contains the story of the founding and flourishing of Majapahit during the reign of King Hayam Wuruk and his minister Gajah Mada. (The *Pararaton* has been translated into Indonesian by Drs. R. Pitono Hardjowardoja (Jakarta: Bhratara, 1965.)

c. Mardi Kawi, Volume 3

A reader in Kawi, the literary language of the Javanese courts, the medium of the traditional *pujangga*, and the language of most of the early Javanese writings.

6. Wasisto Surjodiningrat, *Gamelan, Dance and Wayang in Jogjakarta* (Yogyakarta: University of Gadjah Mada Press, 1970), p. 55.

7. All quotes are from the manuscript of the composition. Prologue I gives the credits of the performance accompanied by the rebab, gendèr, gambang, and suling playing Pathetan Sléndro Manyura. Prologue II is in Kawi, the literary language of Old Java.

Aummmmmmmmmm!
Mastungkara kraneng swingkara,
ring Hjwang Suksma wasa, Awignamastu,
mwatta winengan dirga-haju,
Mastuna-Purnamasiddi.
Aummmmmmmmmm

8. Kahuripan is an eleventh-century East Javanese kingdom believed to have been situated near the delta of the river Brantas, and therefore in the general area of present-day Surabaya. The text is:

Prologue III. Honoto tjitraning kakawin
kang dingin pinurwokolo, aran djaman Kretojogo,
Sri Maha Prabu Erlangga, binataringrat Nuswo
Djowo, ing Kahuripan Pradjaniro, mengkono
sinengkalan 'Nir (Nir Gatining Wiworo)'.

The last phrase 'Nir (*Nir Gatining Wiworo*)' is a *candrasangkala*. The explanation below was written by A. L. Becker.

Candrasangkala is a system for representing the date of a lunar (*candra* = moon) year in the words of a sentence which has some oblique reference to the events so dated, for example, the composition of a poem, the death of someone (marked on his gravestone), the erection of a house (marked over the door), and so forth. Besides being a convenient way of remembering dates, the system has deeper significance for people who believe in the efficacy of verbal formulation and verbal manipulation as a way of discovering hidden truths and controlling events. The word *sangkala* is the Sanskrit Çaka *kala*, time of Çaka, the ancient king whose name is given to the old Indian calendrical system. (Çaka *kala* > *çakala* > *sangkala*). According to Javanese tradition, King Çaka (Ajisaka) came to Java and taught writing and the reckoning of time to the Javanese people. The year one dates his arrival in Java (A.D. 78).

Indirect references, often extremely subtle, are common in Javanese literature. Words of similar meaning (e.g., world-earth), similar sound (e.g., tree-three), or common association (e.g., light-lamp, giant-wild) may substitute for one another in an oblique reference. In song these are referred to as *wangsalan* (returnings). For example, a singer might refer to "the son of Anjani" when she wanted to refer to young men and also when she wanted to use the *sinom* verse form: the son of Anjani = Hanuman, which rhymes with *anom*, "youth," and also with *sinom*, the name of a verse form. In mystical works such oblique references hide mysteries of great subtlety.

In the *candrasangkala* system each number has a set of words associated with it. These words have some connection with the number: 1, for instance, is represented by the moon (*candra*, *wulan*, *sasi*), the navel (*nabi*), the earth (*bumi*) or man (*janma* < Sanskrit *janma* 'born'). The words for zero refer to the invisible heaven, (*boma* < *byoma*), emptiness (*sonya* < *cunya*), or something lost (*nir*). Thus in the sentence referring to the date of the beginning of Erlangga's reign (A.D. 950 or 1028), *Nir Gatining Wiworo*: *Nir*, (empty, lost) means zero (cf. nirvana), *gati* means five (cf. *tatagata*, Sanskrit and Old Javanese for wind, referring to the *five* directions—north, east, south, west, and center—from which the winds come), and *wiworo* means nine (wiworo = door, hole, referring to the nine holes in the body). As a sentence, *Nir gatining wiworo* is open to interpretation, meaning, perhaps, "Destroyed (*nir*) truly (*gati*) is the gate (*wiworo*)," referring to King Erlangga's military victory over the previous kingdom. This interpretation is, however, just a guess. Most *candrasangkala* are amenable to multiple interpretations.

Two other *candrasangkala* are referred to in *Jaya Manggala Gita*:

$$\frac{\text{Karaseng Djalmo Tataning Ratu}}{6 \qquad 1 \qquad 5 \qquad 1} = \text{A.D. 1516 or 1594}$$
essence   man   titled   king

$$\frac{\text{Karengat Tri Wisiking Djanmo}}{6 \qquad 3 \qquad 5 \qquad 1} = \text{A.D. 1536 or 1614}$$
Hear   three   teaching   man

These have oblique reference to the reigns of Sultan Hadiwijoyo and Prince Sutowijoyo in Mataram.

For a fuller description of the *candrasingkala* system see Radèn Bratakesawa, *Katrangan Tjandrasangkala* (Jakarta: Balai Pustaka, 1952).

9. The kingdom of Singosari followed that of Kahuripan. Its capital was near the slopes of the East Javanese mountains Arjuna, Wilirang, and Penanggungan, probably close to the present-day town of Singosari, on the road between Surabaya and Malang.

10. Prologue IV. Pinetung witing djaman Singosari, ono satus tridoso warso, Nuswo Djowo datansah kambah-kambuhing parangmuka. Nengno tekèng wahjo kalané, samengko teteping djojo-djojo widjanjanti abad kentjananing Nuswo Djowo timbul Ratuné ratu utomo, kalokèngrat Sri Hajamwuruk, binatara ing Madjopahit kang kapindo, kanti tuwanggana papatihé patih linuwih, tengran Harjo Gadjahmada, pan pranjoto kumarané nagri Madjopahit angebeki Nusantoro, sumarambahing ngamontjo prodjo.

11.   Tatkala Sri Narendro Kretanegara
             Mulih ring Budabawana
             Trosangrat, duh, Kaharo hara
             Kadi maluja reh nyan kaliyuga.

12. Prologue V. Satus hastho doso warso wus kapungkur, samantara obah djamané, obah ... sojo obah ... owah ... temahan ngglewang! Assalamu 'alaikum Wa rachmatu'llah Wa barakatuhu.

13. "Once a year the old gamelan Sekati is brought from its place in Srimenganti hall inside the Jogja kraton to be played for a week inside the compound of the Great Mosque.

Only after intensive rehearsals may the court musicians from the Kawedanan Hageng Krida Mardawa play the gamelan Sekati. For according to tradition from the Demak era about 500 years ago, the gamelans Sekati are to be played during the Sekaten week from the night of the sixth to the twelfth of the third Javanese month, Mulud, except on Thursday night and Friday morning. This celebration precedes the Garebeg Mulud which is on the twelfth Mulud, the date of the Maulid, or the birthday of the Prophet Muhammad." From Wasisto Surjodiningrat, *Gamelan, Dance and Wayang in Jogjakarta*, p. 1.

14. Prologue VI. Ono barat luwih gedé, nempuh saka mbang kaloran, ing Demak pinangkané, nggowo sworo kaliwat gumuruh, [in Arabic] "Ashadhu Allah Illa ha Ilalah, Wa 'ashadhuanna Moehamada Rosullullah." (This refers to the penetration of Islam into Java originating from the trading ports of the north coast, especially Demak.)

15. Prologue VII.   Subechanalahu Wabichamdi
                                Subechanalahu Wabichamdi

16. This is a religious hymn, called *Santiswaran* in Java, the theme of which is praise of the Prophet Mohammad. This hymn is recited in unison by Moslems on several occasions; festivals, the Prophet's Birthday, and after Friday Prayer. (Notes on and translation of this hymn are the courtesy of Dr. Ragi Rammuny, Department of Near Eastern Languages, University of Michigan.)

17. The Wali are Moslem saints who are believed to have brought Islam to Java.
Prologue VIII. Sangsojo ngrebdo karamaté poro Wali, wus waroto rumesep anèng sanubarining wong, Sa-enggon² kapijarso umjunging kidung sasanti.

18. Prologue IX. Mungkur djaman ka-Walen, ing mbang kidul ana wahju tumurun, ing Padjang lunggwané. Tan ono lijo amung nDjeng Sultan Hadiwidjojo kang wenang sinembah, Sinengkalan "Karaseng Djalmo Tataning Ratu."

19. Prologue X. Kraton Padjang wus gumingsir, mangulon ontjating wahju. Temen nora kalijo pentjoké marang putro déwé. Dijan Sutowidjojo winenang mbawani ing Mataram, adjedjuluk Panembahan Senopati, ono déné sengkalanira: "Karengat Tri Wisiking Djanmo."

20. *Gendhing Gambir Sawit*, Pathet Sléndro Sanga, kethuk loro kerep, minggah papat. (2 kethuk (t)/kenong for first section, 4 kethuk/kenong for second section.) The Javanese symbol ⌠ means that the section so marked is to be repeated many times.

```
                    t                   t          N
 ⌠. 3 5 2   . 3 5 6   2 2 . .   2 3 2 1
   . . 3 2   . 1 2 6   2 2 . .   2 3 2 1 →
   . . 3 2   . 1 6 5   . . 5 6   . 6 5 3
   2 2 . 3   5 3 2 1   3 . 1 2   . 1 6 ⑤ ⌡

(transition                                        N
 to Dawah)   → . 2 . 1   . 6 . 5   . 6 . 5   . 3 . 2
               . 6 . 5   . 2 . 1   . 2 . 1   . 6 . ⑤
                 t          t          t          t    N
 ⌠. 6 . 5   . 1 . 6   . 5 . 6   . 2 . 1
   . 2 . 1   . 2 . 6   . 5 . 6   . 2 . 1
   . 2 . 1   . 6 . 5   . 1 . 6   . 3 . 2
   . 6 . 5   . 2 . 1   . 2 . 1   . 6   ⑤ ⌡
```

21. Betawi is the old Javanese term for Batavia or Jakarta. V. O. C. refers to The Dutch East India Company. For a good discussion of this period in Javanese history see the chapter, "Indonesia in the Days of Sultan Agung and Jan Pieterszoon Coen," in Vlekke, *Nusantara*, pp. 121–144.

22. Kancil is a mouse deer, a character in Javanese folk tales. He usually overcomes his opponents by trickery and is similar to the American folkstory figure Brer Rabbit.

23. Prologue XI. Mataram—mataram kang kaping telu, kedaton anèng Pleret. Sewu num atus tri welas, petungi tahun Masehi, nDjeng Sultan Agung Hanjokrokusumo, kasusro Ratu linuwih ing salwiring rèh, sajeg sabojo pati kalawan kawulané, mulo tan longko, tanah Djowo tatkalanjo ngambah ing djaman ke emasan, je djaman Kawidjajan.

Ajem   Ajem   tentrem

Nanging . . . donja tan ana barang kang langgeng sipaté. Apa kang dadi memalani tanah Djowo? Pro nakodo Walondo, kang sakawit luru² pametuné bumi Nusantoro kang rupa: tjengkèh, mritjo, pala sapanunggalané; gung ngumbar kamurkané, nedijo ngerup hasil V. O. C. madeg ing Betawi!! Uniné sakuton dagang, lawas² gawé bèntèng—bandjur ngganggo mrijem.

Lho . . . ngendi ana wong dagang teka nggowa mrijem; salah kedadèn, dudu tjarané wong dagang, nanging wudjudé wong ndjadjah, panguwasané digaraké, kekerasan di tjakaké, akal kantjil di anggo; luput alus di kasar, ora kenèng di kasar, binudjuk, tan ngétung sangsarané wong tjilik, waton awaké déwé untung. Mula wola-wali ginetjak ing prang dening Mataram sanjoto tan ana hasilé.

24. *Ladrang Gonjang-Ganjing*, Sléndro Pathet Sanga

<pre>
        t   t N   t   t N
    . 2 . 1   . 6 . 5   . 2 . 5   . 2 . 1
    . 2 . 1   . 2 . 1   . 2 . 1   . 6 . ⑤
                                . 2 . ①→ 2nd ending

        t   t N   t   t N
    . 3 . 2   . 6 . 5   . 1 . 6   . 5 . 6
    . 3 . 2   . 6 . 5   . 2 . 1   . 6 . ⑤
</pre>

25. This refers to the revolt against the Dutch led by Prince Diponegoro that lasted five years. When the struggle became hopeless Diponegoro agreed to negotiate terms. He was invited to the Dutch military headquarters and was treacherously arrested and exiled to the Celebes (Sulawesi), where he lived the last twenty-five years of his life. See Vlekke, *Nusantara*, pp. 284–287.

26. This passage refers to a flying white ant, *sulung*, not a moth, entering the fire. I have translated *sulung* as moth, as it is moths that carry the same metaphor in English.

27. The word *rawé-rawé* literally means a curtain made of strips of banana leaves.

28. Prologue XII. Kumpeni sojo ngangseg, ngangseg . . . ngendih panguwasané Ratu Djowo, wiwit ndjeng Sultan Agung Sinuhun Amang-kurat sapisan, Sinuhun Amangkurat ping pindo, ping telu ja Sunan Emas, tekèng Sunan Pakubuwono sapisan ing Kartosuro, sinambung kang kaping pindo, nuli kang djumeneng ping telu ing Surakarta.

Kradjan Mataram petjah dadi 2: Surakarta lan Ngajogjokarta, Pangeran Mangkubumi djedjuluk Sinuwun Hamangkubuwono sapisan, nuli kang djumeneng ping pindo, ping telu . . . Samantoro Pangeran Diponegoro tan kuwowo mireng pandjeriting wong tjilik, temah kojo bantèng kanin mirudo soko pawarangkan.

Wong tjilik bijuk! Tut wuri nDjeng Pangeran Tahun 1825. Amuk ... amuk ... amuk ... amuk ... amuuuuk!!! Adja nganti mundur sadjangkah, kontjo! Ajo, sulung melebu geni! Rawi² rantas, malang² putung! Amuuuk!

29.   Nora njana nora duga
                        Walondo angapus krama
                        Tumindaké tan prasadja
                        Pangran temah pinusara.

                        Dening sang hangkara murka,
                        sagung rakjat sru duhkita
                        dahat deniro aminta
                        siking Widdi pinaringna.

30. Prologue XIII. Duh ndjeng Pangeran Diponegoro, sesotijaning bangsa baban-tènging Nuswa Djowo, paduko kalorobing apus, kapikut ing pendjadjah. ...

31. Prologue XIV. Rakjat, rakjat! Bola bali rakjat kang nandang sangsarané!

Jo, jo, jo, tutugno nggonmu sukan² hondrowino! Tutugno!

Prologue XV. (Gudjeng tjukakaan wongsal wangsul.)

32. Prologue XVI. Apa trimo mung mengkéné iki? Ah ora! Temen² ora! Bongso Indonesia wiwit gumragah, wong pinter mundak akèh, Pergerakan Kebangsaan! Persatuan kang kuwat, saeka- projo- Jo, eling² wetjaning para leluhur, kang wis pinatjak ing djongko² jen ing tembé bakal ana kang tetulung, ngréwangé mbérat memalaning Indonesia, jen mula njata mbandjur besuk kapan tekané?

"Djago wiring kuning, tjébol kepalang."

33. Prologue XVII. Banzai! (Japanese war cry meaning "hurray.")

34. Personal communication from Hardjo Susilo, University of Hawaii.

35. Prologue XVIII. Omulo njoto, iki babaring djongko! ... Hakko Itjiu = Kemakmuran bersama ing Asia Raja. Wis pratjojo marang tuntunaning sadulur tuwo mugo² kang murbèng Dumadi ngidènana marang gegajuhan kang luhur iki!

36. Kaja ngené, kaja mangkéné rasané. Luwih abot, luwih abot parentahé.

37. Prologue XIX. Elo, Elo! Lha endi buktiné? Djaré Hakko Itjiu? Uniné kemakmuran bersama, kok kojo mangkéné dadiné. Sojo suwé, sojo ... Aduh, bangsaku!

38. Prologue XX. Durung uwis² nggoné nandang popotjintroko. Aduh mbuwang pendjadjah dadi malah oleh panindes. Romusha! Katok goni! Slendang rami! Gogik, Bekitjot, wekasan = Beri²!! Kekes rasané, atis, panes, perih! Malah wong pinter² akèh sing podo ditumpesi.

39. Prologue XXI. Saking mèpèt² ing panandang, rakjat dadi tukul waniné, nanging tansah madju-mundur, monga-mangu, awit durung mangerti dalané. Kono kéné ana gerakan dedemitan, pembrontakan Suprijadi petjah ing Blitar! Djepang wiwit kosèk, ngawang glagat wis katatir.

40. Prologue XXII. Dumadakan ... Bom atom ing Hiroschima. Djepang nungkul marang Sekutu. Rakjat Indonesia sojo kempleng tekadé, tan keno ora kudu Merdiko. Proklamasi

Kami bangsa Indonesia, dengan ini menjatakan kemerdekaan Indonesia. Hal² jang mengenai pemindahan kekuasaan dan lain² diselenggarakan dengan tjara saksama, dan dalam tempo jang sesingkat-singkatnja.

Jakarta 17 Agustus 1945
Sukarno—Hatta.

Titi pamedaring gito, pinungkas ing sasanti djojo² Republik Indonesia. Haju. Luhur-Widodo. niring sambékolo.

41. In traditional Javanese drama, any episode may be expanded into a full evening's theater. Whatever the plot, it is molded into the *lakon* structure of Javanese drama. The structural rules of the *lakon* form are as rigid as the structural rules of musical forms and result in all plays sharing a basic similarity. See A. L. Becker, "Textbuilding, Epistemology, and Aesthetics in Javanese Shadow Theater," in *The Imagination of Reality: Essays in Southeast Asian Coherence Systems*, eds. A. L. Becker and Aram Yengoyan (Norwood, N.J.: Ablex, 1979).

42. For a discussion of the "noncompulsive" aspects of Asian drama, of how the viewer is not forced into any fixed degree of attentiveness, see A. L. Becker, "Journey Through the Night," *The Drama Review* 15, no. 3, (Winter 1971): 83.

43. Herbert Luethy, *Indonesia in Travail*, pp. 27, 29.

44. "Early in 1960 the central message of the celebrated speech was stated as consisting of five ideas—the 1945 constitution, Socialism a la Indonesia, Guided Democracy, Guided Economy, and Indonesian Personality—and the first letter of these five phrases were put together to make the acronym USDEK. With 'political Manifesto' shortened to 'Manipol,' the new creed became known as 'Manipol-USDEK'. . . . And for members of some Indonesian communities, notably for many Javanese, there was real meaning in the various complex schemes which the President presented in elaboration of Manipol-USDEK, explaining the peculiar significance and tasks of the current stage of history." Quoted from Herbert Feith, "Dynamics of Guided Democracy," in *Indonesia*, ed. Ruth McVey (New Haven: Human Relations Area File Press, 1963), pp. 367–368.

45. For example, the tambourine pattern in the song *Ngunda Layangan*, by Ki Nartosabdho, on the Lokananta record, *Gara-gara*, BRD–014.

46. *Ki Nartosabdho, Gending² Djawi saha Dolanan gagrak enggal* [New style Javanese pieces] (Semarang: Ngesti Pandowo Wayang Orang, 1969), p. 7.

47. The song *Suara Suling*, Lokananta recording *Ki Nartosabdho*, ARD–037.

48. Some scholars might feel that the deletion of kempul in the first kenong unit of Lancaran, Gangsaran, and Ladrang forms is a traditional way of creating the same effect. This explanation is possible, but inadequate as it cannot explain the many other instances of kempul deletion in other gamelan gong structures. (See chart, Appendix I.)

Notes to Chapter 5

1. Bernard H. M. Vlekke, *Nusantara: A History of Indonesia* (The Hague: W. Van Hoeve, 1965), p. 371.

2. Wasisto Surjodiningrat, *Gamelan, Dance and Wayang in Jogjakarta* (Yogyakarta: University of Gajah Mada Press, 1970), p. 50.

3. Sulaiman Gitosaprodjo, *Ichtisar Theori Sindènan* (Published in stencil form, Malang, East Java, 1971), p. 5.

4. Lokananta recording, *Ki Nartosabdho*, ARD–039.

5. *Adja Lamis* on Lokananta, *Ki Nartosabdho*, ARD–039, is another example of the vocal style of American show tunes of the 1930s as found in gamelan music.

6. According to Hardjo Susilo, University of Hawaii, Ki Wasitodipuro and Ki Nartosabdho were not the first composers to write gamelan compositions in three-four meter. That distinction belongs to Ki Hardjosoebroto who wrote a series of compositions with the general title *Langensekar*. When first introduced, these compositions gave considerable difficulty to Javanese musicians who did not know how to adjust duple-

quadruple subdivisions to a triple meter. Ki Hardjosoebroto is also believed to have introduced the *suara bersama* vocal technique, sometime in the early 1950s.

7. The composers of Christian compositions given by Sumarsam in the booklet *Perkembangan Seni Karawitan* (Published in stencil form, Akademi Seni Karawitan Indonesia, Surakarta, 1971), are R. C. Hardjosoebroto, Darsono, and R. L. Marto-pangrawit. A recording of a mass with gamelan, entitled *Missa Javanica*, has been produced by Philips, No. 840 278 BY. The composers listed on this recording are Marsudi, Sumar-tono, Hardjosoebroto, Atmadarsana, and Sukodi.

8. The concert, which began with *Kawiwitan Meditasi/Konsentrasi* and continued with *Kagok Pangrawit*, took place in May 1968, at the Bangsal Kepatihan, Yogyakarta.

9. For a description of Javanese mysticism see Clifford Geertz, *The Religion of Java* (Glencoe, Illinois: Free Press, 1960). See chapter entitled "The Mystical Sects," p. 339. For a critical review of the book by a Javanese, see "The Religion of Java: A Commentary," by Harsja W. Bachtiar, *Bhratara* [Indonesian journal of cultural studies] 5, no. 1 (January 1973): 85–118.

10. *Gendhing (bonangan) Pangrawit*, Pélog Pathet Lima, kethuk 8 kerep, minggah kethuk 16. (Surakarta style.)

```
         t                    t
. . 3 1   . 3 . 2   3 . 3 5   6 5 3 2
. 3 2 1   . 3 . 2   3 . 3 5   6 5 3 2
. 3 2 1   . 3 . 2   3 . 3 5   6 5 3 2
3 . 3 5   2 3 2 1   . . 1 2   3 5 6 5N
. . 5 7   5 6 7 6   7 7 6̅5̅3   6 5 2 3
5 5 . 7   5 6 7 6   7 7 6̅5̅3   6 5 2 3
5 5 . 7   5 6 7 6   7 7 6̅5̅3   6 5 3 2
5 2 . 3   6 5 3 2   . 4 . 2   4 5 2 1N
. . 1 3   . 2 1 2   3 . 3 5   6 5 3 2
. 3 2 1   . 3 . 2   3 . 3 5   6 5 3 2
. 3 2 1   . 3 . 2   3 . 3 5   6 5 3 2
3 . 3 5   2 3 2 1   6 6 . .   2 3 2 1N
. 2 1 6   . 2 . 1   . 2 1 6   . 2 . 1
2 3 . .   6 5 3 2   3 2 1 6   2 1 6 5
1 5 . 6   2 1 6 5   1 5 . 6   2 1 6 5
6 6 . .   6 6 7 6   . 5 3 2   . 5 . 3N/G
```

Umpak Minggah:
```
. . 5 6   7 7 5 6   . 7 5 6   7 7 5 6
. 7 5 6   7 7 5 6   . 5 3 2   . 5 . 3N/G
```

Minggah:
```
    t         t         t         t
. 6 3 5   6 7 5 6   . 5 3 2   . 5 . 3
. 6 3 5   6 7 5 6   . 5 3 2   . 5 . 3
. 6 3 5   6 7 5 6   . 5 3 2   . 5 . 3
. 4 . 2   . 4 . 1   . . 1 2   3 5 6 5N
. 3 . 6   . 3 . 5   . 3 . 6   . 3 . 5
. 3 . 6   . 3 . 5   3 2 1 3   1 2 3 2
3 2 1 6   5 3 6 5   3 2 3 .   3 2 3 5
3 2 3 .   3 2 3 5   6 5 4 2   4 5 2 1N
3 2 3 .   3 2 3 5   6 5 4 2   4 5 2 1
```

```
3 2 3  .   3 2 3 5   6 5 4 2   4 5 2 1
3 2 3  .   3 2 3 5   6 5 4 2   4 5 2 1
6 6  . .   6 6 5 6   7 7 6 7   5 6 7 6N
5 3 2 5   2 3 5 2   5 3 2 5   2 3 5 6
5 3 2 5   2 3 5 6   7 . 7 6   5 4 2 1
6 5 6  .   6 5 2 1   6 5 6  .   6 5 2 1
. . 5 6   . 1 . 6   . 1 . 6   5 4 2 4N/G
6 5 4 6   4 5 6 1   2 3 2 1   6 5 4 4
6 5 4 6   4 5 6 1   2 3 2 1   6 5 4 4
6 5 4 6   4 5 6 1   2 3 2 1   6 5 4 4
6 5 6 1   6 5 4 4   . 3 . 2   . 3 . 5N
. 3 . 6   . 3 . 5   . 3 . 6   . 3 . 5
. 3 . 6   . 3 . 5   3 2 1 3   1 2 3 2
3 2 1 6   5 3 6 5   3 2 3  .   3 2 3 5
3 2 3  .   3 2 3 5   6 5 4 2   5 4 2 1N
3 2 3  .   3 2 3 5   6 5 4 2   4 5 2 1
3 2 3  .   3 2 3 5   6 5 4 2   4 5 2 1
3 2 3  .   3 2 3 5   6 5 4 2   4 5 2 1
6 6  . .   6 6  . .   2 2  . .   2 3 2 1N
. 2 1 6   . 2 . 1   . 2 1 6   . 2 . 1
2 3  . .   6 5 3 2   3 2 1 6   2 1 6 5
. . 5 6   7 7 5 6   . 7 5 6   7 7 5 6
. 7 5 6   7 7 5 6   . 5 3 2   . 5 . 3N/G³
```

11. *Ladrang Sumingin*, Sléndro Pathet Sanga

```
          t         t  N
6 5 3 5   3 2 3 5
2 1 2 6   2 1 2 6
2 1 2 6   2 1 2 6
2 3 1 2   3 5 3 ②

          t         t  N
1 2 3 2   3 5 3 2
5 6 1 6   5 3 2 1
5 6 1 6   5 3 2 1
2 3 2 1   6 5 3 ⑤
```

Ladrang Kagok Sumingin, Sléndro Pathet Nem

```
          t         t  N
6 5 3 5   3 2 3 5
2 1 2 6   2 1 6 5
2 1 2 6   2 1 6 5
2 5 2 3   5 6 3 ⑤   (1st ending)
          5 6 1 ⑥   (2nd ending)

          t         t  N
5 6 1 6   5 3 5 6
1 1 3 2   6 3 5 6
1 1 3 2   6 3 5 6
5 3 2 3   5 6 1 ⑥   (1st ending)
          5 6 3 ⑤   (2nd ending)
```

```
           t        t   N
. . 5 1  5 6 1 6
2 3 5 .  5 1 5 6
2 3 5 .  5 1 5 6
5 3 2 3  5 6 3 ⑤
```

12. *Ladrang Kagok Madura*, Sléndro Pathet Sanga

```
           t        t   N
1 6 1 2  1 6 1 5
1 6 1 2  1 6 1 5
1 6 1 2  1 6 1 5
3 2 3 .  3 6 3 ⑤
```

```
           t        t   N
1 1 . .  1 1 2 1
3 2 1 2  . 1 6 5
1 6 3 2  5 6 1 6
3 5 6 1  6 5 3 ⑤
```

```
           t        t   N
1 6 5 6  5 3 2 1
5 6 1 6  5 3 2 1
5 6 1 6  5 3 2 1
6 6 3 2  . 1 6 ⑤
```

```
           t        t   N
3 2 3 .  3 6 3 5
3 2 3 .  3 6 3 5
3 2 3 .  3 6 3 5
1 6 1 2  1 6 1 ⑤
```

Notes to Chapter 6

1. Pélog Pathet Bem and Pélog Pathet Manyura/Nyamat are not included. Pélog Patet Bem is the Yogyanese term for those *pélog* modes using pitch levels 1, 2, 3/4, 5, 6,: i.e., Pathet Lima and Pathet Nem as opposed to Pathet Barang, which uses pitch levels 4/5, 6, 7, 2, 3. Pélog Pathet Manyura/Nyamat is said to be like Pathet Barang except that pitch level 1 is substituted for pitch level 7.

2. The temporal associations of the *pélog pathet* given are taken from *Ichtisar Teori dan Praktek Gamelan*, by Sulaiman Gitosapradjo. In a personal communication, summarized below, Sumarsam gives a different arrangement for *pélog* as well as daytime sequence for *sléndro*. According to Sumarsam, the associations are not so much temporal as they are sequential, based on the progression of the mood of the pieces from solemn, quiet, *regu*, to more lively, exciting, *prenes* pieces.

Daytime:

Sléndro Manyura or Pélog Barang; Quiet, solemn pieces played in Irama I/II with kendhang kalih or kendhang satunggal.

Sléndro Sanga or Pélog Nem; Pieces played in Irama I/II/III/IV with kendhang satunggal, kendhang kalih, or kendhang ciblon.

Sléndro Manyura or Pélog Barang; Pieces played in Irama I/II/III/IV with kendhang satunggal, kendhang kalih, or kendhang ciblon.

Sléndro Nem and Pélog Lima are introduced only at nighttime, in the first part of the performance. However, the sequence given above is used for all weddings, whether in daytime or nighttime.

3. "R. T. Djojodipuro almarhum mengatakan bahwa patet itu ialah tempatnja suatu gending," *and* "Tuan[2] Djakub dan Wignjorumekso mengatakan bahwa patet itu dipakai untuk memberi tempat kepada gending." Quote from Professor Ir. Purbodiningrat, "Gamelan," *Sana-Budaja* 1, no. 4 (December 1956) p. 200. Published by the museum Sana-Budaya, Yogyakarta.

4. "Tuan Sastrosuwignjo mengatakan bahwa patet itu ialah njanjian dalang (pemain wajang) dengan pengantaran rebab, gender, gambang, suling, kendang dan (kadang[2]) gong." Purbodiningrat, "Gamelan," p. 200.

5. Sulaiman Gitosaprodjo. *Ichtisar Theori Karawitan dan Teknik Menabuh Gamelan* (Published in stencil form, Malang, East Java, 1971), p. 6.

6. Purbodiningrat, "Gamelan," p. 201.

7. "R. M. Sarwoko mengatakan bahwa perbedaan antara satu patet dengan lainnja berdasar atas suatu perbedaan tjèngkok." Purbodiningrat, "Gamelan," p. 200.

8. "Pada hakekatnja tjèngkok itu bersifat individual, djadi dengan sendirinja djuga lokal. Oleh karenanja maka banjaknja tjèngkok itu theoretis tidak terbatas. Tapi orang mudah mengerti, bahwa tjèngkok itu terikat oleh watak[2] instrumen, oleh hukum[2] mengenai laras, mengenai patet, dan sudah barang tentu mengenai keindahan."

9. Kunst's theory of *pathet* is set forth in his book *Music in Java*, 2 vols. (The Hague: Martinus Nijhoff, 1949). This theory focuses upon the ending pitches of gong phrases and the "5th" relationship between what are defined by Kunst as the principal pitches of each *pathet*. Kunst's theory is the basis of the analysis presented in *The Nuclear Theme as a Determinant of Paṭet in Javanese Music* by Mantle Hood (Groningen: J. B. Wolters, 1954) with the additions by Hood of (1) an analysis of the introductory phrases (*buka*) of many pieces, (2) a classification of commonly found gong contours, and (3) an analysis of the role of each pitch level within each *pathet*. For a critical review of this theory and the conclusions drawn from it by both authors, see Judith Becker, *Traditional Music in Modern Java*, Ph.D. dissertation, University of Michigan, 1972 (Ann Arbor: University Microfilms), pp. 163–173 and pp. 256–259.

10. Kunst, *Music in Java*, p. 90.

11. Mantle Hood, *The Nuclear Theme as a Determinant of Pathet in Javanese Music*, p. 242.

12. I do not accept the usage of the term "nuclear theme" for the saron part, and it was for quite other reasons that the saron part was chosen for analysis. Sometimes the saron is prominent and dominating, other times it is in the background. Some instruments sometimes focus their melodic patterns to coincide with the saron part, others never do. The division of the gamelan into three parts, "nuclear theme," "colotomic," and "elaborating" parts is a theory invented by Kunst (never used by Javanese), which helped him and many since to organize mentally and listen to gamelan music. In the sense that it is a limiting way of listening to gamelan, placing undue emphasis on the saron part, which may or may not be prominent in a given gendhing, and especially since the tripart division of the gamelan instruments is foreign to the native sensibilities of the Javanese, the "nuclear theme," "colotomic," and "elaborating part" theory should be viewed only as a tool, not as a dogma, to be discarded when the listener can comprehend the melodic importance of all the parts of the gamelan.

Kunst himself recognized alternate ways of viewing gamelan structure: Quoting a Javanese musician, he says: "The gong, the kenong, the kethuk and the kempul he counts, in this subdivision, amongst the kalowongan (outlines) as well as the demung (a nuclear-theme instrument), from which it is clear that he does not feel any essential difference—quite a defensible view, too—between colotomy and the nuclear theme." (*Music in Java*, p. 248.)

13. Ki Sindoesawarno, "Factor Penting dalam Gamelan," *Sana-Budaja* 1, no. 3 (1956), p. 138.

"Bagian² lagu jang terketjil jang sudah mengandung maksud disebut gatra, atau satusan [unit]."

14. Actually, two different hierarchical principles operate on the *gatra* (and every other) structural level. The overwhelmingly favored approach to the final pitch of the *gatra* is stepwise, ascending or descending. This fact marks the penultimate pitch as an important structural point. On the other hand, the principle of subdivision of all units marks the second pitch level of the *gatra* as important. For example, the *gatra* 6 5 3 5 when subdivided produces two end stresses, 6 5/3 5. Both these hierarchies are reflected in the Javanese terminology for the four digits of the *gatra*:

6	5	3	5
small dhing	small dhong	large dhing	large dhong.

15. Many contours having only two or three occurrences in the whole collection of data are not included in this study, but they indicate that it is possible for just about any contour to occur occasionally.

16. A close examination of the charts will reveal that pitch level 7 will, on rare occasions, occur in Pélog Pathet Nem and Pélog Pathet Lima. For a discussion of this phenomenon see Hood, *The Nuclear Theme as a Determinant of Pathet in Javanese Music*, pp. 167 and 193.

17. Like all the *pélog pathet*, it is possible to find any pitch level in gong position in Pélog Barang. However, certain pitch levels are much more frequent in gong position in specific *pathet* than are others.

18. For an informational analysis based on the data in Appendix 4, see Appendix 5, "An Informational Analysis of *Pathet*" by Alan R. Templeton, Department of Biology, Washington University, St. Louis, Missouri.

19. A good example of these added tones can be seen in Mantle Hood, *The Ethno-musicologist* (New York: McGraw-Hill, 1971), illustrations 2–7, pp. 60, 62, and 63. Also hear the aural presentation on the accompanying record Side I, Band 2.

Notes to Chapter 7

1. Soedjatmoko, "Art and Modernization," Address given at the Southeast Asian Institute, Saint Joseph College, Emmitsburg, Maryland, November 1968. Distributed by the Information Section, Embassy of Indonesia, Washington, D.C.

2. Clifford Geertz, *The Religion of Java* (Glencoe, Illinois: Free Press, 1960), p. 235.

Note to Appendix 1

1. Other examples can be found for gamelan music in the following: Jaap Kunst, *Music in Java*, vol. 1 (The Hague: Martinus Nijhoff, 1949); Mantle Hood, *The Nuclear Theme as a Determinent of Patet in Javanese Music* (Groningen, Djakarta: Wolters, 1954); Wasisto Surjodiningrat, *Gamelan dan Komputer* (Yogyakarta: Universitas Gadjah Mada, 1977); and R. A. Sutton, "Notes Toward a Grammar of Variation in Javanese Gendèr Playing", *Ethnomusicology* 21, no. 2 (May 1978).

Notes to Appendix 5

1. Jaap Kunst, *Music in Java*, 2 vols. (The Hague: Martinus Nijhoff, 1949); Mantle Hood, *The Nuclear Theme as a Determinant of Pathet in Javanese Music* (Groningen and Djakarta: J. B. Wolters, 1954)

2. Ki Sindoesawarno, "Factor Penting dalam Gamelan," *Sana-Budaja* 1, no. 3 (1956): 138. Published by the museum Sana-Budaya, Yogyakarta.

3. *Associations* here are meant in a very broad sense and do not preclude the acquisition or formulation by the listener of more abstract "rules" or "laws" for judging *pathet*. For the purposes of this analysis, associations will later be equated with the conditional probabilities, but this does not indicate how a human listener would store and/or use the information gained from listening to a large number of gamelan pieces. Although certain features of this analysis were motivated by considering how the listener judges *pathet*, the means by which this analysis is accomplished cannot be equated to the psychological processes occuring in the human mind.

4. The logarithm of a number is always defined in terms of some "base" number. Let this base number be designated by a, then the logarithm of the number x, designated by "$\log x$," is defined as the number which satisfies the relation

$$a^{\log x} = x.$$

For example, if $x = 4$ and $a = 2$, $\log x = 2$ because $2^2 = 2 \cdot 2 = 4$. If $x = 8$, then the logarithm to the base 2 is 3 because $2^3 = 2 \cdot 2 \cdot 2 = 8$. The logarithm is dependent upon the base chosen; for example, the logarithm of 16 to the base 2 is 4 ($2^4 = 16$), but to the base 4 it is 2 ($4^2 = 16$). The question of which base to choose is irrelevant for the purposes of this appendix because the information measure that is ultimately used is rescaled to a zero-to-one range; hence, the information measure is invariant with respect to the base of the logarithm.

5. The categories of descending, ascending, and remaining *gatra* once again refer to the type of end cadence. Because of the insertion of pitch levels 4 and 7 into the *pélog* system, the definitions are slightly modified from the *sléndro* case to yield a numerical breakdown of *gatra* more like the one used in *sléndro*. Descending cadences now refer both to end cadences in which the third pitch is one level above the end-pitch level and to those end cadences in which the third pitch is two pitch levels above the end-pitch level, with the intermediate pitch level being either 4 or 7. For example, *gatra* ending with 4 3, 5 3, 7 6, and 1 6 are classified as descending *gatra*. Similarly, *gatra* ending with 7 1, 6 1, 3 5, 4 5, and so forth, are classified as ascending *gatra*. Remaining, once again, refers to all gatra that are not either descending or ascending.

Bibliography

*Indicates that the translation listed in the entry will appear in *Karawitan: Source Readings in Javanese Music*, edited by Judith Becker (Ann Arbor: Center for South and Southeast Asian Studies, University of Michigan, in press).

Abdulgani, Roeslan. *"Manipol" and "USDEK": The Political Manifesto of the Republic of Indonesia and its Basic Elements*. Djakarta: Department of Information, Republic of Indonesia, 1960.

Amir, Dr. M. "Pertukaran dan Pertikaian Pikiran" [Exchange of ideas and controversy]. In *Polemik Kebudajaan*, edited by Achdiat Ki Mihardja. Djakarta, 1950. Translated by Claire Holt in *Art in Indonesia: Continuities and Change*.

Anderson, Benedict R. *Mythology and the Tolerance of the Javanese*. Ithaca: Modern Indonesian Project, Cornell University, 1965.

Apel, Willi, ed. *Harvard Dictionary of Music*. 2d rev. ed. Cambridge, Mass: Harvard University Press, 1969.

Bachtiar, Harsja W. "The Religion of Java: A Commentary." *Bhratara* [Indonesian journal of cultural studies] 5, no. 1 (1973): 85–118.

Becker, A. L. "Journey Through the Night: Notes on Burmese Traditional Theater." *The Drama Review* 15, no. 3, (1971): 83–87.

Becker, Judith. "Anatomy of a Mode." *Ethnomusicology* 13 (1969): 267–279.

———. "The Migration of the Arched Harp from India to Burma." *The Galpin Society Journal* 20 (1969): 17–23.

Belo, Jane. *Traditional Balinese Culture*. New York: Columbia University Press, 1970.

Brandon, James R. *On Thrones of Gold*. Cambridge, Mass.: Harvard University Press, 1970.

———. *Theatre in Southeast Asia*. Cambridge, Mass.: Harvard University Press, 1967.

Bratakesawa, Radèn. *Katrangen Tjandrasangkala*. Jakarta, Balai Pustaka, 1952.

Chevé, Emile. *Methode Galin-Paris-Chevé: Methode Elémentaire de Musique Vocale*. Paris: Chez Les Auteurs, 1884.

Coedès, G. *The Indianized States of Southeast Asia*. Edited by Walter F. Vella. Translated by Susan Brown Cowing. Honolulu: East-West Center Press, 1968.

Covarrubias, M. *Island of Bali*. New York: Alfred A. Knopf, 1950.

Dewantara, Ki Hadjar. *Sari Swara*. Djakarta: Pradnjaparamita, 1964.

Direcktorat Djenderal Kebudajaan. *Peladjaran Bawa Gerong* [Study course in bawa and gérong]. Manuscript in stencil form. Djawa Timur, 1967.

Dungga, J. A., and Manik, L. *Musik di Indonesia dan Beberapa Persoalannja* [Music in Indonesia and some of its problems]. Djakarta: Balai Pustaka, 1952.

Echols, John M., and Shadily, Hassan. *An Indonesian-English Dictionary*. Ithaca: Cornell University Press, 1970.

Feith, Herbert. "Dynamics of Guided Democracy." In *Indonesia*, edited by Ruth McVey, pp. 309–409. New Haven: Human Relations Area File Press, 1963.

Geertz, Clifford. *Agricultural Involution: The Process of Ecological Change in Indonesia*. Berkeley: University of California Press, 1963.

———. "Deep Play: Notes on the Balinese Cockfight." *Daedalus*, (Winter 1972), 1–37.

———. *Peddlers and Princes*. Chicago: University of Chicago Press, 1963.

———. *Person, Time and Conduct in Bali: An Essay in Cultural Analysis*. Cultural Report Series no. 14, Southeast Asian Studies. New Haven: Yale University, 1966.

———. *The Religion of Java*. Glencoe, Illinois: Free Press, 1960.

Geertz, Hildred. "Indonesian Cultures and Communities." In *Indonesia*, edited by Ruth McVey, pp. 24–97. New Haven: Human Relations Area File Press, 1963.

———. *The Javanese Family*. New York: Free Press of Glencoe, 1961.

Gitosaprodjo, Sulaiman. Translated by Judith Becker. *Ichtisar Theori Karawitan dan Teknik Menabuh Gamelan* [A summary of the theory of music and the technique of playing the gamelan]. Published in stencil form. Malang, East Java, 1971.

———. Translated by Stanley Hoffman. *"Ichtisar Theori Sindenan" [A summary of the theory of singing]. Manuscript. Malang, East Java, 1971.

———. "Peladjaran Dasar Gender" [A beginning study course for the gender]. Manuscript. Malang, East Java, 1970.

———. "Peladjaran Dasar Kendang" [A beginning study course for the kendhang]. Manuscript. Malang, East Java, 1970.

———. "Peladjaran Dasar Rebab" [A beginning study course for the rebab]. Manuscript. Malang, East Java, 1970.

Hadisoeseno, Harsono. *Education and Culture*. Djakarta: Ministry of Education and Culture, Republic of Indonesia, 1955.

Hall, Daniel G. E. *A History of South-East Asia*. 2d. ed. New York: St. Martin's Press, 1964.

Hatch, Martin F., Jr. "Vocal Pictures: Transcribed Songs of Central Java." Master's thesis, World Music Program, Wesleyan University, Middletown, Conn., 1969.

Heine-Geldern, R. *Conceptions of State and Kingship in Southeast Asia*. Southeast Asia Program, Data Paper no. 18. Ithaca: Cornell University, 1956.

Heins, E. L. "Music of the Serimpi 'Anglir Mendung.'" *Indonesia* 1 (1966): 135–151. Modern Indonesia Project, Cornell University.

Holt, Claire. *Art in Indonesia: Continuities and Change*. Ithaca: Cornell University Press, 1967.

———, ed. *Culture and Politics in Indonesia*. Ithaca: Cornell University Press, 1972.

Hood, Mantle. "The Effect of Medieval Technology on Musical Style in the Orient." *Selected Reports*, vol. 1, no. 3, pp. 148–170. Los Angeles: University of California.

———. "The Enduring Tradition: Music and Theater in Java and Bali." In *Indonesia*, edited by Ruth McVey, pp. 438–471. New Haven: Human Relations Area File Press, 1963.

———. *The Ethnomusicologist*. New York: McGraw-Hill, 1971.

———. *Javanese Gamelan in the World of Music*. Jogjakarta: Kedaulatan Rakjat, 1958.

———. "Music of the Javanese Gamelan." *Festival of Oriental Music and the Related Arts*. Los Angeles: University of California, 1960, 17–23.

———. *The Nuclear Theme as a Determinant of Pathet in Javanese Music*. Groningen and Djakarta: J. B. Wolters, 1954.

———. "Slendro and Pelog Redefined." *Selected Reports*, vol. 1, no. 1, pp. 28–48. Los Angeles: University of California, 1966.

Hood, Mantle, and Susilo, Hardja. *Music of the Venerable Dark Cloud*. Booklet accompanying record of same name. Los Angeles: Institute of Ethnomusicology, University of California, 1967.

Hughes, John. *Indonesian Upheaval*. New York: Fawcett Publications, 1967.

Humardani, Drs. S. D. "Drama Tari Ramajana Gaja Surakarta" [The dance-drama Ramayana, Surakarta style]. Paper read at the Seminar Drama Tari Ramajana Nasional [The national seminar on the dance-drama Ramayana]. Jogjakarta: September 1970.

———. "Seni Tari" [Art dance]. *Udan Mas* (a periodical devoted to the arts), 1959, pp. 115–117.

Ijzerdraat, Bernard. *Bentara Senisuara Indonesia* (an illustrated dictionary of Indonesian musical instruments). Djakarta: J. B. Wolters, 1954.

———. "Rhythm and Dance in Java." In *Dance and Literature in Java*, edited by R. M. Koentjaraningrat. Jogjakarta: Tunggal Irama, 1959.

Jacobson, Edward, and Van Hasselt, J. H. *De Gong-Fabricatie Te Semarang*. Leiden: E. J. Brill, 1907. Translated by Andrew Toth, "The Manufacture of Gongs in Semarang." *Indonesia* 19 (1975): 127–172. Modern Indonesia Project, Cornell University.

Jay, Robert R. *Religion and Politics in Rural Central Java*. Southeast Asia Studies Cultural Report Series no. 12. New Haven: Yale University, 1963.

Kartomi, Margaret. "Conflict in Javanese Music." *Studies in Music*, no. 4 (1970), pp. 62–80. University of Western Australia Press, Nedlands, Western Australia.

———. "Music and Trance in Central Java." *Ethnomusicology* 17 (1973): 163–208.

Kaufmann, Walter. *Musical Notations of the Orient*. Bloomington, Indiana: Indiana University Press, 1966.

Kempers, A. J. Bernet. *Ancient Indonesian Art*. Amsterdam: Van Der Peet, 1959.

Koentjaraningrat, R. M., ed. *Tari dan Kesusasteraan di Indonesia* [Dance and literature in Indonesia]. Jogjakarta: Pertjetakan Taman-Siswa, 1959.

———., ed. *Villages in Indonesia*. Ithaca, N.Y.: Cornell University Press, 1967.

Kroeber, A. L. *Culture Patterns and Processes.* New York: Harcourt, Brace and World, 1923, 1948.

Kunst, Jaap. "Around Von Hornbostel's Theory of the Cycle of Blown Fifths." *Journal of the Royal Institute for the Indies* 27 (1948): 3–35.

————. *The Cultural Background of Indonesian Music.* Amsterdam: Uitgave van het Indisch Instituut, 1949.

————. *Hindu-Javanese Musical Instruments.* The Hague: Martinus Nijhoff, 1968.

————. *Music in Java.* Translated by Emile van Loo. 2d rev. ed., 2 vols. The Hague: Martinus Nijhoff, 1949.

Leach, E. R. *Political Systems of Highland Burma.* London: G. Bell and Sons, 1954.

Lelyveld, Th. B. van. *La Danse dans le Theatre Javanais.* Paris: Librarie Floury, 1931.

Lentz, Donald. *The Gamelan Music of Java and Bali.* Lincoln: University of Nebraska Press, 1965.

Lord, Albert B. *The Singer of Tales.* Cambridge, Mass: Harvard University Press, 1960. Reprint, New York: Atheneum, 1965.

Luethy, Herbert. *Indonesia in Travail.* New Delhi: Congress for Cultural Freedom, 1966.

Malm, William P. *Music Cultures of the Pacific, The Near East and Asia.* Englewood Cliffs, New Jersey: Prentice-Hall, History of Music Series, 1967.

Mangkunagara VII of Surakarta. *On the Wajang Kulit (Purwa) and Its Symbolic and Mystical Elements.* Translated by Claire Holt. Southeast Asia Program, Data Paper no. 27. Ithaca: Cornell University, 1957.

Martopangrawit, R. L. "Tetembangan" [Singing]. Manuscript. Akademi Seni Karawitan Indonesia, Surakarta, 1967.

————. Translated by Martin Hatch. *"Pengetahuan Karawitan" [Musical knowledge]. Manuscript. Akademi Seni Karawitan Indonesia, Surakarta, n.d.

McLuhan, Marshall. *The Gutenberg Galaxy.* Toronto: University of Toronto Press, 1962.

————. *Understanding Media: The Extensions of Man.* New York: McGraw-Hill, 1965.

McPhee, Colin. "Angkloeng Gamelans in Bali." *Djawa* 16 (1936): 322–333.

————. "The Balinese Wajang Koelit and Its Music." *Djawa* 16 (1936): 1.

————. "Children and Music in Bali." *Djawa* 18 (1938): 1–14.

————. *Music in Bali.* New Haven: Yale University Press, 1966.

McVey, Ruth, ed. *Indonesia.* New Haven: Human Relations Area File Press, 1963.

Mellema, R. L. *Wayang Puppets: Carving, Colouring and Symbolism.* Translated by Mantle Hood. Amsterdam: Royal Tropical Institute, 1954.

Meyer, Leonard B. *Emotion and Meaning in Music.* Chicago: University of Chicago Press, 1956.

————. *Music, the Arts, and Ideas.* Chicago: University of Chicago Press, 1967.

Moebirman. *Wajang Purwa: The Shadow Play of Indonesia.* The Hague: Van Deventer-Maastichting, 1960.

Moerdowo, R. *Reflections on Indonesian Arts and Culture.* Surabaja: Permata, 1958.

————. *Seni Tari Bali* [Balinese art dance]. Manuscript in stencil form. Denpasar: Penerbit Jajasan Melati, n.d.

Moertono, Soemarsaid. *State and Statecraft in Old Java: A Study of the Later Mataram Period, 16th to 19th Century.* Ithaca: Modern Indonesia Project Monograph Series, Cornell University, 1968.

Morton, David. *The Traditional Music of Thailand: Introduction, Commentary and Analyses.* Los Angeles: Institute of Ethnomusicology, University of California, 1968.

Muhadjir. "Lenong," *Kompas,* 28 July 1970.

Onghokom. "The Wayang Topeng World of Malang." *Indonesia* 14 (1972): 111–124. Modern Indonesia Project, Cornell University.

Paauw, Douglas S. "From Colonial to Guided Economy." In *Indonesia,* edited by Ruth McVey, pp. 155–247. New Haven: Human Relations Area File Press, 1963.

Pararaton. Translated into Indonesian by Drs. R. Pitono Hardjowardojo. Djakarta: Bhratara, 1965.

Peacock, James L. *Rites of Modernization: Symbolic and Social Aspects of Indonesian Proletarian Drama.* Chicago: University of Chicago Press, 1968.

Pigeaud, Th. G. *Java in the Fourteenth Century: A Study in Cultural History. The Nagara-Kertagama by Rakawi Prapanca of Majapahit, 1365 A.D.* 5 vols. The Hague: Martinus Nijhoff, 1960, 1963.

Poerbapangrawit, R. M. Kodrat. Translated by Judith Becker. *Gendhing Jawa.* Jakarta: Harapan Masa, 1955.

Poerbatjaraka, R. M. Ng. Translated by Stanley Hoffman. *"Raden Inu Main Gamelan: Bahan Untuk Menerangkan Kata Patet," [Prince Inu plays gamelan: Material for explaining the word *pathet*]. *Bahasa dan Budaja* [Language and culture] 5 (1957): 3–25. Djakarta: Fakultas Sastra, Universitas Indonesia.

Poerbatjaraka, R. M. Ng, and Hadidjaja, Tardjan. *Kepustakaan Djawa* [Javanese literature]. Djakarta and Amsterdam: Penerbit Djambatan, 1952.

Poerwadarminta, W. J. S. *Baoesastra Djawa*. Groningen and Batavia: J. B. Wolters, 1939.

Prawiroatmodjo, S. *Bausastra Djawa-Indonesia*. Surabaya: Penerbit Express and Marfiah, 1957.

Proyek Pelita, Departemen Pendidikan dan Keguruan. *Pergelaran Karawitan* [Musical presentation]. Manuscript in stencil form. Pengembangan Pusat Kesenian: Djawa Tengah, 1971.

Purbodiningrat, Prof. Ir. Translated by Stanley Hoffman. *"Gamelan," *Sana-Budaja* 1, no. 4 (1956): 185–206. Published by the museum Sana-Budaja, Yogyakarta.

Rabin, Barbara W. "The Preservation of Melodic Content with Rhythmic Variations in Javanese Wajang Melodies 'Ajak-ajakan,' 'Srepegan' and 'Sampak.'" Master's thesis, World Music Program, Wesleyan University, Middletown, Conn., 1969.

Rassers, W. H. *Panji, The Culture Hero: A Structural Study of Religion in Java*. The Hague: Martinus Nijhoff, 1959

Selosoemardjan. *Social Change in Jogjakarta*. Ithaca: Cornell University Press, 1962.

Sindoesawarno, Ki. Translated by Stanley Hoffman. *"Factor Penting dalam Gamelan" [Important factors in gamelan]. *Sana-Budaja* 1, no. 3 (1956): 136–148. Published by the museum Sana-Budaja, Yogyakarta.

———. Translated by Martin Hatch. *Ilmu Karawitan* [The science of music]. Published in stencil form. Akademi Seni Karawitan Indonesia, Surakarta, 1955.

———. Translated by Stanley Hoffman. *"Menerangkan kata Patet" [To explain the word *pathet*]. *Udan Mas* 1, no. 7 (1960): 151–154. Periodical published by Jajasan Lektur Kesenian Kebudajaan Nasional "Kemudawati," Surakarta.

———. "Pendidikan Kesenian" [Art education]. *Udan Mas* 1, no. 1, (1959): 4–6.

———. "Radyapustaka dan Nut-Angka" [Palace documents and cipher notation]. *Radyapustaka* (1960): 57–63. Yogjakarta: Pertjetakan Taman-Siswa.

Soebardi. "Calendrical Traditions in Indonesia." *Madjalah Ilmu Sastra Indonesia* [Journal of Indonesian cultural studies] 3, no. 1 (1965): 49–62.

Soedarsono. "Classical Javanese Dance: History and Characterization." *Ethnomusicology* 13 (1969): 498–506.

Soedjatmoko, His Excellency. "Art and Modernization." Address given November 1968 and distributed by the Information Section, Embassy of Indonesia, Washington D.C.

Soekanto. "Konservatori Karawitan dan Kebudajaan Nasional." [The music conservatory and national culture] *Sana-Budaja* 2 (1953): 21–25. Published by the museum Sana-Budaja, Yogyakarta.

Soekardi, Kris. "Seluk beluk Gending Bondet." [Complications of *gendhing bondet*]. Master's thesis, Akademi Seni Karawitan Indonesia, Surakarta, n.d.

Soerjatmadja, K. M. "Konservatori Karawitan Indonesia" [The Indonesian Music Conservatory]. *Sana-Budaja* 1, no. 5 (1957): 207–215. Published by the museum Sana-Budaja, Yogyakarta.

Soeseno, Kartomihardjo. "Speech Levels as Indicators of Social Classes in Javanese Novels." Master's thesis, Cornell University, 1971.

Soetandija. "Gending Emeng minggah Ladrang Nalongsa dan Ladrang Wreda-Muspra" [The composition Emeng minggah Ladrang Nalongsa and the composition Ladrang Wreda-Muspra]. Master's thesis, Akademi Seni Karawitan Indonesia, Surakarta, n.d.

Soetrisno. *Sedjarah Karawitan Indonesia* [The history of Indonesian music]. Published in stencil form. Akademi Seni Karawitan Indonesia, Surakarta, n.d.

Solheim, Wilhelm G. "New Light on a Forgotten Past." *National Geographic* 139 (1971): 330–339.

Sumarsam. *Perkembangan Seni Karawitan* [The development of the musical arts]. Address presented at Pusat Kesenian Djawa Tengah, February 1971. Published in stencil form. Akademi Seni Karawitan Indonesia, Surakarta, 1971.

———. *Tjengkok Genderan* [Melodic patterns for gender]. Published in stencil form. Akademi Seni Karawitan Indonesia, Surakarta, 1971.

Supandi, Atik. "Titilaras" [Notation]. Senior paper, Akademi Seni Karawitan Indonesia, Surakarta, 1969.

Surjodiningrat, Wasisto R. M. *Gamelan, Dance and Wajang in Jogjakarta*. Yogyakarta: University of Gadjah Mada Press, 1970.

———. *Penjelidikan Dalam Pengukuran Nada Gamelan-gamelan Djawa Termuka di Jogjakarta dan Surakarta* [Research on Javanese gamelan intervals especially in Yogyakarta and Surakarta]. Yogyakarta: University of Gadjah Mada Press, 1967.

Susilo, Hardja. "Drumming in the Context of Javanese Gamelan." Master's thesis, Institute of Ethnomusicology, University of California at Los Angeles, 1967.

Sutherland, Heather. "Pudjangga Baru: Aspects of Indonesian Intellectual Life in the 1930's." *Indonesia* 6 (1968): 106–127. Modern Indonesia Project, Cornell University.

Sutigna, Daeng. "Sedikit Tentang Huruf Musik" [A brief essay about music notation]. *Indonesia* 2 (1951): 15–18. (Periodical in the Indonesian language.)

Tedjohadisumarto, R. *Mbonbong Manah.* 5 vols. Djakarta: Penerbit Djambatan, 1958.

Teeuw, A. *Modern Indonesian Literature.* The Hague: Martinus Nijhoff, 1967.

Tirtaamidjaja, N. "A Bedaja Ketawang Dance Performance at the Court of Surakarta." *Indonesia* 1 (1966): 31–61. Modern Indonesia Project, Cornell University.

Tobing, W. Lumban. "Adakah mungkin synthese antara seni-musik pelog dan slendro dengan seni-musik Barat?" [Is a synthesis possible between pélog and sléndro and Western music?] *Indonesia* 2 (1951): 19–23 (Periodical in the Indonesian language.)

Van Niel, Robert. "The Course of Indonesian History." In *Indonesia*, edited by Ruth McVey, pp. 272–308. New Haven: Human Relations Area File Press, 1963.

Vlekke, Bernard. *Nusantara: A History of Indonesia.* The Hague: W. van Hoeve, 1965.

Wagner, Fritz A. *Indonesia: The Art of an Island Group.* New York: Greystone Press, 1967.

Wallis, Richard. "Poetry as Music in Java and Bali." Master's thesis, University of Michigan, 1973.

Wertheim, W. T. *Indonesian Society in Transition: A Study of Social Change.* 2d rev. ed. The Hague and Bandung: W. van Hoeve, 1959.

Wojowasito, Soewojo. *Kamus Kawi (Djawa Kuna) Indonesia* [Dictionary Kawi (Old Javanese)-Indonesian]. Malang, East Java: Team Publikasi Ilmiah Fakultas Keguruan Sastra dan Seni, Institute Keguruan dan Pendidikan (IKIP), 1970.

Zoete, B. de, and Spies, Walter. *Dance and Drama in Bali.* London: Faber and Faber, 1952.

Glossary and Index of Javanese and Indonesian Terms

General Index

About the Author

JUDITH BECKER is associate professor of musicology at the University of Michigan and since 1967 has been director of the University of Michigan gamelan ensemble. She spent more than two years doing fieldwork in Java on gamelan music. In 1967, she received the Society for Ethnomusicology's Charles Seeger award.